# The New
# Joy
## of
# Eating

• • • • ♥ ♥ ♥

## Renny Darling

♥ ♥ ♥ • • • • ♥ ♥

*The New Fast & Fancy Favorites*
*Leaner, Lighter & More Luscious*

Other Simply Delicious Cookbooks
by Renny Darling

*The Joy of Eating*
*The Love of Eating*
*The Joy of Entertaining*
*The Joy of Eating French Food*
*Great Beginnings & Happy Endings*
*With Love from Darling's Kitchen*
*Easiest & Best Coffee Cakes & Quick Breads*
*Entertaining! Fast & Fancy*
*Cooking Great! Looking Great! Feeling Great!*
*The Moderation Diet*

Cover art and borders by the distinguished artist
Christina Ladas

**First Edition**

Published by    Royal House Publishing Co., Inc.
P.O. Box 5027
Beverly Hills, CA 90210

Printed in the United States of America
Library of Congress Catalog Card Number:  91-90078
ISBN: 0-930440-32-3

# The Contents

To my dearest friends,
and friends of friends,
and friends of friends of friends...
My ever-loving thanks.

# The Introduction

The world of food has undergone several major revolutions in the past 25 to 30 years. Americans started traveling to the farthest reaches of the world and were dining on the finest international cuisines. From basic, down-home regional cooking, Americans were introduced to the great cuisines of Europe.

They returned from their travels with the memories of these great meals and the desire to recreate these dishes in their homes. American appetites for ethnic cookbooks and cooking schools, teaching these exotic cuisines, seemed insatiable. Cookbooks and cooking schools specializing in foreign cuisines sprung up everywhere. Gourmet shops mushroomed in every nook and cranny, featuring the latest and newest kitchen gadgetry. Americans developed a more refined and sensitive palate, and became more and more knowledgeable about food. I do believe there are more creative and inventive cooks in our nation today than there are anywhere else in the world.

However, with this increased knowledge of international cuisines, on the other side of the spectrum, Americans were becoming more and more concerned with being slim and trim. Now gyms and exercise boutiques were sprouting up all over; running, jogging and fast walking became the order of the day. At this same time, the increased knowledge between the relationship of diet and health was evolving. Slowly, but very insistently, Americans were becoming more and more health conscious, reading labels and health books, along with government reports on diet and health. Reports and surveys abounded and results were centered around lowering calories, cholesterol, fats and salt intake. However, these reports very often were inconclusive and further, contradictory to earlier findings.

True to my belief in moderation, in use of ingredients and size of portions, (my last cookbook "Cooking Great! Looking Great! Feeling Great! - The Moderation Diet" spells this out in detail), there is a marked decrease nowadays in cooking with salts, fats and oils. In this "New Joy..." I have tried to maintain the integrity of a dish, while reducing fat and cholesterol content as much as possible. This new philosophy based on the relationship between diet and health, I do believe, is here to stay.

There are many wonderful ingredients on the market today that are the biggest help in achieving this. Low-fat sour cream is an excellent substitute as is half and half. Non-fat cottage cheese is amazingly good and worked well with all the recipes I tried. I use it exclusively now. Frozen non-fat yogurts and ice milk are wonderful desserts for the dieter, and the fat content is definitely not missed. I don't want to dwell on the numerous products in the market, ranging from pastries to beef, that feature low-fat, low-cholesterol content. The list is endless. Suffice it to say that the quest for good health and a good-quality-long-life is paramount today and from all indications this is not a fad, but a trend that will be with us for a long time to come.

"Designer" ingredients that were new and exciting become dated quickly. Old-fashioned dishes like meat loafs, once disregarded in favor of patés and mousselines, are now coming back into popularity. Lately, Marscapone and Chevre create more excitement than Swiss or Cheddar. Brie was really popular for a while, but is now a fading star. I just read an article stating that sun-dried tomatoes were "out" and sun-dried cherries were "in" but that was a frivolous remark and should be discounted. That's like saying tomatoes are "out."

In "The New Joy..." I have tried to incorporate many of "what's new" and "what's in" with new treasures that will not fail to please. I attempted to reduce the fat and sugar as much as possible, and to the point where to reduce them further would be to diminish the taste. However, many recipes, that were abundant with butter or cream, have been trimmed down to fit our present lifestyle, and are still delicious and satisfying.

The dessert section has been trimmed down wherever possible. Rather than take the heart out of a dessert, it would make more sense to eat and enjoy a smaller portion. As I wrote (around 1969) in my first food article for our local paper (and this concept has only strengthened during the years),

> "A dish should delight in its taste...for it's the pleasure of the TASTE that delivers THE JOY OF EATING."

So, in the case of desserts, learn to keep the portions small and moderate and you won't feel deprived and left wanting. Bland, boring food is a true culprit and not worth the time or the calories spent.

In closing, the more I read, the more I travel, the more I learn about the great cuisines, the more similarities I find that unite them. It seems every nation has a counterpart of some basic. Consider stuffed pasta...ravioli, wontons, kreplach...all representing different nationalities. Consider crepes, blini, pancakes, palascintas, different ways of expressing flat circles of dough. Most cultures have a dough wrapped specialty...piroshkis, empañadas, calzones, turnovers, coulibiacs...and more. Cuisines are multi-national.

Dear friends, I close with the hope that peace and harmony will abound in our land...that we can devote our time to sharing, with family and friends, the things that enrich our lives and elevate our spirits...good times with love and friendship. For, when you think of it, that is all there is...anywhere.

Your loving friend,


Renny Darling

## A Personal Memoir

The world of food is the world of love. For the past 36 years, I have dedicated myself to sharing with others one of life's loving pleasures. I have never been able to keep a culinary secret...and I never will. My life is an open cookbook...so to speak. But so many of you have written asking about my personal life, how I started, where I get my inspiration, I thought, perhaps, some of my fans spanning these 36 years would like to hear a few words about how it all began.

My love affair with food started with my earliest memories. I was born into a family where food played a central role. My Mom, who never had a cooking lesson, was the most incredible and consistent cook and baker. Born in Greece, she cooked in the style of the Mediterranean with a strong emphasis on Greek, Spanish, French and Italian cuisines. (She was also fluent in these languages, which never failed to amaze me.)

How she developed such a varied repertoire that spanned the continent of Europe, is a wonder for me. How she instinctively knew about the chemistry of food, what to combine and how to combine it, still amazes me. She was the perfect cook and baker. Her breads were always perfect, her pastries divine, her filos to dream about, her vegetables always interesting and complex, combined with rhythm and <u>pertinence</u>. If you wonder what I mean by pertinence...she never added an ingredient because "it was there", but rather orchestrated a dish with a thought to balancing flavors and textures, and to create harmony.

She never added gourmet touches, unless they FIT and enhanced the dish. No frivolous touches like chopped almonds here, or a dash of cream there. Every ingredient she used was essential to the tapestry she wove. And all this came from the roots of her being, for she never used a recipe or a cookbook, that I recall. As I wrote in one of my cookbooks, she truly had "golden hands and loving arms." My Dad, deeply loved good food, too, and as he owned a restaurant, food was central to his life. He ran the restaurant, but my mother reigned over the chefs and she shared with them all her exquisite recipes. My, that was a long time ago.

In the early 50's, I became a fanatic about food. I don't know why, but I was driven to make every dish I had ever tasted...with one important difference. I was dedicated to simplifying the preparation to make life easier for the cook.

My Mom made everything from scratch and worked so hard in the kitchen. She never used canned vegetables or made tuna fish sandwiches. (Often I wondered what it was that most of the children ate at school, something brownish, with purple jelly, between slices of white bread.) I often craved to taste a peanut butter and jelly sandwich...which I finally did, but as an adult...but I "deleted the jam, added honey, sliced bananas, yellow raisins and a faint sprinkling..." (I always had to improve a recipe.) We almost always had to come home for lunch...to lunches like lamb chops with creamed spinach and roasted potatoes. Dinner always included a salad course, fish course and a meat course with at least 3 desserts to choose from. Two huge refrigerators and 2 cavernous freezers were always stocked and filled to the brim.

But my Mom had no time for herself and I always felt very guilty and sad to see her work so hard. Yet eating was always such a pleasure for our incredibly large family and many friends. And these two ideas were the seeds that formed my philosophy about cooking easy and eating grand.

The opening lines in the original "Joy of Eating" were

> "I must confess I do not like to chore in the kitchen one bit more than necessary...but I do love and adore delicious food prepared in an exciting and different manner.

> "THE JOY OF EATING originated out of these two notions...the desire for exquisite tasting dishes, that could prepared in the minimum amount of time. This book is dedicated to the preparation of delectable dishes with minimum technique.

> "The main emphasis is TASTE...rich, glorious and pleasurable...with recipes that promise to get you out of the kitchen in a hurry."

And to this day, 36 years and 15,000 recipes later, my work still reflects this philosophy...delicious food prepared in the least amount of time, or simply stated,

COOKING EASY      EATING GRAND

My original recipe for souffles came about by a rather humorous occurrence. It was in August of 1954. (I remember the date, not because I have a good memory, but because that was the month I made the first breakfast for my friend, Harry, who is now my husband.) But it is a cute story and and worth telling because my very glamorous Chocolate Souffle and Souffle au Grand Marnier and Souffle au Cappuccino really had a humble beginning.

Harry came to our home early one morning, and it was easy to see he hadn't eaten breakfast. He answered "Oh yes." before I finished the question "Would you like a little breakfast...?"

Well, now what to do!!! I didn't exactly know how my Mom prepared her omelets...but I did know she used cream cheese so often with eggs... So, I whipped together 5 eggs (3 for Harry and 2 for me), 1/2 pound of cream cheese, loosened the mixture with milk and then wondered, whether to cook the omelet on top of the stove or in the oven. I thought for a minute and decided on the oven, just in case there was a mess, no one would see it, but me...and I could always clean it up, later.

Lo! and behold, what emanated out of the oven was the most gorgeous, delicious souffle, and to this day, it is the basis of all my souffles. No separating eggs, no making a white sauce, no beating egg whites separately and at the last minute, and best of all, with later experimenting, I found it could be assembled in advance and baked before serving. Harry says, to this day, that it was the best omelet he ever tasted and it was then, he decided to marry me. We were married later that year.

Anyway, to go on, since August of 1954 I started to cook a storm. My first dinner party in 1954 was the u-l-t-i-m-a-t-e gourmet discovery, an Indian Curry Dinner. My second was German Sauerbraten with Dumplings and Red Cabbage. Everybody thought they were on another planet. When I made an Indonesian Rice Table everybody fainted. I kept copious notes and these menus appeared 14 years later, in 1968, the first year of the ROMC . And oddly enough, they were pretty advanced for 1968, also.

During this same time, I was blessed with 3 treasures, Joey, Jeffy and Debby, who are the joys of my life and whom I love very, very much. I must have been a very good person in a past life to have been so lucky to have them.

In 1964, my girlfriend, Sheila Howard, asked me for a menu for a dinner party she was having. I gave her my recipes for Stuffed Chicken Breasts with Mushroom Wine Sauce, Spiced Apricots with Walnuts, and a simple Steamed Broccoli with Butter. The next day she called to say that dinner was the biggest hit, and someone at her party wanted to call me for a menu for a brunch she was having. And that is how it all began.

For the next 5 years I received calls from friends, and then friends of friends, and then friends of friends of friends, asking for recipes and menus. I never minded and was happy to share my recipes and menus with total strangers. And it was Sheila who gave me the idea for the Recipe Club. She thought I should print up my recipes and share them through a club for a nominal amount. Please accent the word "nominal" because I first charged $1.00 for a 3-month membership. Needless to say, it was a very expensive hobby. But I loved the fan letters and the raves, and all the happiness they expressed, and I was very content with that arrangement.

When I started the Recipe Club in 1968, I had 14 years of intense dedication to food. I was very creative at that time, young and energetic, and my mind was ablaze with new and exciting variations of the classics. Even in my sleep, it would not stop. The title for "The Joy of Eating" came about in my sleep. One morning, I found the title written on the pad, next to my bed. Below it was a scribble for an incomplete Lamb Glaze. I saved that little bit of paper all these years, for as you probably have guessed, I am intensely sentimental and I save every little memento, so as not to trust my memory.

The recipes that appeared in the original "Joy of Eating" were actually first created during 1954 to 1968 and first appeared in 1968, when the Recipes-of-the-Month Club first started. "The Joy of Eating" and "The Love of Eating" contained the best recipes that appeared in that newsletter, so beloved to me and to thousands of my fans, from 1968 to 1975...plus lots of new recipes, too. It was a very personal newsletter and many of the members corresponded with me regularly after each issue.

The newsletter continued until 1988, when the cost to produce it became prohibitive. I recall how sad I felt when the letters were sent out advising the members that we were not going to visit together each month. And then, the letters so many of you wrote, urging me to continue, really saddened me, too. I received thousands of letters stating the same sentiment. That the newsletter made them feel happy, and they felt as if I was there, in their kitchen, visiting with them every month.

To this day, I still receive letters with checks, asking me to start the club again. Each month, the ROMC newsletter, contained 16 to 20 pages and about 30 recipes, plus cooking tips, food tips, special lessons and whatever else I felt the members would benefit by knowing.

During those 20 years, I offered over 7500 recipes, which were not compiled, but carefully created, to be quick and easy to prepare, and a pure joy to eat, and I do not believe I duplicated myself more than a handful of times.

When I look back at those early issues, I must admit, the recipes were really ahead of their time. Imagine, 36 years ago, Creme Fraiche made easy, souffles and breads in minutes, croissants and puff pastry made quick and easy, magnificent cakes and tortes to stir and bake...the concept of a Quick & Easy Cuisine was unheard of in the 50's, and quite innovative for the 60's. And now everybody, everywhere (including the people I spoke to in every nation in Europe) want to COOK EASY AND EAT GRAND. The idea of Quick Cook, Fast Cook, Cooking in Minutes is very prevalent today. And most major cookbook authors have included this concept in their writings. But when I first started simplifying the great cuisines in the early 50's, it was very new, indeed.

During that time, regional food was the mainstay of American kitchens, and roast turkey, ham or beef were the hallmarks of holiday dinners...pot roast and meat loaf were the family traditions.

For the past 36 years, I have dedicated myself to sharing with others, the joy, the excitement I feel about one of the loving pleasures of life. I could never, never abandon the world of food. And I shall consider it fitting and divine, if on my deathbed, my last words would be those of Pierette, sister of Brillat Savarin...who died at the table shortly after her hundredth birthday...

"Bring on the dessert...I think I am about to die."

As I have stated so many times before, cooking is a labor of love, but when you take away the labor, all that's left is LOVE.

And love is what I feel, for the tens of thousands of you, who have written me the most "unabashed love letters", and who have brought joy into my days and happiness into my life. How happy I am that I have been able to touch upon your life, and bring you some pleasure and joy as well. My dearest friends, and friends of friends, and friends of friends of friends...I embrace you...all.


Renny Darling

# A Few Basics:

## INGREDIENTS

**Cottage Cheese**
Non-fat cottage cheese is a new and wonderful ingredient that I use most frequently. It worked exceedingly well in all the recipes I tested.

**Eggs**
Large Grade AA eggs were used throughout.

**Flour**
To sift or not to sift? I do not sift, but I do spoon the flour loosely into a measuring cup and then level it with a spatula. Do not tamp the flour down or you will increase the amount of flour substantially.

**Nuts**
The flavor of nuts is greatly enhanced by toasting. Toast them in a single layer in a 350° oven for 8 to 10 minutes, or until they begin to take on color. Do not wait until they are golden brown, for they continue to cook for a short while after removing from the oven and could become lightly overdone.

**Orange or Lemon, Grated**
When an ingredient calls for "grated orange" or "grated lemon", it indicates the grating of the whole fruit which includes, fruit, juice and peel. Remove any large pieces of membrane. **Of course, use a thin-skinned orange.** A smallish orange will yield about 6 tablespoons. To grate the fruit, you must use the 3rd largest side of a four-sided grater. Use short strokes. You cannot use a food processor to grind the fruit as it will release too much of the bitter white (the pith.) Grating by hand is the only way to avoid this.

**Orange or Lemon Zest**
When "orange zest" or "lemon zest" is called for, it refers to the grating of only the outer peel of the fruit. The zest is the thin orange or lemon layer that contains the essence of the orange or lemon flavor. "Orange zest" does not include the white part (the pith.) "Orange peel" does contain some pith.

**Raisins**
The flavor of raisins is improved if they are (plumped) soaked for a while (overnight) in orange juice or sherry or some liqueur. If you need to plump them instantly, then place them in a bowl and pour boiling water to cover. Allow to stand for 5 minutes and then drain and pat dry.

**Salt**
The amounts of salt is left to your personal preference. I do not add salt except in the rarest instances. I try to enrich the flavor of the dish with pure, natural ingredients. After a while, you do not miss the salt.

### Sour Cream
The new low-fat sour cream, or the "sour half and half" is another excellent substitute for its richer cousin. It was very reliable when used in most recipes. It is noted as "low-fat sour cream" in the recipes. Where "sour cream" is indicated, it refers to the regular sour cream. In a few instances, where the original recipe would have been diminished, (like the Velvet Cheesecake), the full-strength sour cream was used.

### Sugar
Always sift powdered sugar to remove unsightly lumps.

### Vegetables
Often, frozen vegetables are used. This is a time convenience. In certain soups or stews where 3 or 4 vegetables are used, the time saved is marked. Frozen vegetables come peeled, cut and trimmed in perfect sizes. As a general rule, fresh is better than frozen and frozen is better than canned. If you have the time, of course, fresh is recommended.

## GENERAL BASICS

### Pans
Whenever a "tube pan" or "angel cake pan" is called for, AND THIS IS IMPORTANT, it refers to a pan with a "removable bottom." I am making this extra notation, just in case the description of "removable bottom" is not included in the recipe. This is also true of layer pans, tart pans, and the like. As a general rule, if a pan is made with a removable bottom, then that is the one to buy.

### Cooking or Baking Times
Cooking times are approximate, due to variations in ovens and oven temperatures. In most cases I try to include 2 descriptions to help you know when a dish is finished cooking or baking. The first is the approximate cooking or baking time and the second is some hint as to how the dish should look.

### Numbers Served
The number of people a recipe will serve is approximate. It will, of course, depend on the number of courses you are serving.

### Preheating Oven
In all recipes, oven should be preheated.

### Unmolding Gelatins
To remove gelatin from a mold, start by sprinkling a few drops of cold water on the serving platter. This will help to slide the mold to the center. Run a knife along the edge to loosen the sides. Now, place the mold into hot water (up to the height of the gelatin, being careful not to let water go over the top) for 5 seconds. Shake the mold to loosen the bottom. Place platter over the mold, then quickly invert mold over the platter. Shake gently until mold settles onto the platter.

# Breads & Muffins

Heirloom Fruit & Nut Bread, 16
Apricot, Raisin & Currant Nut Bread, 16
Date & Fig Nut Bread, 16
Banana Chocolate Chip Bread, 17
Banana Date Nut Bread, 17
Pumpkin Raisin Walnut Bread, 18
Pumpkin Apricot Bread, 18
Pumpkin Date Nut Bread, 18
Pumpkin Fig Nut Bread, 18
Zucchini Orange Bread with Nuts & Raisins, 19
Carrot Orange Bread, 19
Pumpkin Orange Spice Muffins with Orange Glaze, 20
Apple Orange Bran Muffins, 21
Crispy Sweet Raisin Corn Muffins, 21
Best Whole Wheat Apricot Bran Muffins, 22
Orange Bran Muffins with Raisins & Walnuts, 22
Honey Oat Bran Muffins with Currants, 23
Instant Monkey Bread with Dill & Cheese, 23
Best Greek Sweet Biscuit Bread with Currants, 24
French Bread with Garlic, Pimiento & Cheese, 24
Easy, Easy Garlic Cheese Bagels, 25
Light Orange Butter Spread, 25
Garlic, Rosemary & Raisin Bread, 26
French Loaf with Goat Cheese & Sun-Dried Tomatoes, 26
Pita Crisps with Honey & Sesame Seeds, 27
Pita Crisps with Parmesan Cheese, 27
Pita Pizzas with Fresh Tomatoes & Mozzarella, 27
2-Minute Flatbread with Garlic & Rosemary, 28
Flatbread with Sun-Dried Tomatoes & Onions, 28
Flatbread with Green Onions & Parsley, 28
Flatbread with Chiles & Cheese, 28
Old-Fashioned Chewy Pretzels, 29
Cream Cheese with Peaches, 29
Old-Fashioned Sticky Raisin Pecan Buns, 30
Sour Cream Biscuits with Dill, 31
Biscuits with Chiles & Cheese, 31
Easiest & Best Brunch Danish Crescents, 32
Onion & Cheese Crescents for Soup & Salad, 33
Westphalian Pumpernickel with Parmesan, 34
Low-Calorie Cottage Cheese & Chive Spread, 34
Whipped Honey Cream Cheese, 34
Sour Cream Corn Bread with Chiles & Cheese, 35
Wimbledon Cream Scones with Currants, 35
Quick & Easy Maple Oatmeal Pudding, 36
Old-Fashioned Country Marmalade, 36

# Heirloom Fruit & Nut Bread

| | |
|---|---|
| 1/2 | pound glazed cherries, coarsely chopped |
| 1/2 | pound glazed mixed fruits, coarsely chopped |
| 1 1/2 | cups walnuts or pecans, coarsely chopped |
| 1/2 | cup flour |
| | |
| 1/4 | cup butter or margarine (1/2 stick), softened |
| 1 | cup sugar |
| 3 | eggs |
| | |
| 1 1/4 | cups whole wheat pastry flour (or all-purpose flour) |
| 1 | teaspoon baking powder |
| 1/2 | teaspoon baking soda |
| | |
| 2 | teaspoons vanilla |
| 1 | small orange, grated. (Use fruit, juice and peel.) |
| | sherry |

Preheat oven to 275°. Lightly oil and flour 6 aluminum foil baby loaf pans, 6x3x2-inches. In a bowl, toss together first 4 ingredients until mixture is evenly coated. Set aside.

Beat butter with sugar until blended. Add eggs, one at a time, beating well after each addition. Beat in next 3 ingredients until blended. Stir in dried fruit mixture, vanilla and grated orange until blended.

Divide batter into the 6 prepared pans. Bake at 275° for about 1 hour and 30 minutes or until a cake tester inserted in center comes out clean. Cool bread in pans. While cooling, paint with sherry 2 or 3 times. When cool, wrap in plastic wrap and foil. Refrigerate or freeze. To serve, cut into 1/2-inch slices and please use a very sharp knife. Yields 72 slices.

**To Make Heirloom Apricot, Raisin & Currant Nut Bread:**
Substitute 1 pound of mixed apricots, raisins and currants for the glazed fruits.

**To Make Heirloom Date & Fig Nut Bread:**
Substitute 1/2 pound, each, of chopped pitted dates and figs for the glazed fruits.

# Banana Chocolate Chip Bread

This is one of the best chocolate chip breads made a little lighter and a little less sweet. It is very easy to prepare, but it can be ruined by overbeating. To be certain to avoid this, stir the ingredients by hand...the less stirring the better. Overstirring the bananas can make the bread gummy, and baking time will increase ad infinitum. This can also be baked in one 8x4-inch pan for about 55 minutes.

1 1/2    cups flour, sifted

1    teaspoon baking soda
4    tablespoons light sour cream

6    tablespoons softened butter (3/4 stick)
3/4    cup sugar

2    eggs

1    cup coarsely mashed bananas (about 2 medium bananas)
1/2    cup (3 ounces) semi-sweet chocolate chips
1    teaspoon vanilla
    pinch of salt (optional)

Sift flour and set aside. Mix together soda and sour cream and set aside. Cream butter with sugar until light and fluffy. Add eggs, one at a time, beating well after each addition. Stir in flour and sour cream mixture alternately to butter mixture, stirring only until combined. Stir in bananas, chocolate chips, vanilla and optional salt.

Divide batter between 4 lightly greased mini-loaf pans (6x3x2-inches) and bake at 350° for about 35 minutes or until a cake tester inserted in center comes out clean. Yields 4 mini-loaves.

**To Make Banana Date Nut Bread:**
Eliminate chocolate chips and add 1/2 cup chopped pitted dates and 1/2 cup chopped walnuts.

# Pumpkin Raisin Walnut Bread

*This is a nice little bread to consider making around Thanksgiving. The sugar and butter have been reduced markedly, but it still is a tasty loaf. This can be prepared in 4 mini-loaf pans (6x3x2-inches). Bake for 40 minutes. Many different dried fruits can be substituted. Some are listed below.*

| | |
|---|---|
| 1 | cup canned pumpkin puree |
| 3/4 | cup sugar |
| 1/2 | cup orange juice |
| 2 | eggs |
| 1/4 | cup butter, softened (1/2 stick) |

| | |
|---|---|
| 2 | cups whole wheat pastry flour (or all-purpose flour) |
| 2 | teaspoons baking powder |
| 1/2 | teaspoon baking soda |
| 1 | teaspoon cinnamon |
| 2 | teaspoons pumpkin pie spice |

| | |
|---|---|
| 1/2 | cup raisins, plumped in orange juice and drained |
| 3 | tablespoons grated orange peel |
| 1/2 | cup chopped walnuts |

In your mixer, beat together the pumpkin, sugar, orange juice, eggs and softened butter until well blended. Add the next 5 ingredients all at once, stirring until they are moistened. Stir by hand and do not overmix. Add raisins, peel and walnuts and stir quickly until combined.

Place batter into two 4x8-inch loaf pans, that have been lightly greased and floured. Bake in a preheated 350° oven for about 45 to 50 minutes or until a cake tester inserted in center comes out clean. Yields 2 loaves.

**To Make Pumpkin Apricot Bread:**
Add 1/2 cup chopped dried apricots when you add the raisins.

**To Make Pumpkin Date Nut Bread:**
Delete the raisins and add 1/2 cup chopped pitted dates.

**To Make Pumpkin Fig Nut Bread:**
Add 1/2 cup chopped soft figs when you add the raisins.

# Zucchini Orange Bread with Nuts & Raisins

*To peel or not to peel the zucchini? Well, if the green flecks do not bother you, as they do me, leave the zucchini unpeeled. I, personally, do not mind green onions or chives in savory breads. But in sweet breads, I always peel the zucchini, as I find green spots less than appetizing.*

| | |
|---|---|
| 1/3 | cup butter or margarine, softened |
| 2 | eggs |
| 3/4 | cup sugar |
| 1 | teaspoon vanilla |

| | |
|---|---|
| 1 | cup peeled and grated zucchini |
| 1 | small orange, grated. (Use peel, fruit and juice, about 6 tablespoons.) |

| | |
|---|---|
| 1 1/2 | cups whole wheat flour or all-purpose flour |
| 1 | teaspoon baking powder |
| 1 | teaspoon baking soda |
| 2 | teaspoons cinnamon |
| 1/3 | cup yellow raisins |
| 1/3 | cup chopped walnuts |

Beat together first 4 ingredients until blended. Stir in zucchini and orange until blended. Combine the remaining ingredients and add, all at once, stirring until blended. Divide batter between 4 mini-loaf pans (6x3x2-inches); place pans on a cookie sheet, and bake at 325° for 45 minutes, or until a cake tester, inserted in center, comes out clean.

Allow to cool for 15 minutes, and then remove from pans and continue cooling on a rack. Yields 4 mini-loaves.

**Carrot Orange Bread:**
Simply substitute grated carrots for the grated zucchini.

# Pumpkin Orange Spice Muffins
## with Orange Glaze

*These muffins are dark and dense and super-moist. While they are not sweet, they are fruity and nutty, and a delicious choice for breakfast or brunch.*

| | |
|---|---|
| 1/2 | cup oil |
| 1/2 | cup sugar |
| 2 | eggs |
| 1 | cup canned pumpkin puree |
| 1/4 | cup molasses |
| 3 | tablespoons grated orange |
| 1 | teaspoon vanilla |
| | |
| 2 | cups whole wheat pastry flour |
| 2 | teaspoons pumpkin pie spice |
| 1 1/2 | teaspoons baking soda |
| 1/4 | cup plumped raisins |
| 1/4 | cup black currants |
| 1/2 | cup chopped walnuts or pecans |

Beat together first 7 ingredients until blended. Mix together the remaining ingredients and add, all at once, stirring until blended. Do not overmix. Divide batter between 12 paper-lined muffin cups and bake at 350-degrees for about 25 to 30 minutes, or until a cake tester, inserted in center, comes out clean.

Allow to cool in pan for 10 minutes, and then remove from pan and continue cooling on a rack. When cool, brush tops with Orange Glaze (optional). Yields 12 muffins.

Orange Glaze:
Stir together 1 tablespoon orange juice and 1/3 cup sifted powdered sugar until blended.

*Note:* ♥ *Muffins freeze beautifully. However, if you plan to freeze, do not glaze until defrosted.*

## Apple Orange Bran Muffins

*You will love these bran muffins. They are moist and fragrant with the flavors of orange and apple. These can be frozen in double plastic bags.*

| | |
|---|---|
| 2 | cups Raisin Bran Cereal Flakes |
| 3/4 | cup milk |
| 1 | egg, beaten |
| 1/4 | cup (1/2 stick) softened butter |
| | |
| 1 | apple, peeled, cored and grated |
| 1 | medium orange, grated (remove any large pieces of membrane, but use the peel, juice and fruit, about 6 tablespoons) |
| | |
| 1 | cup flour |
| 2 1/2 | teaspoons baking powder |
| | pinch of salt (optional) |
| 1 1/2 | teaspoons cinnamon |
| 6 | tablespoons sugar |

Combine cereal, milk, egg and softened butter and mix well. Add the apple and the orange and stir to combine. Add all the dry ingredients at once and stir until blended. Do not overmix. Divide batter between 12 paper-lined muffin cups and bake at 400° for 25 minutes or until a cake tester inserted in center comes out clean. Yields 12 muffins.

## Crispy Sweet Raisin Corn Muffins

*If you enjoy muffins that are crisp and crunchy, you will love this little treasure. These are on the sweet side and are delicious served warm for breakfast with a little cream cheese and jam. These, also, are a nice accompaniment to a Mexican soup or salad.*

| | |
|---|---|
| 3/4 | cup sugar |
| 1 | egg |
| 1/3 | cup melted butter |
| 1 1/2 | cups milk |
| | |
| 2 | cups flour |
| 2/3 | cup yellow cornmeal |
| 2 1/2 | teaspoons baking powder |
| 3/4 | cup yellow raisins |

Beat together first 4 ingredients until blended. Beat in the remaining ingredients until blended. (Do not overbeat.) Divide batter between 12 paper-lined muffin cups and bake in a 350-degree oven for about 35 minutes, or until a cake tester, inserted in center, comes out clean. Allow to cool in pan for 10 minutes, and then, remove from pan and continue cooling on a rack. Yields 12 muffins.

# The Best Whole Wheat Apricot Bran Muffins

*These healthy muffins are filled with all manner of good things...and most of all, taste. Good for breakfast or snacking. I like to store these in the refrigerator in a plastic bag. If storing for more than 4 days, freeze in double plastic bags.*

| | |
|---|---|
| 2 | cups 100% all-bran cereal |
| 1 1/4 | cups orange juice |
| 1/4 | cup oil |
| 1 | egg |

| | |
|---|---|
| 1 1/3 | cups whole wheat flour |
| 1/4 | cup sugar |
| 1 | teaspoon baking powder |
| 1 | teaspoon baking soda |
| 1 | teaspoon cinnamon |

| | |
|---|---|
| 1/2 | cup coarsely chopped apricots |
| 1/3 | cup coarsely chopped walnuts or pecans |

In the large bowl of an electric mixer, soak bran in orange juice for 5 minutes. Beat in oil and egg. Combine the next 5 ingredients and add, all at once, beating until blended. Do not overmix. Stir in apricots and nuts. Divide batter between 12 paper-lined muffin cups and bake at 350° for 25 minutes, or until a cake tester, inserted in center, comes out clean. Allow to cool in pan. Yields 12 muffins.

# Orange Bran Muffins with Raisins & Walnuts

*This is a great muffin to serve for breakfast, for it is filled with lots of fiber, fruit, raisins and walnuts. The flavors of cinnamon and orange add the right sparkle.*

| | |
|---|---|
| 1 1/2 | cups 100% all-bran cereal |
| 1 | cup milk |
| 1/3 | cup oil |
| 1 | egg |
| 1/3 | cup sugar |
| 1 | medium orange, grated. Use fruit, juice and peel, (6 tablespoons.) |

| | |
|---|---|
| 1 1/3 | cups flour |
| 3 | teaspoons baking powder |
| 2 | teaspoons cinnamon |
| 1/2 | cup, each, chopped walnuts and yellow raisins |

Beat together first 6 ingredients until blended. Add the remaining ingredients and beat until blended. Do not overbeat. Divide batter between 12 paper-lined muffin cups and bake at 400-degrees for 20 minutes, or until a cake tester, inserted in center, comes out clean. Allow to cool in pan for 10 minutes, and then remove from pan and continue cooling on a rack. Yields 12 muffins.

# Honey Oat Bran Muffins with Currants

| | |
|---|---|
| 1 | cup low-fat milk |
| 1/4 | cup oil |
| 1 | egg, beaten |
| 1/2 | cup honey |
| 3 | tablespoons grated orange |
| | |
| 1 | cup oat bran cereal |
| 1 1/2 | cups whole wheat flour |
| 1 | teaspoon baking powder |
| 1 | teaspoon baking soda |
| 2 | teaspoons cinnamon |
| | |
| 1/2 | cup dried currants |
| 1/2 | cup chopped pecans |

In the large bowl of an electric mixer, beat together first 5 ingredients until blended. Combine next 5 ingredients and add, all at once, beating until blended. Stir in currants and pecans. Divide batter between 12 paper-lined muffin cups and bake at 350° for 25 minutes, or until a cake tester, inserted in center, comes out clean. Allow to cool in pan. Yields 12 muffins.

**To Make with Apricots, Figs, Dates or Raisins:**
Currants can be substituted with either apricots, figs, dates or raisins.

# Instant Monkey Bread with Dill & Cheese

*This is nice bread to bring along on a picnic or to serve at a barbecue. It is informal, casual and a tasty accompaniment to barbecued chicken. This is a basic recipe. Any combination of herbs and seasonings can be used to match your dinner. Thyme, oregano, onions, garlic, sesame seeds, are all good.*

| | |
|---|---|
| 2 | packages refrigerated biscuits (10 each), separated |
| 2 | tablespoons butter or margarine, melted |
| 1/4 | cup Parmesan cheese, grated |
| 4 | tablespoons chopped chives |
| 1 | teaspoon dried dill weed |

In a 10-inch tube pan, place 5 rolls evenly around the bottom. Brush lightly with melted butter. Sprinkle with 1 tablespoon of the Parmesan cheese and about 1 tablespoon chopped chives and 1/4 teaspoon dried dill weed. Repeat this three times. (Place rolls in a staggered fashion and not directly on top of each other.)

Bake in a preheated 400° oven until golden brown. Remove from pan and serve hot. Serve in a ring and let your family or guests pull off a roll at a time. Yields 20 biscuits.

## Best Greek Sweet Biscuit Bread with Currants

*This is a variation of my Mom's breakfast bread. I know it contains a large amount of cream, but it also serves a large number of people. It is moist, tender and delicious and serves well with sweet or savory spreads. It is good served with cream cheese, sliced strawberries and a sprinkling of pecans. And also great to serve with cheese and wine.*

| | |
|---|---|
| 4 | cups flour |
| 2 | teaspoons baking powder |
| 1/4 | teaspoon salt |
| 1/2 | cup sugar |
| 1/2 | cup cold butter or margarine, cut into 4 pieces |
| 1/2 | cup dried currants |
| 3 | eggs |
| 1 1/8 | cups cream |

In the large bowl of an electric mixer, beat together first 5 ingredients until butter is finely dispersed. Beat in currants. Thoroughly beat together eggs and cream and, with the motor running, slowly add to the flour mixture just until blended. Do not overbeat. Spread dough evenly into a greased 10-inch springform pan. Bake at 350° for 35 to 40 minutes or until top is golden brown. To serve, cut into thin wedges. Yields 16 slices.

## French Bread with Garlic, Pimiento & Cheese

| | |
|---|---|
| 1 | French bread, (1 pound), cut into 32 thin slices (about 1/2-ounce, each) |
| 1/4 | cup low-fat mayonnaise |
| 1 | jar (2 ounces) pimiento strips, chopped or mashed |
| 6 | cloves minced garlic |
| 1/2 | cup grated Parmesan cheese |
| | paprika |

Place bread slices on a cookie sheet. Stir together mayonnaise, pimiento and garlic and brush a thin coating of mayonnaise mixture on each slice of bread. Sprinkle tops with grated cheese and paprika. Broil for a few seconds until tops are browned. Serve with soup or salad. Yields 32 slices.

# Easy, Easy Garlic Cheese Bagels

*These chewy breads are a cinch to make. Taste can be varied in many ways. Onion powder, onion flakes, Parmesan cheese, poppy seeds, sesame seeds are all good. Serve warm with a little light cream cheese. These freeze beautifully in double plastic bags. Remove from the bags while defrosting.*

**Bagels:**

- 1 package dry yeast
- 1/2 cup lukewarm water (105°)
- 1 teaspoon sugar

- 1 cup lukewarm water (105°)
- 1 tablespoon sugar
- pinch of salt
- 4 cups flour

**Topping:**
- 1 egg white, beaten
- garlic powder
- 2 tablespoons grated Parmesan cheese

In the large bowl of an electric mixer, stir together first 3 ingredients, until yeast starts to bubble. Add the remaining bagel ingredients and beat until blended. With a dough hook, or by hand on a lightly floured board, knead until dough is soft and smooth, about 2 minutes. Dough doesn't have to rise.

Divide dough into 12 pieces. Roll each piece of dough into a 1/2-inch thick rope, pinch ends together to form a circle and place dough on a lightly greased cookie sheet. Brush tops with beaten egg white and sprinkle with garlic powder to taste. Sprinkle tops with 1/2 teaspoon grated cheese. Bake in a preheated oven at 400° for about 15 minutes or until tops are golden. Makes 12 yummy bagels.

# Light Orange Butter Spread

- 1/2 cup butter (1 stick), unsalted and slightly softened. (If butter is too soft, it will become oily.)
- 1/2 cup sifted powdered sugar
- 1 teaspoon orange zest
- 2 tablespoons concentrated orange juice

Beat butter until light. Slowly beat in powdered sugar, orange zest and orange juice Place butter in a crock and refrigerate before serving. Makes about 1 cup flavored butter.

# Garlic, Rosemary & Raisin Bread

*I hope you make this bread soon. It is extremely delicious and easy to prepare. Dough is a little denser than a batter bread, but not designed for kneading. Kneading is done by beating in a mixer. The raisins add the perfect touch of sweetness.*

| | |
|---|---|
| 1 | envelope yeast |
| 1/2 | cup warm water (105°) |
| 1 | teaspoon sugar |
| | |
| 4 | cups flour |
| 1 | teaspoon salt |
| 1 | tablespoon crushed dried rosemary |
| 1 | teaspoon coarse-grind garlic powder |
| | |
| 1 1/2 | cups warm water (105°) |
| 1/2 | cup olive oil |
| | |
| 1/3 | cup raisins |

In a bowl, soften yeast in water and sugar, until yeast starts to foam. In the large bowl of an electric mixer, stir together next 4 ingredients. Beat in yeast mixture and additional water and olive oil to form a soft dough. Continue beating for 4 minutes. Beat in raisins.

In an oiled 12-inch baking pan, spread dough evenly, and drizzle a little oil on top. Cover loosely with plastic wrap and allow dough to rise in a warm place until dough doubles in bulk. Remove plastic wrap and bake at 350° for 40 minutes or until top is nicely browned. Serves 12.

# French Loaf with
# Goat Cheese, Sun-Dried Tomatoes & Chives

| | |
|---|---|
| 1 | French bread, about 1 pound, cut in half, lengthwise |
| 1/4 | cup melted butter or margarine, (1/2 stick) |
| 1/4 | pound goat cheese, softened |
| 1/2 | cup chopped chives |
| 2 | sun-dried tomatoes, chopped |

Brush cut side of bread lightly with butter or margarine. Spread softened goat cheese on top and press chopped chives and tomatoes over the cheese. Wrap each half of the loaf in aluminum foil. Heat in a 400° oven for about 15 minutes. Open foil and broil for a few seconds until lightly browned. Cut each half into 8 slices. Yields 16 slices.

*The following are 2 very delicious accompaniments to soups or salads. Whenever I prepare them, everyone enjoys them immensely. They disappear like magic. The amounts of honey or Parmesan Cheese can be increased for a more pronounced flavor.*

## Pita Crisps with Honey & Sesame Seeds

6   6-inch pita breads, cut along the edge and opened flat
12   teaspoons honey or more to taste
12   teaspoons sesame seeds

Spread 1 teaspoon honey on each cut side of pita bread. Sprinkle with 1 teaspoon sesame seeds. Bake at 350° for 3 to 4 minutes or until bread is crisped. Careful, for there are only a few seconds between crisp and burned. Serve with soup or salads. Can be prepared earlier in the day and covered with plastic. Serve at room temperature. Yields 12 servings.

## Pita Crisps with Parmesan Cheese

6   6-inch pita breads, cut along the edge and opened flat
12   teaspoons butter
12   teaspoons grated Parmesan cheese or more to taste

Spread 1 teaspoon butter on each cut side of pita bread. Sprinkle with 1 teaspoon grated Parmesan. Bake at 350° for 3 to 4 minutes or until bread is crisped. Careful, for there are only a few seconds between crisp and burned. Serve with soup or salads. Can be prepared earlier in the day and covered with plastic. Serve at room temperature. Yields 12 servings.

## Pita Pizzas with Fresh Tomatoes & Mozzarella

*Split pita breads can be used as a base for any number of fillings. It is a light, low-calorie crust. It is very thin, so don't expect a chewy crust.*

3   6-inch pita breads, cut along the edges and opened flat
1   cup diced tomato
4   ounces grated Mozzarella cheese
3   tablespoons grated Parmesan cheese
6   tablespoons finely chopped green onions
1/2   teaspoon Italian Herb Seasoning
     pinch of hot pepper flakes

Lay pitas, cut side up, on a cookie sheet. Stir together the remaining ingredients and divide among the pitas, spreading evenly to the edges. Bake at 350° for 5 minutes, or until cheese melts. Broil for a few seconds to brown tops. Yields 6 servings.

# 2-Minute Flatbread with Garlic & Rosemary

*This is a variation of the popular beer bread, but heightened with the addition of garlic and rosemary. The cheese rounds out the taste beautifully. This is a great bread to serve with a meal in an Italian mood. If preparing bread earlier in the day, leave it in the pan and wrap pan securely with plastic wrap. The first 3 ingredients are basic and flavorings can be mixed and matched. Match the spices to your dinner, or add sesame seeds, poppy seeds, caraway seeds, etc. for a bread with a totally different character.*

**Basic Bread:**

| | |
|---|---|
| 3 | cups self-rising flour |
| 3 | tablespoons sugar |
| 1 | can (12 ounces) beer, cold or at room temperature. (I have found no difference in results using either.) |
| 3 | tablespoons crumbled rosemary |
| 6 | cloves minced garlic |
| 4 | teaspoons oil |
| 2 | tablespoons grated Parmesan cheese |

In the large bowl of an electric mixer, beat together first 3 ingredients until blended. Do not overbeat. Beat in rosemary and garlic. Spread 2 teaspoons oil in a 12-inch round baking pan. Spread batter evenly in pan, drizzle 2 teaspoons oil on top and sprinkle with grated Parmesan cheese.

Bake at 350° for 40 to 45 minutes, or until top is golden brown. Allow to cool in pan. To serve, cut into wedges or serve whole and let everybody tear off a piece or two (mostly two.) Quite delicious served warm or at room temperature with soup or salad. Serves 12.

**To Make 2-Minute Flatbread with Sun-Dried Tomatoes & Onions:**
To the Basic Bread, omit garlic and rosemary and add 4 chopped sun-dried tomatoes and 1/3 cup chopped green onions. Everything else remains the same.

**To Make 2-Minute Flatbread with Green Onions & Parsley:**
To the Basic Bread, omit garlic and rosemary and add 1/2 cup chopped green onions and 2 tablespoons minced parsley. Everything else remains the same.

**To Make 2-Minute Flatbread with Chiles & Cheese:**
Omit the rosemary and add 1 can (4 ounces) diced green chiles and 1/2 cup (2 ounces) grated Jack cheese. Everything else remains the same.

# Old-Fashioned Chewy Pretzels

*Children love these old-fashioned pretzels with the different toppings. As the dough does not need to rise, these can be prepared in, literally, minutes.*

1 envelope dry yeast
1/2 cup lukewarm water (105°)
1 teaspoon sugar

1 cup lukewarm water (105°)
1 teaspoon sugar
1/4 teaspoon salt
4 cups flour

Topping:
1 egg, beaten
onion flakes, poppy seeds, grated Parmesan cheese, or sesame seeds

In the large bowl of an electric mixer, soften yeast in 1/2 cup lukewarm water and 1 teaspoon sugar until yeast starts to bubble. (If yeast does not bubble, it is inactive and should be discarded.) Beat in the remaining water, sugar, salt and flour until blended. With a dough hook, knead the dough until it is soft and smooth, about 2 minutes.

Dough does not need to rise. Divide dough into 16 pieces and roll each piece into a 1/4-inch thick rope. Shape into a pretzel, pinch ends down and place, seam side down, on a very lightly greased cookie sheet. Brush tops with beaten egg and sprinkle with topping of your choice.

Bake in a 400° preheated oven for about 15 minutes or until lightly browned. Makes 16 fun pretzels.

# Cream Cheese with Peaches

1/2 pound light cream cheese, softened
1 cup canned, drained sliced peaches, pureed in blender or processor
1 tablespoon light sour cream

In your electric mixer bowl, beat together all the ingredients until blended. Place in a crock or bowl and refrigerate. Yields about 2 cups.

# Old-Fashioned Sticky Raisin Pecan Buns

*Over the years, I thought of giving you this recipe, but decided against it each time. So many are intimidated with using yeast, and of course, it does take a little more time. In this recipe, I knead the dough at the very soft stage with the mixer and then add a little additional flour to make a soft dough. Results have always been excellent. Why am I including it now? Because this is a true comfort food and I thought you should at least have the recipe, if and when the spirit moves you.*

| | |
|---|---|
| 1 | package dry yeast |
| 1/2 | cup warm water (105°) |
| 1 | teaspoon sugar |
| | |
| 1/2 | cup warm milk (105°) |
| 1/2 | cup butter, melted |
| 1/2 | cup sugar |
| 1/2 | teaspoon salt |
| 2 | eggs |
| | |
| 4 1/2 | cups flour |

In the large bowl of an electric mixer, soften yeast in water and sugar and allow to rest for 5 or 10 minutes or until yeast starts to foam. (If the yeast does not foam, it is inactive and should be discarded.) Beat in the next 5 ingredients until blended. Beat in 4 cups of flour, 1 cup at a time, and continue beating for 4 minutes. Beat in the last 1/2 cup of flour to form a soft dough. Place dough in an oiled bowl and turn to oil top. Allow to rest in a warm place until doubled in bulk, about 1 hour.

Meanwhile, prepare Sticky Topping and spread evenly into a 9x13-inch baking pan. Punch dough down and roll out to a 12x18-inch rectangle. Spread dough with Cinnamon Raisin Filling and roll up tightly, on the 18-inch side, like a jelly roll. With a sharp knife, cut into 12 buns (1 1/2-inches, each) and place evenly into prepared pan. Cover pan with plastic wrap and allow to rise again, in a warm place, until doubled, about 1 hour.

Remove plastic wrap. Bake at 350° for about 30 minutes, or until top is lightly browned. Allow to cool in pan for 15 minutes, and then invert onto a cookie sheet, to get the syrup on top. Cut into 12 large buns.

Sticky Topping:
| | |
|---|---|
| 1/2 | cup melted butter |
| 3/4 | cup dark brown sugar |
| 1 | cup chopped pecans |

Heat together all the ingredients until sugar is melted, about 1 minute.

Cinnamon Raisin Filling:
| | |
|---|---|
| 1/3 | cup sugar |
| 2 | teaspoons ground cinnamon |
| 1/2 | cup yellow raisins |

Toss together all the ingredients until blended.

# Sour Cream Biscuits with Dill

| | |
|---|---|
| 1 3/4 | cups all-purpose flour |
| 2 | teaspoons baking powder |
| 1 | teaspoon baking soda |
| | pinch of salt and sugar |
| 4 | tablespoons butter |
| | |
| 1 | teaspoon dried dill weed |
| 2/3 | cup sour cream |
| 1/4 | cup milk |

In the large bowl of an electric mixer, beat together first group of ingredients, until mixture resembles coarse meal. Stir together the remaining ingredients, and add, all at once, stirring lightly, until mixture forms a soft dough. Do not overmix.

On a floured pastry cloth, pat dough out into a 1/2-inch thick circle. Cut into rounds with a 3-inch biscuit cutter. Gather scraps and cut into additional rounds. Place rounds on an ungreased cookie sheet and bake at 425° for about 15 minutes, or until biscuits are golden. Yields 8.

# Biscuits with Chiles & Cheese

| | |
|---|---|
| 1 1/2 | cups all-purpose flour |
| 2 | teaspoons baking powder |
| 1 | teaspoon baking soda |
| | pinch of salt |
| 3 | tablespoons butter |
| | |
| 1 | can (4 ounces) diced green chiles |
| 3 | ounces sharp cheddar cheese, grated |
| 1 | cup sour cream |

In the large bowl of an electric mixer, beat together first group of ingredients, until mixture resembles coarse meal. Stir together the remaining ingredients, and add, all at once, stirring lightly, until mixture forms a soft dough. Do not overmix.

On a floured pastry cloth, pat dough out into a 1/2-inch-thick circle. Cut into rounds with a 3-inch biscuit cutter. Gather scraps and cut into additional rounds. Place rounds on an ungreased cookie sheet and bake at 425° for about 15 minutes, or until biscuits are golden. Yields 8.

# Easiest & Best Brunch Danish Crescents with Raisins & Walnuts

*These are the most delicious little Danish that are great with coffee. They do not contain yeast but they taste and look as if they did. The dough is versatile as it can be used for savory pastries when made with onions and cheese. (See following recipe for Onion & Cheese Crescents.)*

**Basic Dough:**
- 1    cup cottage cheese
- 3    ounces butter (3/4 stick), softened
- 1    cup flour

**Walnut Raisin Filling:**
- 1/2    cup finely chopped walnuts
- 1/2    cup sugar
- 1/2    cup finely chopped raisins
- 1    teaspoon cinnamon

     cinnamon sugar for topping

Beat together cottage cheese and butter until blended. Beat in flour until blended. Remove dough to floured wax paper and shape into a ball. Divide dough into three parts. On a floured pastry cloth, roll each part out to measure a 10-inch circle.

Combine filling ingredients until blended. Sprinkle 1/3 the filling evenly over the dough. Cut dough into 8 triangular wedges, by cutting in half, again and again. Roll each triangle from the wide end toward the point and curve into a crescent. Sprinkle with cinnamon sugar and place on a lightly buttered cookie sheet. Repeat with remaining dough.

Bake at 350° for about 30 to 35 minutes, or until tops are golden brown. Remove from pan and allow to cool on a brown paper bag. Yields 24 crescents.

**To Make Cinnamon Sugar:**
In a glass jar with a tight-fitting lid, shake together 1 cup sugar and 4 teaspoons cinnamon. Unused cinnamon sugar can be stored for months. Nice to keep on hand to sprinkle on pancakes, waffles, fresh fruit, etc.

# Onion & Cheese Crescents for Soup and Salad

*This is a delightful bread to accompany soup or salad. Serve these warm and no need to serve with butter.*

| | |
|---|---|
| 1 | cup cottage cheese |
| 3 | ounces butter (3/4 stick), softened |
| 1 | cup flour |
| | |
| 2 | tablespoons grated Parmesan cheese |
| 1 | tablespoon dried onion flakes |

**Topping:**

| | |
|---|---|
| 2 | tablespoons melted butter |
| 3 | tablespoons grated Parmesan cheese |

Beat together cottage cheese and butter until blended. Beat in flour until blended. Beat in cheese and onions until blended. Remove dough to floured wax paper and shape into a ball. Divide dough into three parts. On a floured pastry cloth, roll each part out to measure a 10-inch circle.

Cut dough into 8 triangular wedges, by cutting in half, again and again. Roll each triangle from the wide end toward the point and curve into a crescent. Brush lightly with melted butter and sprinkle with a little grated cheese. Place crescents on a lightly buttered baking sheet and repeat with the remaining dough.

Bake at 350° for about 30 to 35 minutes, or until tops are golden brown. Remove from pan and allow to cool on a brown paper bag. Yields 24 crescents.

**Variations:**
Sprinkle top with poppy seeds, sesame seeds or rye seeds in addition to cheese.

# Westphalian Pumpernickel with Parmesan

*I first tasted this, it seems eons ago, at the old Brown Derby in Beverly Hills. It still is a lovely accompaniment to soups or salads. This pumpernickel is as thinly sliced and as dark as you could ever want.*

- **12** slices Westphalian pumpernickel (from the refrigerated section in your market. It is very, very thinly sliced.)

- **6** teaspoons butter
- **12** teaspoons grated Parmesan cheese
- **12** teaspoons finely chopped chives

This is marvellous with salads and soups. Simply butter the bread. Sprinkle each slice with 1 teaspoon Parmesan cheese and 1 teaspoon chives. Broil for a few seconds until cheese is bubbly and bread crisped. Yields 12 slices.

# Low-Calorie Cottage Cheese & Chive Spread

*Cottage cheese can be whipped up to the texture of sour cream. It is a very benign spread. It will sparkle a slice of bread or a baked potato or a raw vegetable. The non-fat cottage cheese is the biggest boon. It is every bit as tasty as the regular or low-fat cottage cheese with the plus, it is very low in calories. Other herbs can be used but chives are a must.*

- **1** cup non-fat cottage cheese
- **1** tablespoon lemon juice
- **1/4** cup chopped chives

In a food processor, beat cottage cheese and lemon juice until mixture is smooth. Add the chives and blend until chives are very finely chopped. Yields 1 1/4 cups.

# Whipped Honey Cream Cheese

- **4** ounces light cream cheese, softened
- **2** tablespoons light sour cream
- **1/4** cup orange honey
- **1** teaspoon grated orange zest (the orange part of the peel)

Beat cream cheese and sour cream until creamy and light. Add honey and orange zest and beat until fluffy. Refrigerate in a bowl or a crock. Yields about 1 1/4 cups.

## Sour Cream Corn Bread with Chiles & Cheese

*To the basic bread can be added 3/4 cup of corn kernels, fresh or frozen. This adds a little texture to the bread. Chiles and cheese can also be omitted, if you are looking for a simple, basic corn bread.*

| | |
|---|---|
| 2 | eggs |
| 1 | cup low-fat sour cream |
| 1 3/4 | cups milk |
| 1/4 | cup sugar |
| 6 | tablespoons melted butter |
| | |
| 2 | cups yellow cornmeal |
| 3/4 | cup flour |
| 1 | tablespoon baking powder |
| | |
| 1 | can (4 ounces) diced green chiles |
| 1 | cup grated Jack cheese |

Beat together first 5 ingredients until blended. Combine next 3 ingredients and add, all at once, beating until blended. Stir in the chiles and cheese. Pour batter into a greased 9x13-inch baking pan and bake at 350° for 45 minutes or until top is golden brown. Serves 12.

## Wimbledon Cream Scones with Currants

*This is a variation of my Victorian Cream Scones. Serve it with Devonshire Cream and Strawberries for an English breakfast treat. This recipe is a little more moist and tender than the traditional scone. Chopped dried apricots can be substituted for the currants. As a variation, add 2 tablespoons of toasted chopped almonds.*

| | |
|---|---|
| 3 | cups flour |
| 2 | teaspoons baking powder |
| 1/4 | teaspoon salt |
| 1/2 | cup sugar |
| 1/2 | cup cold butter or margarine, cut into 4 pieces |
| | |
| 1/3 | cup dried currants |
| | |
| 2 | eggs |
| 1 | cup cream |

In the large bowl of an electric mixer, beat together first 5 ingredients until butter is finely dispersed. Beat in currants. Thoroughly beat together eggs and cream and, with the motor running, slowly add to the flour mixture just until blended. Do not overbeat. Spread dough evenly into a greased 10-inch springform pan. Bake at 350° for 30 minutes or until top is golden brown. To serve, cut into thin wedges. Yields 12 slices.

# Quick & Easy Maple Oatmeal Pudding

*Here's a brand new recipe for you. I have given you many noodle puddings, bread puddings and rice puddings in the past, but I have never given you an oatmeal pudding...partly because I just thought this one up. My Mom used to make farina pudding when we were young, (I must confess it was not one of my favorites) but the idea is a good one. Here I make it with oats, serve it with fresh, stewed or dried fruits or with just a hint of maple syrup. Raisins are optional, but a nice addition. Other dried fruits can be substituted. Depending on how much nutrition you wish to pack, water can be substituted for the milk. This is a solid breakfast.*

|       |                                        |
|-------|----------------------------------------|
| 2     | cups quick-cooking oats                |
| 2     | eggs                                   |
| 2     | cups non-fat milk                      |
| 4     | tablespoons sugar (more or less to taste) |
| 1/3   | cup raisins (optional)                 |
| 1     | teaspoon pure maple extract            |
| 1/2   | teaspoon vanilla                       |
|       |                                        |
| 1     | teaspoon cinnamon sugar                |

Beat together first group of ingredients until blended. Pour mixture into a lightly greased 10x2-inch round baking pan, sprinkle with cinnamon sugar, and bake at 350° for 30 to 35 minutes, or until pudding is set and top looks dry. To serve, spoon into cereal bowls, and serve with a little milk and fresh or stewed fruit, applesauce, strawberries with a dollup of yogurt or with just a drizzle of maple syrup. Serves 6.

# Old Fashioned Country Marmalade

*I made up this little recipe when I was a Brownie leader years ago. I wanted something easy for my Brownie girls to make as a little gift for their families for the holidays. The girls squeezed the lemons, broke the walnuts by hand, stirred the marmalade, spooned it into pretty jars and made the labels. I cut the cherries. In a few days, so many parents called asking for the recipe, I decided to make it a bonafide recipe. It is still one of my favorites.*

|       |                                             |
|-------|---------------------------------------------|
| 3     | pounds orange marmalade                     |
| 1     | jar (8 ounces) Maraschino cherries, drained and cut into pieces |
| 3     | tablespoons fresh lemon juice               |
| 1/2   | cup walnuts, coarsely broken                |
| 1/2   | cup golden raisins                          |
| 1/2   | cup currants                                |

Simply mix all the ingredients together and spoon the mixture into pretty jars. Yields about 8 cups.

# Casseroles

# Easy, Easy Tamale Casserole

*This is a tasty dish for lunch or dinner. Also, it travels well, and is a good choice for a pot luck supper. Assemble it earlier in the day and bake it before serving.*

| | |
|---|---|
| 1 | large onion finely chopped |
| 3 | cloves garlic, minced |
| 1 | teaspoon butter or margarine |
| | |
| 1 | pound ground beef or ground turkey |
| 1 | can (1 pound 12 ounces) crushed tomatoes in tomato puree |
| 2 | tablespoons chili powder (or more to taste) |
| 1/2 | teaspoon cumin powder (or more to taste) |
| | pepper to taste |
| | |
| 12 | frozen tamales (about 3 ounces, each) defrosted and cut in half |
| 1/2 | cup low-fat sour cream |
| 1/2 | cup grated cheddar cheese (2 ounces) |
| 1/2 | cup chopped green onions |

Saute onion and garlic in butter until onion is soft. Add ground beef and continue sauteing, crumbling the beef, until the meat is cooked through. Add tomatoes and seasonings. Cook sauce for 20 minutes.

In a 9x13-inch baking pan, place the tamale slices. Cover tamales evenly with the sauce. Mix sour cream, cheddar cheese and green onions and drop by tablespoonful over the sauce. Bake casserole in a 350° oven for 30 or 35 minutes or until mixture is piping hot and cheese is melted. Serves 6 for dinner, 12 for lunch.

# Red Hot Lentil Chili

*Lentils are becoming more popular in recipes other than soup. Here, I spice them with chili, cumin and cayenne pepper. An interesting dish and simple to prepare.*

| | |
|---|---|
| 1 | package (1 pound) lentils, rinsed and picked over for particles |
| 2 | large onions, chopped |
| 6 | cloves garlic, minced |
| 3 | carrots, grated |
| 1 | can (28 ounces) crushed tomatoes in puree |
| 8 | cups chicken broth |
| 4 | tablespoons chili powder |
| 2 | teaspoons ground cumin |
| 2 | teaspoons sugar |
| 1 | teaspoon oregano flakes |
| 1/8 | teaspoon cayenne pepper |
| | salt and pepper to taste |

In a Dutch oven casserole, stir together all the ingredients and bring to a boil. Lower heat, cover pan and simmer mixture for about 1 hour or until lentils are tender. Serve in deep bowls with corn bread or biscuits. Serves 8.

# Paella Darling

*This is a very delicious paella more in the Mexican mood than its Spanish cousin. This can be prepared with cooked chicken pieces. Roast 1 fryer chicken (about 2 1/2 pounds), cut into serving pieces and well-seasoned with onion, garlic and paprika, for 1 hour 10 minutes, or until tender. Bury the chicken into the rice mixture and heat through before serving. I prefer roasting the chicken separately for better flavor. Cooking the chicken in the broth gives it a soupy taste.*

|       |                                            |
|-------|--------------------------------------------|
| 2     | large onions, chopped                      |
| 1     | tablespoon oil                             |
| 1     | can (4 ounces) diced green chiles          |
| 2     | tomatoes, chopped coarsely                 |
|       |                                            |
| 1 1/2 | cups raw rice                              |
| 1 1/2 | cups chicken broth                         |
|       | pepper to taste                            |
| 1/4   | teaspoon ground cumin                      |
| 1     | teaspoon ground turmeric                   |
|       |                                            |
| 3     | cups cooked chicken or turkey, cut into 3/4-inch dice |

In a Dutch oven casserole, saute onions in oil until onions are transparent. Do not brown. Add chile and tomatoes and heat through. Add next 5 ingredients, cover pan and cook over low heat until rice is tender and liquid is absorbed, about 30 minutes. Stir in the chicken and heat through. Fluff with a fork and serve. Serves 6.

*Note:* ♥ *To the basic recipe, you can add 1 package (10 ounces) hot, cooked green peas over the top.*

# Easy Boston Baked Beans

*This is a nice, easy casserole to serve for a backyard picnic or barbecue. The flavor is really delicious even though I have omitted the bacon.*

| | |
|---|---|
| 1 | onion, chopped |
| 1 | tablespoon oil |
| | |
| 1/4 | cup dark molasses |
| 1/4 | cup dark brown sugar |
| 1/2 | cup chili sauce |
| 1/4 | cup beef broth |
| 2 | tablespoons spicy brown mustard |
| 4 | cans (1 pound, each) oven baked beans |

In an ovenproof Dutch oven casserole, saute onion in oil until onion is transparent. Stir in the remaining ingredients until blended. Cover pan with its lid (if it's ovenproof), or tightly with foil, and bake at 350° for 30 minutes. Remove cover and stir. (Add a little more broth if beans appear to be dry.) Continue baking for another 30 minutes. Serves 12 to 16.

# Red Beans & Pink Rice

*Often, my Mom would make this casserole into a complete meal with the addition of cubes of chuck. These were cooked separately with the beans. Rice was also cooked separately and then combined with the beans. Using the canned kidney beans saves hours of preparation time. This is also excellent with garbanzos.*

| | |
|---|---|
| 1 | onion, chopped |
| 3 | cloves garlic, minced |
| 2 | tablespoons oil |
| | |
| 1 | can (1 pound) red kidney beans, rinsed and drained |
| 2 | tomatoes, fresh or canned, chopped |
| 2 | tablespoons tomato sauce |
| 3 | cups chicken broth |
| 1 1/2 | cups long grain rice |
| | salt and pepper to taste |

In a Dutch oven casserole, saute onion and garlic in oil until onion is soft. Stir in the remaining ingredients, cover pan, and simmer mixture until rice is tender and liquid is absorbed, about 30 minutes. Serves 8.

**To Make Garbanzos with Pink Rice:**
Substitute 1 can (1 pound) garbanzos, rinsed and drained, for the red beans.

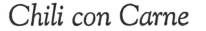

# Chili con Carne

*Who doesn't love a "bowl of red?" There are probably as many recipes for chili as there are cooks. It has been made with any number of ingredients and spices. Many have battled over what should or should not be included. Purists believe beans are an "abomination." This is a great recipe, with or without the beans.*

|       |                                                      |
|-------|------------------------------------------------------|
| 3     | onions, chopped                                      |
| 6     | cloves garlic, minced                                |
| 2     | tablespoons oil                                      |
| 3     | pounds boneless chuck steak, coarsely ground ("chili grind") |
|       |                                                      |
| 2     | cans (10 1/2 ounces, each) beef broth                |
| 3     | tablespoons Masa Harina (finely ground corn meal)    |
|       |                                                      |
| 4     | tablespoons chili powder (or more to taste)          |
| 1     | tablespoon cumin powder                              |
| 1     | tablespoon paprika                                   |
| 1     | tablespoon dried oregano flakes                      |
| 1     | can (16 ounces) tomato sauce                         |
| 2     | teaspoons sugar                                      |
| 1/4   | teaspoon red pepper flakes, (or more to taste)       |
| 1     | can (1 pound) red kidney beans, rinsed and drained   |
| 1     | can (7 ounces) diced green chiles                    |

In a Dutch oven casserole, saute onions and garlic in oil until onions are softened. Add the beef and cook until the meat loses its pinkness. Stir beef broth with Masa Harina and add to casserole. Stir in the remaining ingredients and simmer mixture, partially uncovered, for 45 minutes, or until meat is tender and mixture is thickened. Serve with Biscuits with Chile & Cheese or Corn Bread. Serves 8.

# Baked Beans in Sweet & Hot Barbecue Sauce

|       |                                                      |
|-------|------------------------------------------------------|
| 3     | cans (1 pound, each) white beans, rinsed and drained |
| 1     | cup ketchup                                          |
| 1     | cup chili sauce                                      |
| 1/2   | cup beef broth                                       |
| 1/2   | cup brown sugar                                      |
| 1/4   | cup dark molasses                                    |
| 3     | tablespoons vinegar                                  |
| 1     | tablespoon Dijon mustard                            |
| 3     | shakes cayenne pepper, or to taste                   |

In an oven-proof Dutch oven casserole (with an oven-proof lid,) stir together all the ingredients, cover pan and bake at 350° for about 1 hour. Check about half-way through baking and add a little broth, if casserole appears dry. Nice with barbecued chicken or ribs. Serves 8.

# Old-Fashioned Noodle Pudding
## with Apples, Raisins & Orange

*Here, the old-fashioned noodle pudding is heightened with the tasty addition of apples, raisins and orange. It is an informal dish and great to serve with roast chicken on a Sunday night when family and friends are visiting.*

| | |
|---|---|
| 8 | ounces medium noodles, cooked and drained |
| 6 | tablespoons butter, melted |
| | |
| 3 | eggs |
| 3/4 | cup sugar |
| 1 | cup low-fat sour cream |
| | |
| 2 | medium apples, peeled, cored and grated |
| 3 | tablespoons grated orange |
| 1/3 | cup yellow raisins |
| 1/2 | teaspoon vanilla |
| | |
| 1 | tablespoon cinnamon sugar |

In an 8x12-inch baking pan, toss cooked noodles with melted butter. Beat together next 3 ingredients until blended. Stir in next 4 ingredients until blended. Pour mixture over the noodles and toss until evenly mixed. Sprinkle top with cinnamon sugar. Bake at 350° until custard is set and top is browned. Serves 10.

# Noodle Casserole with Tomatoes and Onions

| | |
|---|---|
| 1/2 | pound wide noodles, cooked tender and drained |
| 2 | tablespoons melted margarine |
| | |
| 1 | can (1 pound) stewed tomatoes, drained. Reserve juice. |
| 1/2 | cup of reserved tomato juice |
| 8 | green onions, finely minced |
| 3 | cloves garlic, minced |
| 2 | tablespoons parsley leaves (fresh), chopped |
| 1 | cup Jack cheese, grated (4 ounces) |
| 1/4 | cup Parmesan cheese, grated |
| | pepper to taste |

Cook noodles al dente (tender but still firm). Toss noodles in melted margarine. Set aside. Stir together remaining ingredients. In an 8x12-non-stick pan, layer 1/2 the noodles and 1/2 of the tomato mixture. Top with remaining noodles and tomato mixture. Bake in a 350° oven for 30 minutes or until heated through and top is browned. Serves 8.

# Orange Sweet Potato Pudding with Pecans

*Sweet potato puddings are not low in calories, but for a very special holiday dinner, you can splurge a little. Keep the portions small. This is just for tasting.*

- 3    eggs
- 1/2   cup low-fat sour cream
- 1/2   cup frozen orange juice concentrate, defrosted
- 1/4   cup sugar
- 1/4   cup orange fruit spread or orange marmalade

- 1    can (1 pound) sweet potatoes, drained and mashed

- 1    cup vanilla wafer crumbs
- 1/4   cup chopped pecans

Beat eggs with sour cream, orange juice concentrate, sugar and orange fruit spread until mixture is blended. Beat in mashed sweet potatoes and vanilla wafer crumbs until blended.

Place mixture in a buttered 8x12-inch baking dish. Sprinkle top with chopped pecans and gently press them into the top. Bake in a 350° oven for about 50 minutes or until puffed and golden. Serves 12.

#  Cheese Blintze Casserole

*Actually, cheese blintzes are good for breakfast, lunch or a light dinner. They are truly satisfying with a little low-fat sour cream and finely chopped fresh fruit.*

- 12   frozen cheese blintzes, thawed

- 4    eggs
- 1    pint low-fat sour cream
- 1    teaspoon vanilla
- 1/4   cup sugar
- 1/2   cup golden raisins, plumped in orange juice
- 1/2   small orange, grated. Use fruit, juice and peel.
-     cinnamon

Place blintzes in a lightly oiled 9x13-inch non-stick baking pan. Beat eggs with sour cream, vanilla and sugar. Add raisins and orange. Pour mixture over blintzes. Sprinkle top with cinnamon to taste. Bake in a 350° oven for 45 minutes, until custard is set and top is golden. Serve with a dollup of low-fat sour cream and sliced strawberries. Strawberry fruit spread is good too. Serves 6.

# Noodle Pudding with Cottage Cheese & Chives

*This can be assembled earlier in the day and stored in the refrigerator. Bring to room temperature before heating. A good choice for a light meatless dinner.*

- 1/2 pound wide noodles, cooked tender and drained
- 2 tablespoons melted butter or margarine

- 4 eggs
- 1 cup low-fat sour cream
- 1 cup non-fat cottage cheese

- 1/4 cup grated onion
- 2 tablespoons finely chopped parsley
- 1/2 cup chopped chives
- 1/3 cup Parmesan cheese, grated
- pepper to taste

Toss noodles in melted butter. Beat eggs with sour cream and cottage cheese until well blended. Add remaining ingredients and beat until blended. Combine noodles and egg mixture and toss to mix well. Place mixture into a buttered 9x13-inch baking pan and bake in a 350° oven for about 45 minutes or until pudding is set and top is browned. Serve with Quick-Cook Tomato Sauce on the side. Serves 6 for dinner or 12 as an accompaniment.

Quick-Cook Tomato Sauce:
- 1 can (1 pound 12 ounces) crushed tomatoes in tomato puree
- 2 tablespoons onion flakes
- 1/8 teaspoon coarse ground garlic powder
- 1 teaspoon sugar
- 1 teaspoon olive oil
- 1 teaspoon, each, sweet basil flakes and Italian Herb Seasoning

In a saucepan, cook together all the ingredients for 5 minutes.

# Cabbage Rolls in Sweet & Sour Tomato Sauce

*I recommend using the ground turkey instead of the beef. It reduces the calories and fat content with very little change in taste. Stuffed cabbage is one of the true comfort foods, very delicious and satisfying. I hope your children like it, too.*

| | |
|---|---|
| 1 | head cabbage (1 pound) |
| 1 | pound lean ground beef or ground turkey |
| 2 | cups cooked rice |
| 1 | large onion, grated |
| 1 | clove garlic, minced |
| 1 | egg |
| 1/4 | cup cold water |
| | pepper to taste |

Wash cabbage and remove the core. In a saucepan, stand it up and cook it in boiling water for 10 to 12 minutes. Remove and refresh under cold water. Carefully remove the outer leaves. When the leaves get too small to roll, chop them finely and place them in a large Dutch oven casserole.

Combine the remaining ingredients and mix until blended. Place about 2 tablespoons meat mixture on bottom of cabbage leaf. Tuck in the sides and roll it up. Place rolls in Dutch oven, seam-side down. Pour Sweet and Sour Tomato Sauce over the rolls, cover pan and simmer for about 1 hour over low heat, or until cabbage is tender. Makes about 12 cabbage rolls and serves 6 generously.

Sweet & Sour Tomato Sauce:

| | |
|---|---|
| 1 | teaspoon oil |
| 1 | can (1 pound) stewed tomatoes, chopped. Do not drain. |
| 2 | cans (8 ounces, each) tomato sauce |
| 1 | can (10 1/2 ounces) beef broth |
| 4 | tablespoons lemon juice |
| 1 | tablespoon sugar |
| | salt and pepper to taste |

Stir together all the ingredients until blended.

# New Orleans Bread Pudding with Apricots & Pecans & Bourbon Street Sauce

|       |                                                              |
|-------|--------------------------------------------------------------|
| 3     | eggs                                                         |
| 1 1/2 | cups sugar                                                   |
| 4     | teaspoons vanilla                                           |
| 4     | tablespoons melted butter                                  |
| 3     | cups milk                                                   |
|       |                                                             |
| 12    | slices stale (or toasted) raisin bread, crusts removed and cubed, about 12 ounces |
| 4     | ounces chopped dried apricots (1 cup)                      |
| 1/2   | cup chopped pecans                                         |
| 1     | tablespoon cinnamon sugar                                 |

In a large bowl, beat together first 5 ingredients until blended. Toss in bread and allow to stand until liquid is evenly absorbed. Stir in apricots. Place mixture into a buttered 9x13-inch baking pan and sprinkle top with pecans and cinnamon sugar. Press pecans gently into the top to avoid burning. Bake at 325° for about 1 hour or until pudding is set and golden brown. To serve, cut into squares and serve with a spoonful of Bourbon Street Sauce on top. Whipped Creme Fraiche Vanilla is also delicious. Serves 10.

Bourbon Street Sauce:

|     |                      |
|-----|----------------------|
| 1   | cup sugar            |
| 1/2 | cup butter           |
| 2   | tablespoons water    |
|     |                      |
| 1   | egg, well beaten     |
| 1/4 | cup Bourbon whiskey  |

In the top of a double boiler, over hot water, heat together first 3 ingredients until sugar is melted. Stir in beaten egg and bourbon and cook and stir until sauce is slightly thickened and mixture reaches 170° on a candy thermometer. Do not over cook. Yields about 1 1/4 cups sauce.

Whipped Creme Fraiche Vanilla:

|     |                                                     |
|-----|-----------------------------------------------------|
| 3/4 | cup cream, whipped                                  |
| 1   | tablespoon sugar                                    |
| 1   | teaspoon vanilla                                    |
| 1/4 | cup sour cream                                      |
| 2   | teaspoons Bourbon. (Rum is also good with other desserts.) |

Beat cream with sugar and vanilla until stiff. Beat in sour cream and bourbon until blended.

# Artichoke, Tomato & Potato Frittata

*Frittatas are densely filled omelets that can be made with an infinite variety of fillings. They can take on the character of any cuisine and can be adapted to fit any menu. I can write a whole cookbook on frittatas. They are so versatile as they can be served for breakfast, brunch, lunch or dinner and are also fine for snacking. Frittatas are easy to prepare and are great when you are serving a large group.*

|     |     |
| --- | --- |
| 2   | jars (6 1/2 ounces, each) marinated artichoke hearts, drained |
| 1   | can (1 pound) baby sliced potatoes, rinsed and drained |
| 2   | cups non-fat cottage cheese |
| 1/3 | cup grated Parmesan cheese |
| 2   | eggs, beaten |
| 1/3 | cup minced chives |
| 4   | tablespoons dried bread crumbs |
| 1   | tablespoon chopped parsley |
| 1/2 | teaspoon dried rosemary, crumbled |
|     |     |
| 1   | large tomato, very thinly sliced |
| 1   | tablespoon grated Parmesan cheese |

In a large bowl, stir together first group of ingredients until blended. Spread mixture evenly into an oiled 9x13-inch baking pan. Place tomatoes evenly on top and sprinkle cheese over all. Bake at 350° for 55 to 60 minutes, or until frittata is set and top is browned. To serve, cut into 24 2-inch squares. Yields 12 generous servings.

**To make a Greek-Styled Frittata:**
Add 3 or 4 ounces of crumbled feta cheese and substitute dill weed for the rosemary.

**To make a French-Style Frittata:**
Add 3 or 4 ounces of crumbled chevre cheese and substitute thyme for the rosemary.

# Noodle Lasagna Italienne

*Making lasagna with egg noodles gives a totally different character to this dish. Entire casserole can be assembled earlier in the day and stored in the refrigerator. Bring to room temperature before reheating.*

3/4 pound wide egg noodles, cooked until tender and drained

1 onion, finely chopped
2 cloves garlic, minced
1 teaspoon oil
1 pound ground beef or ground turkey

1 can (1 pound 12 ounces) crushed tomatoes in puree
1 teaspoon sugar
1 teaspoon Italian Herb Seasoning
  pepper to taste

1 pound low-fat Ricotta cheese
3 eggs
1/2 cup grated Parmesan cheese
1 teaspoon sweet basil flakes
1/4 cup chopped chives

Saute onion and garlic in oil until onion is soft. Add ground beef (or turkey) and continue sauteing, crumbling the beef, until beef is cooked through. Add tomatoes, sugar and seasonings and simmer gently for 20 minutes. Set sauce aside.

Beat together the Ricotta cheese and next 4 ingredients until blended.

Spread a thin layer of sauce in a 9x13-inch porcelain baking pan. Place half the noodles over the sauce. Follow with half the cheese mixture and half the sauce. Repeat, layering the remaining noodles, cheese mixture and sauce. Sprinkle top with a little more grated Parmesan cheese. Bake casserole at 350° for about 35 minutes or until piping hot. Serves 8.

# Mexican Strata with Chiles and Cheese

6 eggs
1/2 cup milk
1/2 cup light cream

1 can (4 ounces) diced green chiles
1/2 cup Jack cheese, grated (2 ounces)
2 tablespoons grated Parmesan cheese
1/3 cup chopped chives
pepper to taste

2 medium tomatoes, peeled, seeded and thinly sliced
1 tablespoon grated Parmesan cheese

Beat together first 3 ingredients until blended. Stir in next 5 ingredients until blended. Pour egg mixture into a lightly oiled 8x12-inch non-stick baking pan. Lay tomato slices on top and sprinkle with grated cheese. Bake in a 350° oven for about 40 minutes or until eggs are set and top is puffy and golden brown. Serve with a dollup of low-fat sour cream on top (optional). Serves 6.

# Noodle & Spinach Pudding

*Serving this with Quick-Cook Tomato Sauce, makes this casserole a good choice for an evening when you are planning a vegetarian meal.*

1 package (8 ounces) medium noodles, cooked tender and drained
2 packages (10 ounces each) chopped spinach, defrosted and drained

1 tablespoon butter or margarine
1 medium onion, grated
3 eggs, well beaten
1 cup low-fat sour cream
1 cup non-fat cottage cheese
1/3 cup grated Parmesan cheese
pinch of pepper and nutmeg

Cook noodles and set aside. Defrost spinach, place in a strainer and press to drain. Saute onion in butter until onion is tender. In a large bowl, stir together all the ingredients until blended. Place mixture in a lightly oiled 8x12-inch non-stick baking pan. Cover pan with foil and bake for 30 minutes in a 350° oven. Remove foil and bake for 15 minutes longer, or until top is browned. Serve with a spoonful of Quick-Cook Tomato Sauce (Page 51) on the side. Serves 6 for dinner or 12 as an accompaniment.

# Vegetarian Lasagna Pie with Spinach & Cheese

*Lasagna needs no introduction. It is a long-time favorite. Made with spinach and cottage cheese, it is exceedingly light and delicious.*

  6 lasagna noodles, cooked in boiling water until tender and drained

Spinach Filling:
  2 packages (10 ounces, each) frozen chopped spinach, defrosted
    and pressed in a strainer to drain
  2 cups non-fat cottage cheese
  1/2 cup bread crumbs
  1/2 cup grated parmesan cheese
  2 eggs

Coat the bottom of a 9x13-inch baking pan with 1 cup of 5-Minute Tomato Sauce and place 3 noodles on the top. Mix together Spinach Filling ingredients until blended and spread evenly over the noodles. Place remaining 3 noodles on top and pour 5-Minute Tomato Sauce over all. Sprinkle top with a little extra grated Parmesan cheese. Cover pan with foil and bake at 350° for 40 minutes. Remove foil and continue baking for 20 minutes. Serves 10.

5-Minute Tomato Sauce:
  1 can (1 pound 12 ounces) crushed tomatoes in puree
  1 tablespoon olive oil
  2 tablespoons dried onion flakes
  1/4 teaspoon coarse grind garlic powder
  1 teaspoon sugar
  1 teaspoon, each, sweet basil flakes and Italian Herb Seasoning
    pinch of cayenne pepper
    salt and black pepper to taste

In a covered saucepan, simmer together all the ingredients for 5 minutes.

# Broccoli Frittata with Onions & Cheese

  2 packages (10 ounces, each) frozen chopped broccoli, defrosted
  2 eggs, beaten
  2 cups non-fat cottage cheese
  1/3 cup grated Parmesan cheese
  1/3 cup whole wheat bread crumbs
  1/3 cup chopped chives
    pepper to taste

In a large bowl, stir together all the ingredients. Spread mixture evenly in a 9x13-inch non-stick baking pan which has been lightly oiled. Sprinkle top with a little additional Parmesan cheese. Bake in a 350° oven for about 40 minutes or until frittata is set and top is golden brown. Serves 10 for lunch.

# Eggplant Lasagna Greenfield

*This superb eggplant recipe was given to me by a friend but it used almost 1 cup of olive oil. I have modified the technique and reduced the amount of oil out of deference to reducing calories and oil intake. Instead of frying the eggplant, I bake it. This is easier and uses practically no oil. I believe you will find the end result lighter and more delicious.*

|   |   |
|---|---|
| 2 | eggplants (about 1 pound, each) |
|   | pepper |
| 1 | teaspoon oil |
|   |   |
| 2 | eggs, beaten |
| 1 | pound low-fat Ricotta cheese |
| 1/4 | pound part skim milk Mozzarella cheese, grated |
| 1/2 | cup grated Parmesan cheese |
| 1/2 | teaspoon dried basil |
|   |   |
|   | Quick-Cook Tomato Sauce |
| 1 | tablespoon grated Parmesan cheese |

Peel and slice eggplant in 1/4-inch slices. Sprinkle with pepper. Place eggplant slices on a cookie sheet, brush lightly with oil, cover with foil and bake in a 400° oven for about 20 minutes or until eggplant slices are soft. Remove from oven and set aside.

Beat together eggs, cheeses and basil until blended. Set aside. In a 9x13-inch baking pan, layer Quick-Cook Tomato Sauce, eggplant and cheese mixture, starting and ending with the tomato sauce. Sprinkle top with additional Parmesan cheese. Bake at 375° for about 40 minutes or until piping hot. Serves 8.

Quick-Cook Tomato Sauce:

|   |   |
|---|---|
| 1 | can (1 pound 12 ounces) crushed tomatoes in puree |
| 1 | onion, very finely chopped |
| 3 | cloves garlic, minced |
| 1 | teaspoon, each sweet basil flakes and Italian Herb Seasoning |
| 1 | teaspoon olive oil |
| 1 | bay leaf |

In a saucepan, simmer together all the ingredients for 10 minutes. Remove bay leaf.

*Note:* ♥ *Eggplant can be prepared the day before and stored in the refrigerator.*
      ♥ *Entire casserole can be assembled earlier in the day and cooked in the evening.*

# Thai Rice with Peanuts & Scallions

*This is my translation of the Pad Thai Noodle Casserole made with rice. It is a delicious casserole and can be altered in many ways. Shrimp is a great substitution. When cooking the chicken or shrimp in the sauce, do not overcook. As this dish is an invention, I prepare it with long-grain rice. Sticky rice (short-grain) may not work well.*

- 2 cloves garlic, minced
- 1 tablespoon margarine
- 2 cups chicken broth
- 1 cup long-grain rice
  salt to taste

Chicken & Thai Sauce:
- 4 tablespoons ketchup
- 2 tablespoons sugar
- 3 tablespoons margarine
- 2 tablespoons "nampla" fish sauce. (Can substitute soy sauce but nampla is better.)
- 2 chicken breast halves, (about 4 ounces, each), boned and cut into small dice

- 1/4 cup chopped peanuts
- 1/2 cup chopped green onions

In a saucepan, saute garlic in margarine. Stir in the broth, rice and salt, cover pan and simmer mixture for about 30 minutes, or until rice is tender and liquid is absorbed.

Meanwhile, in a skillet, over high heat, cook together the next 5 ingredients, stirring, until chicken is opaque and sugar is melted, about 2 minutes. When rice is cooked, toss in the Chicken & Thai Sauce, peanuts, and green onions. Serves 4 generously.

# Country Spinach Frittata with Parmesan

- 2 packages (10 ounces, each) frozen chopped spinach, defrosted and drained in a strainer to press out the juice
- 2 cups non-fat cottage cheese
- 2 eggs
- 1/2 cup bread crumbs
- 1/2 cup grated Parmesan cheese

Stir together all the ingredients until blended. Spread mixture evenly in an oiled 9x13-inch baking pan and bake at 350° for about 1 hour or until top is golden brown. Cut into squares to serve. Serves 12.

## Linguini with Artichokes & Red Peppers

*This is an interesting casserole to take to a backyard picnic or barbecue. The colors are smashing and the taste delicious. Casserole can be prepared earlier in the day and stored in the refrigerator.*

- 8 eggs, beaten
- 2/3 cup grated Parmesan cheese
- 2 jars (7 ounces, each) marinated artichokes, cut into fourths. Do not drain.
- 6 marinated red peppers, cut into slivers
- 8 ounces linguini, cooked in boiling water until tender and drained
  salt and pepper to taste

In a large bowl, beat eggs with cheese until blended. Toss in the remaining ingredients until nicely mixed. Spread mixture evenly into a greased 9x13-inch baking pan and bake at 350° for about 50 minutes or until eggs are set and top is golden brown. Cut into squares to serve. Yields 12 servings.

## Baked Pastelle of Fettucine with Goat Cheese

- 1 pound fettucine, cooked in boiling water until tender and drained
- 2 cups crumbled goat cheese (8 ounces)
- 1/3 cup grated Parmesan cheese

- 2 onions, chopped
- 6 cloves garlic, minced
- 1 tablespoon olive oil
- 1 1/2 pounds ground beef

- 1 can (1 pound 12 ounces) Italian-style tomatoes, chopped. Do not drain.
- 1 can (6 ounces) tomato paste
- 1 teaspoon sugar
- 1 teaspoon sweet basil flakes
- 1 teaspoon Italian Herb Seasoning
  pinch cayenne pepper
  salt and black pepper to taste

Toss fettucine with cheeses and place evenly in an oiled 9x13-inch baking pan. In a Dutch oven casserole, saute onion and garlic in oil until onion is soft. Add the ground beef and cook and stir until meat is crumbled and loses its pinkness. Add the remaining ingredients to the casserole and simmer sauce for 20 minutes. Pour sauce evenly over the fettucine and sprinkle a little extra grated Parmesan cheese on top. Bake at 350° until heated through. Broil for a few seconds to brown the top. Serves 6.

## Baked Zitis with Tomato Meat Sauce & Cheese

1 pound zitis, cooked in boiling water until tender and drained
3/4 cup grated Parmesan cheese

Tomato Meat Sauce:
1 onion, chopped
6 cloves garlic, minced
1 tablespoon olive oil
1 pound ground beef

1 can (1 pound 12 ounces) crushed tomatoes in puree
3/4 teaspoon sweet basil flakes
1/2 teaspoon Italian Herb Seasoning
1 teaspoon sugar
pinch of cayenne pepper
salt and black pepper to taste

Toss zitis with cheese and spread evenly in an oiled 9x13-inch baking pan. In a Dutch oven casserole, saute onion and garlic in oil until onion is soft. Add the ground beef and cook and stir until meat is crumbled and loses its pinkness. Add the remaining ingredients to the casserole and simmer sauce for 10 minutes. Pour sauce evenly over the zitis and sprinkle top with a little more grated cheese. Bake at 350° until heated through. Broil for a few seconds to brown the top. Serves 6.

## Chicken with Mushrooms and Pink Rice

*This homey family dish is very much like the Spanish Arroz con Pollo. It is especially attractive and delicious.*

1 onion, finely chopped
4 shallots, minced
4 cloves garlic, minced
2 teaspoons oil
1/2 pound mushrooms, sliced

1 cup raw rice, long-grain
2 cups chicken broth
1/4 cup tomato sauce
1 teaspoon turmeric, 1/2 teaspoon cumin and pepper to taste

1 package (10 ounces) frozen green peas, defrosted
3 cups cooked, diced chicken

In a Dutch oven casserole, saute onion, shallots and garlic in oil until they are transparent. Add mushrooms and continue cooking until mushrooms are tender and liquid is absorbed, about 5 minutes. Add the next group of ingredients to the casserole and stir to mix. Cover pan and simmer mixture over low heat, until rice is tender and liquid is absorbed. Stir in the peas and chicken and heat through. Serves 4 or 5.

# Greek Chicken Casserole with Lemon Rice, Spinach & Feta Cheese

| | |
|---|---|
| 1 | onion, finely chopped |
| 2 | cloves garlic, minced |
| 2 | tablespoons olive oil |
| 1 | cup rice |
| 2 | cups chicken broth |
| | |
| 1 | package (10 ounces) frozen chopped spinach, drained |
| 4 | tablespoons lemon juice |
| 1/4 | cup chopped green onions |
| 1/4 | cup crumbled feta cheese |
| 1/3 | teaspoon dried dill weed |
| 2 | cups diced, cooked chicken |

In a Dutch oven casserole, saute onion and garlic in oil until onion is transparent. Stir in rice and chicken broth, cover pan, and simmer mixture for 30 minutes, or until rice is tender and liquid is absorbed. Meanwhile, in a bowl, toss together the remaining ingredients until nicely mixed. Stir spinach mixture into cooked rice and heat through. Serves 4.

# Ratatouille Howard

| | |
|---|---|
| 1 | tablespoon olive oil |
| 1 | large onion, sliced |
| | |
| 1/3 | cup tomato paste |
| 1 | teaspoon thyme flakes |
| 1 | teaspoon minced garlic |
| 3 | tablespoons flour |
| 1 | can (1 pound) stewed tomatoes, chopped. Do not drain. |
| | |
| 1 | eggplant, (about 1 1/4 pounds), peeled and thinly sliced |
| 1/2 | pound zucchini, peeled and sliced |
| 1 | green pepper, cleaned, seeded and sliced |
| | |
| 1/2 | pound sliced Monterey Jack cheese |

Saute onion in olive oil until transparent. Stir in tomato paste, thyme, garlic, flour and undrained tomatoes. In a 9x13-inch baking pan, layer ingredients. First, layer half of the tomato mixture, then half of the vegetables, then half of the cheese slices. Repeat layering, with remaining tomato mixture, vegetables and cheese. Cover pan tightly with foil. Bake at 400° for 40 minutes, uncover pan, and continue baking until vegetables are cooked and tender. Serves 6.

# Spicy Bread Pudding Pie with Peaches & Raisins with Light Strawberry Sauce

*This is a nice easy way to make a bread pudding pie. A delicious peach and cream filling is sandwiched between slices of egg bread and sparkled with spice. If you do not have pumpkin pie spice, use 3/4 teaspoon cinnamon and 1/8 teaspoon each, ground nutmeg and ground cloves.*

| | |
|---|---|
| 8 | slices stale egg bread, crust removed |
| 1/2 | pound thinly sliced peaches, fresh or frozen |
| 1/3 | cup yellow raisins |
| 3 | eggs |
| 1 1/2 | cups milk |
| 1/2 | cup half and half |
| 1/2 | cup sugar |
| 1 | teaspoon vanilla |
| 1 | teaspoon pumpkin pie spice |

In a 9x9-inch baking pan, place 4 slices of egg bread. Place peaches and raisins evenly on top and cover with remaining bread slices. Beat together the remaining ingredients and pour egg mixture evenly over the bread. Allow to rest for a few minutes until egg mixture is fully absorbed. Bake at 350° for about 40 minutes, or until eggs are puffed and top is golden brown. Spoon into bowls and serve with a spoonful of Light Strawberry Sauce on top. Serves 8.

Light Strawberry Sauce:

| | |
|---|---|
| 1 | pint fresh strawberries, sliced |
| 2 | teaspoons sugar |
| 1 | tablespoon lemon juice |

In a glass bowl, stir together all the ingredients until blended. Cover bowl and refrigerate until serving time. The strawberries will have rendered their juice, producing a light sauce. If strawberries are not in season, defrost a 12-ounce package of frozen strawberries in syrup and stir in 2 tablespoons of lemon juice. This is a little sweeter, but very good, too.

# Hors D'Oeuvres

Royal Crown Russe of Salmon & Caviar, 58
Mousseline of Cream Cheese & Caviar, 58
Smoked Salmon Mold with Chives & Dill, 59
Crabmeat Mold, 59
To Make Green Onion Frills, 59
To Make Toast Points, 59
Piroshkis with Herbed Mushroom Filling, 60
Pork Won Tons with Currant Mustard Sauce, 61
Chevre Cheese Spread with Chives & Dill, 61
Beef Dumplings with Chinese Red Hot Sauce, 62
Pork Dumplings with Hot Plum Sauce, 62
Red Hot Buffalo Wings with Honey Barbecue Sauce, 63
Meatballs in Sweet & Sour Cranberry Sauce, 63
Instant Hors D'Oeuvres with Flaky Biscuits, 64
Petite Pizzas, Miniature Burgers, Cocktail Franks,
Crabmeat with Cream Cheese, Caponata and Mozzarella,
Shrimp with Swiss Cheese, Mushroom & Mozzarella, 64
Giant Calzones with Pizza Filling, 65
Giant Calzones with Spinach & Cheese, 65
Mushrooms Stuffed with Crabmeat & Garlic Cream Cheese, 66
Batter-Fried Shrimp with Hot Plum Sauce, 66
Hummus, 67
Tarama, 67
Oysters Royale with Garlic, Herbs & Cheese, 68
Gravad Lax with Honey Dill Sauce, 69
Salmon with Tomatoes & Onions, 69
Salmon Spread with Lemon & Chives, 69
Baked Brie with Strawberries & Almonds, 70
Baked Brie with Currants & Pine Nuts, 70
Mini-Muffins with Parmesan, 70
Chicken with Apricot, Peanut & Sesame Sauce, 71
Shrimp with Red Hot Cocktail Sauce, 71
Clams Romano Stuffed with Garlic & Herbs, 72
Spinach Dumplings with Lemon Dill Yogurt, 72
Layered Mexican Dip with Chiles & Cheese, 73
Easiest & Best Guacamole with Tomatoes & Chiles, 73
Cold Vegetable Platter with Imperial Sauce Verte, 74
Emerald Sauce Dip with Raw Vegetables, 74

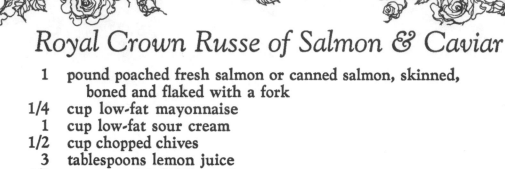

# Royal Crown Russe of Salmon & Caviar

1    pound poached fresh salmon or canned salmon, skinned,
        boned and flaked with a fork
1/4  cup low-fat mayonnaise
1    cup low-fat sour cream
1/2  cup chopped chives
3    tablespoons lemon juice
1/2  teaspoon dried dill weed

1    package unflavored gelatin
1/2  cup water

3/4  cup low-fat sour cream
1    jar (3 1/2 ounces) golden caviar or pink caviar

In a large bowl, stir together first 6 ingredients until nicely mixed. Soften gelatin in water, in a metal measuring cup. Place cup in a pan with simmering water and heat until gelatin is dissolved. Stir gelatin into salmon mixture. Spread mixture into a 4-cup ring mold and refrigerate until firm. Unmold onto a lovely platter and garnish with parsley.

Mask mold with sour cream, creating the effect of draping the sour cream around the mold. Leave some of the mold exposed. Refrigerate until ready to serve. Just before serving, spoon the caviar in a ring around the top. Serve with toast points or 1-inch squares of thinly sliced black bread. Serves 12.

# Mousseline of Cream Cheese & Caviar

1    package (8 ounces) low-fat cream cheese
4    tablespoons low-fat sour cream
3    tablespoons lemon juice

1/3  cup chopped chives
1    jar (3 1/2 ounces) golden, pink or black caviar

Beat together first 3 ingredients until blended. Beat in chives until blended. Line, with plastic wrap, a 1-pint daisy mold or other decorative mold (without a hole in the center). Press cream cheese mixture firmly into the mold and refrigerate. When ready to serve, unmold onto a serving platter and remove plastic wrap. Place caviar in the center (if using a daisy mold) or along the top in a decorative fashion. Serve with small toast points. Yields 1 1/2 cups spread.

# Smoked Salmon Mold with Chives & Dill

*Using the low-fat cream cheese and sour cream does not weaken the taste in any way. This is a favorite among our friends. It could not be simpler to prepare. Use a simple soda cracker if you are serving this as an hors d'oeuvre, or miniature bagels as an accompaniment to a buffet. Using the plastic wrap as a liner in the mold makes unmolding a snap. This technique is a good one to remember with molds with sticky fillings, where it would be impossible to remove the mold without marring the design.*

|   |   |
|---|---|
| 1 | package (8 ounces) low-fat cream cheese |
| 2 | tablespoons low-fat sour cream |
| 1/4 | cup chopped chives or green onions |
| 4 | tablespoons lemon juice |
| 1/4 | pound smoked salmon (lox), cut into 1-inch pieces |
| 1/4 | teaspoon dried dill weed |

In the large bowl of an electric mixer, beat together cream cheese and sour cream until blended. Beat in remaining ingredients until blended. Place a sheet of plastic into a 2-cup decorative mold (one without a hole in the center) and press salmon mixture into the mold. Cover and refrigerate. When ready to serve, invert onto a serving platter, remove plastic wrap and decorate with green onion frills, lemon slices sprinkled with dill, or cherry tomatoes. Yields 2 cups.

### To Make Crabmeat Mold:
Prepare mold as above, deleting lox. Place mold on a large serving platter and surround with 1 1/2 pounds of crabmeat. Decorate with green onion frills and lemon slices. Serve with bland soda crackers.

### To Make Green Onion Frills:
The white bulb and green leaves can be frilled. Cut the green onion in approximate 3-inch pieces. With a sharp knife, cut the thinnest strips lengthwise down 1-inch of each side, leaving the 1-inch in the center intact. Place onions in water and refrigerate for several hours or overnight. The cut edges will curl into attractive frills.

### To Make Toast Points:
Use a good quality, firm-textured, thinly-sliced white bread. Remove the crusts and cut each slice in half, on the diagonal. Cut again on the diagonal, producing 4 small triangles. Toast bread at 350° for 10 minutes, or until the bread is lightly crisped. Spread with a thin layer of butter while still warm. These can be prepared earlier in the day and stored in a cannister with a tight-fitting lid.

# Piroshkis with Herbed Mushroom Filling

*These are a heavenly hors d'oeuvre and are also excellent with soup or salad. The pastry is light and delicate and the filling is lavished with sour cream and sparkled with herbs.*

The Pastry:
- 1    cup butter (2 sticks)
- 1/2   pound cream cheese
- 2    cups flour
-      pinch of salt

- 1    egg, beaten, for brushing on tops
-      grated Parmesan cheese for sprinkling on tops

In your electric mixer, cream butter and cream cheese until the mixture is blended. Add flour and salt and mix at low speed until the flour is incorporated and even. Place dough on floured wax paper and sprinkle top with a little more flour. Shape it into an 8-inch circle and wrap it in the wax paper and then foil and refrigerate it overnight.

Divide dough into four parts. Working one part at a time, roll it out on a floured pastry cloth until the dough is approximately 1/8-inch thick. Cut with a cookie or biscuit cutter into 2 3/4-inch rounds and accumulate scraps in the refrigerator to roll out at the end.

Place 1/2 teaspoon of Mushroom, Sour Cream, Herb Filling in center of each round, moisten the edges and fold over. Press edges down with the tines of a fork. Brush tops with beaten egg and pierce tops with a fork. Sprinkle top with grated Parmesan cheese.

Place piroshkis on a buttered cookie sheet and bake at 350° for about 25 minutes or until tops are lightly browned. Yields about 50 piroshkis.

Mushroom, Sour Cream, Herb Filling:
- 2    tablespoons butter
- 1    onion, finely chopped
- 1/2   pound mushrooms, finely chopped
- 4    tablespoons flour, scanty
- 1/4   teaspoon thyme flakes
- 1/4   teaspoon ground poultry seasoning
-      salt and pepper to taste
- 1    cup sour cream

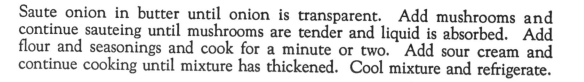

Saute onion in butter until onion is transparent. Add mushrooms and continue sauteing until mushrooms are tender and liquid is absorbed. Add flour and seasonings and cook for a minute or two. Add sour cream and continue cooking until mixture has thickened. Cool mixture and refrigerate.

## Pork Won Tons with Currant Mustard Sauce

- 1 tablespoon oil
- 1/2 pound ground pork
- 1/4 pound minced mushrooms
- 1/4 cup finely minced green onions
- 6 water chestnuts, finely minced
  salt and pepper to taste
  pinch of garlic powder

- 1 package prepared won ton skins (about 45-50 in package)

Heat oil in skillet. Saute together all the ingredients, except the won ton skins, until pork is thoroughly cooked and all the liquid is absorbed.

Place 1 teaspoon of filling on each skin. Moisten edges with water and fold in half, either lengthwise or on the diagonal. Run fingers around the edges, pressing to seal. Fry filled won tons in hot oil until golden brown on both sides. To serve, dip in Hot Plum Sauce (page 62) or Currant Mustard Sauce.

**Currant Mustard Sauce:**
- 1 cup currant jelly
- 2 tablespoons prepared mustard
- 1/2 cup dried currants

Simmer together all the ingredients for about 5 minutes. Yields 1 1/2 cups.

## Chevre Cheese Spread with Chives & Dill

*In this recipe, the old blue cheese ball has been substituted with chevre. Serve this with small, thin slices of French bread, cut from narrow baguettes. Small, bland soda crackers are good, too.*

- 1/2 pound log chevre cheese
- 2 cloves garlic, minced
- 2 tablespoons sour cream
- 1/4 cup chopped chives
- 2 tablespoons chopped parsley
- 1/3 teaspoon dried dill weed

For a textured spread, in a bowl, mash together all the ingredients until blended. For a smoother spread, blend in a food processor, but don't puree. Press cheese into a plastic-lined 1-pint mold, cover and refrigerate. Invert onto a serving platter, remove plastic liner, and surround mold with sprigs of whole chives, lemon slices and bread slices. Yields about 1 1/4 cups.

The following are 2 very delicious sauces for baby dumplings (a nicer way of describing meatballs). Dumplings can be prepared earlier in the day and heated before serving. Hot Plum Sauce can be warmed before serving.

## Beef Dumplings with Chinese Red Hot Sauce

1 1/2   pounds ground lean beef
1   small onion, grated (not chopped) (about 1/2 cup)
1   clove garlic, minced
4   slices bread, crusts removed, soaked in water and squeezed dry
2   eggs
    salt and pepper to taste

In a large bowl, mix together all the ingredients until blended. Shape mixture into 3/4-inch balls. In a large skillet, brown the dumplings on all sides until cooked through and place in a chafing dish to keep warm. Have Chinese Red Hot Sauce close by for dipping.

Chinese Red Hot Sauce:
1/2   cup chili sauce
1/2   cup ketchup
1   teaspoon soy sauce
1/2   teaspoon Coleman's Dry Mustard

Stir together all the ingredients until blended. Serve at room temperature. Yields about 1 cup sauce.

## Pork Dumplings with Hot Plum Sauce

1 1/2   pounds ground lean pork
1   small onion, grated (not chopped) (about 1/2 cup)
1   clove garlic, minced
4   slices bread, crusts removed, soaked in water and squeezed dry
2   eggs
    salt and pepper to taste

In a large bowl, mix together all the ingredients until blended. Shape mixture into 3/4-inch balls. In a large skillet, brown the dumplings on all sides until cooked through and place in a chafing dish to keep warm. Have Hot Plum Sauce close by for dipping. Serve sauce warm.

Hot Plum Sauce:
1   cup plum jam
2   tablespoons, each, vinegar and soy sauce
1/4   cup chili sauce
1   tablespoon brown sugar
    pinch of cayenne pepper

In a saucepan, heat together all the ingredients and simmer sauce for 3 minutes. Allow to cool slightly and serve.

# Red Hot Buffalo Wings
# with Honey Barbecue Glaze

*This is an adaptation of the well-known "Buffalo Wings." Usually deep fried, these are baked, eliminating a lot of calories. Traditionally served with Blue Cheese Dressing, I have chosen to omit it, as the wings stand alone quite well.*

- 3 pounds chicken wings, tips removed and split at the joint. Sprinkle with salt, pepper and garlic powder. Brush lightly with a little butter.

Honey Barbecue Glaze:
- 1/2 cup good quality barbecue sauce
- 1/3 cup honey
- 2 tablespoons vinegar
- 1/4 teaspoon cayenne pepper (or more to taste)

Place chicken in one layer in a 12x16-inch baking pan and bake at 350° for 40 minutes. Stir together glaze ingredients and start basting chicken. Continue baking and basting for 30 minutes, or until chicken is tender and a dark, deep color.

# Meatballs in Sweet & Sour Cranberry Sauce

- 1 1/2 pounds ground beef
- 1 small onion, grated
- 2 eggs
- 1/2 cup herb seasoned stuffing mix, soaked in
    - 3 tablespoons water
- 2 tablespoons dried parsley flakes
- salt and pepper to taste

Combine all the ingredients and shape into 1/2-inch balls. Brown the meatballs in a large skillet, shaking the pan frequently so that the meatballs will brown on all sides. If the meat is very lean, do this in a little butter. Place meatballs and hot Sweet and Sour Cranberry Sauce in a chafing dish. Makes about 50 to 60 meatballs.

Sweet & Sour Cranberry Sauce:
- 1 cup whole berry cranberry sauce
- 1/2 cup ketchup
- 2 tablespoons grated onion
- 1 teaspoon vinegar
- 2 tablespoons brown sugar

Combine all the ingredients and simmer over low heat for 5 minutes. Add meatballs and heat through.

*Here is a simple technique for making hors d'oeuvre or canape bases that will save you hours of preparation. No punching, kneading, rolling or folding--simply use refrigerated Flaky Rolls or Flaky Biscuits as a base. The layers of each roll separate easily and each layer is a perfect base for an hors d'oeuvre or canape.*

## Instant Hors D'Oeuvres with Flaky Biscuits

Separate each flaky roll into 3 layers and place on an ungreased cookie sheet. Top with any of the following or use your favorite combination. Wrap securely with plastic wrap and refrigerate. When ready to serve, bake in a preheated 400° oven for 8 minutes. Serve at once.

1. **PETITE PIZZAS:** Purchase a 6-ounce can of pizza sauce. Place a slice of Mozzarella cheese, 1 teaspoon pizza sauce and a thin slice of sausage on a flaky roll layer.

2. **MINIATURE BURGERS:** Spread a thin layer of ketchup over a flaky round. Top with a thin layer of seasoned ground beef. To make a **Cheeseburger,** top with a thin slice of cheese.

3. **COCKTAIL FRANKS:** Wrap flaky layer around a cocktail-size frank. Serve with **Mustard Mayonnaise Sauce,** (1/2 cup mustard mixed with 1/4 cup mayonnaise.)

4. **CRABMEAT AND CREAM CHEESE:** Spread cream cheese over flaky layer. Top with a small piece of crabmeat. Sprinkle with grated Parmesan cheese.

5. **CAPONATA AND MOZZARELLA:** Purchase a can of the prepared caponata (5 ounces). Place 1/2 teaspoon of caponata on flaky roll layer. Top with a small slice of Mozzarella cheese.

6. **SHRIMP WITH SWISS CHEESE:** Place a baby shrimp on a flaky round. Top with a slice of Swiss cheese and sprinkle with minced chives.

7. **MUSHROOM AND MOZZARELLA:** Place a small mushroom (canned) on a flaky layer. Cover with a slice of Mozzarella cheese and sprinkle with chopped chives.

# Giant Calzones with Pizza Filling

*Calzone, a dough-enclosed pizza, is usually made with pizza dough. In this recipe, it is elevated with the use of puff pastry. This is a great recipe to serve for a backyard picnic or for a light supper. Ground turkey can be substituted for the beef. Using the frozen patty shells, makes this exceedingly easy to prepare and the results will truly surprise you. There is no end to the number of fillings you could use. I am sharing 2 as an example. Chicken, fish, cheese or vegetables can be used.*

- 1 **package frozen patty shells (6 shells), thawed in the refrigerator**
- 1 **egg beaten**
- 6 **tablespoons grated Parmesan cheese**

On a floured pastry cloth, roll out each patty shell to measure 6 inches. Place 2 heaping tablespoons filling on one half of the shell. Fold the other half over and seal edges securely with the tines of a fork. Scallop the edge and prick the top 4 times with the tines of a fork. Place calzone on a greased cookie sheet, brush with beaten egg and sprinkle with grated cheese. Repeat for the other patty shells.

Bake at 400° for 20 to 25 minutes, or until pastry is puffed and a deep golden brown. Serve with fresh fruit or a vegetable salad. Serves 6.

Pizza Filling:
- 1 onion, minced
- 1 teaspoon oil

- 1 pound ground beef or turkey
- 2 tomatoes, seeded and chopped
- 2 tablespoons grated Parmesan cheese
- 4 ounces grated Mozzarella cheese
- 1/2 teaspoon sweet basil flakes
- 1/2 teaspoon Italian Herb Seasoning flakes
  - salt and pepper to taste

In a skillet, saute onion in oil until onion is soft. Add the ground beef and continue sauteing, stirring, until meat loses its pinkness. Drain meat, place in a bowl and stir in the remaining ingredients.

Spinach & Cheese Filling (for 12 calzones):
- 1 package (10 ounces) frozen chopped spinach, defrosted and pressed in a strainer to thoroughly drain
- 1 cup non-fat cottage cheese
- 1 egg
- 1/3 cup grated Parmesan cheese
- 1/3 cup bread crumbs

In a bowl, stir together all the ingredients until blended.

# Mushrooms Stuffed with Crabmeat & Garlic Cream Cheese

*This is one of the most delicious stuffings for mushrooms. These can be assembled earlier in the day and baked before serving.*

    3/4    pound medium-sized mushrooms, cleaned and stems removed
    1/2    pound crabmeat, pick over for bones
    1/2    pound low-fat cream cheese
    1/2    cup garlic croutons, finely crushed
           Parmesan cheese, grated
           paprika

Mix together the crabmeat, cream cheese and croutons until mixture is blended. Mound mixture into mushroom caps. Sprinkle tops generously with grated Parmesan cheese and lightly with paprika. Broil until piping hot. Make extras. They are especially good. Yields about 20.

# Batter-Fried Shrimp with Hot Plum Sauce

    1/2    cup flour
    1/2    cup corn starch
      1    cup cold water
      1    egg
    1/8    teaspoon salt

      2    pounds medium shrimp, shelled and deveined, lightly dusted
           with flour

With a rotary beater, beat together first 5 ingredients until thoroughly smooth. Dip shrimp in batter and fry in a thin layer of hot oil until browned on both sides. Remove from oil and drain on paper towelling. Serve warm with Hot Plum Sauce for dipping. Yields about 40 to 44 bite-size servings.

Hot Plum Sauce:
    1/2    cup plum preserves
      2    tablespoons brown sugar
      2    tablespoons vinegar
      2    tablespoons ketchup

Combine all the ingredients and cook for 5 minutes. Allow to cool a few minutes and serve. Makes about 3/4 cup sauce.

# Hummus

*This Middle Eastern chick pea dip is delicious served with small wedges of fresh pita bread. The "tahini" can be purchased in most supermarkets and health food stores. This can be prepared in minutes using the food processor. Also, it can be prepared 2 days in advance and stored, covered, in the refrigerator.*

|       |                                                      |
|-------|------------------------------------------------------|
| 2     | cans (15 ounces, each) chick peas, rinsed and drained |
| 4     | cloves garlic                                        |
| 2/3   | cup lemon juice                                      |
| 1/2   | cup olive oil                                        |
| 3/4   | cup tahini (sesame seed paste)                       |
|       | pinch of salt, black pepper and cayenne pepper       |

Place all the ingredients in the bowl of a food processor and blend until mixture is pureed, creamy and smooth. Cut 6-inch fresh pita breads into 1-inch wedges or squares. Place Hummus in a crystal bowl and surround with fresh pita.

# Tarama

*I hesitated to share this recipe because it has a very strong, assertive taste. But it is exotic and there may be a time you could use it. This is an adaptation of my mother's recipe. Tarama is sold packed in a casing (which must be removed) or in glass jars without the casing (which I recommend). This can be prepared several days earlier and stored in the refrigerator. Serve it with pita bread, toast points, raw vegetables or thin slices of Greek sesame bread. "Tarama Caviar" and Greek sesame bread can be purchased in most Continental or Greek markets.*

|       |                                                      |
|-------|------------------------------------------------------|
| 6     | slices white bread, crusts removed, dipped in water and squeezed dry |
| 1/3   | cup carp roe (also known as "Tarama Caviar")         |
| 6     | tablespoons lemon juice, or more to taste            |
| 4     | cloves garlic, peeled and sliced                     |
| 1/2   | small onion, chopped, about 4 tablespoons            |
| 1     | cup vegetable oil                                    |

In a food processor bowl, blend together first 5 ingredients. Gradually beat in the oil, in a steady stream, until oil is incorporated. Place mixture in a glass bowl and serve with lightly buttered toast points or wedges of pita. Raw vegetables are good, too. Yields 3 cups.

# Oysters Royale with Garlic, Herbs & Cheese

*This is an incredibly delicious small entree, that I fashioned after a dish we enjoyed in New Orleans. We still rapture over the memory. However, the original brought tears to our eyes. Mine is milder, with only a faint bite. A little extra red pepper can be added, but I do not recommend it. This can be prepared in large individual oyster shells or ramekins. Simply layer crumb mixture, oysters, crumb mixture and a generous sprinkling of grated Parmesan cheese on top. Heat for about 20 minutes at 350-degrees until heated through. Casserole, or individual ramekins, can be prepared earlier in the day, stored in the refrigerator and heated before serving.*

- 6 cloves garlic, minced
- 1 onion, finely chopped
- 4 shallots, minced
- 1/2 cup butter (1 stick)

- 1/4 cup dry white wine
- 1/2 teaspoon paprika
- 1/2 teaspoon thyme flakes
- 1/4 teaspoon oregano flakes
  salt and pepper to taste

- 3 cups fresh egg bread crumbs, about 8 slices of bread, crusts removed and made into crumbs in food processor
- 1/2 cup grated Parmesan cheese
- 1/8 teaspoon cayenne pepper

- 2 cans (8 ounces, each) whole oysters packed in water, drained. Reserve juice.
- 2 tablespoons grated Parmesan cheese

In a Dutch oven casserole, saute garlic, onion and shallots in butter until onion is soft, but not browned. Add the next 6 ingredients and simmer mixture until wine is almost evaporated. Toss in the crumbs, cheese and cayenne pepper until blended. Now add enough of the drained oyster juice until crumbs hold together.

In a 9-inch round porcelain baker, layer half the crumb mixture, the drained oysters and then the remaining crumbs on top. Sprinkle top with the 2 tablespoons grated Parmesan. Bake in a 350-degree oven for about 20 to 25 minutes, or until piping hot. Spoon directly from the porcelain baker onto individual small plates. Serves 8.

# Gravad Lax with Honey Dill Sauce

Serving small squares of lox on wafer-thin slices of black bread with a dab of Honey Dill Sauce, transforms basic lox into Gravad Lax, an excellent hors d'oeuvre taken from the Swedish smorgasbord.

**Honey Dill Sauce:**

| | |
|---|---|
| 1/4 | cup vinegar |
| 2 | tablespoons honey |
| 1/2 | cup salad oil |
| 1/2 | teaspoon dried dill weed (or to taste) |
| | salt and pepper to taste |

| | |
|---|---|
| 1/2 | pound lox, cut into 1-inch squares |

Beat together the vinegar and the honey. Gradually beat in the oil, beating until mixture is thickened. Add dill and taste for salt and pepper. Serve lox with Honey Dill Sauce on wafer-thin slices of black bread. Makes a little more than 3/4 cup sauce.

# Salmon with Tomatoes & Onions (Lomi Lomi)

| | |
|---|---|
| 1/4 | pound lox, shredded |
| 1 | large tomato, peeled, seeded and finely chopped |
| 3 | green onions, finely chopped, use the green tops too |
| 1 | tablespoon salad oil |
| 1 | tablespoon vinegar |
| | salt and pepper to taste |

Combine all the ingredients and mix well. Serve with cocktail size slices of rye bread or pumpernickel.

# Salmon Spread with Lemon & Chives

| | |
|---|---|
| 1 | package (8 ounces) low-fat cream cheese |
| 2 | tablespoons low-fat sour cream |

| | |
|---|---|
| 1/4 | cup chopped chives |
| 4 | tablespoons lemon juice |
| 1/4 | pound lox |

Beat together cream cheese and sour cream until blended. Beat in the remaining ingredients until blended. Serve with miniature bagels or soda crackers. Yields about 1 3/4 cups spread.

## Baked Brie with Strawberries & Almonds

1    wheel of brie (8-inch circle) weighing about 2 pounds.
       remove the outer rind of mold from the top.  Place brie
       in an 8-inch round quiche dish or porcelain baker.

1/2  cup chopped almonds

1    cup sliced fresh strawberries

Mark the top of the brie into 4 wedges.  Fill alternate wedges with almonds and leave alternate wedges unfilled.  Place brie in a 350° oven and bake for about 20 minutes, or until brie is soft.  Fill unfilled wedges with sliced strawberries.  Serve at once with small toast points or pale soda crackers.

## Baked Brie with Currants & Pine Nuts

1    wheel of brie (8-inch circle) weighing about 2 pounds.
       remove the outer rind of mold from the top.  Place brie
       in an 8-inch round quiche dish or porcelain baker.

3/4  cup currants
3/4  cup pine nuts

Mark the top of the brie into 4 wedges.  Fill alternate wedges with currants and pine nuts.  Place brie in a 350° oven and bake for about 20 minutes, or until brie is soft.  Serve at once with small toast points or pale soda crackers.

## Mini-Muffins with Parmesan

2    eggs
1    cup small curd cottage cheese
2    tablespoons sour cream
1    tablespoon oil
1    teaspoon sugar
1/2  cup grated Parmesan cheese
1/2  cup Bisquick

Beat eggs.  Add remaining ingredients and beat together until blended.  Grease hors d'oeuvre-size teflon-lined muffin pans.  Fill 1/2 full with batter.  Bake in a preheated 350° oven for 25 minutes or until puffed and lightly browned.  Serve warm with a dollup of sour cream and caviar or sour cream and a thin slice of smoked salmon.  Yields 24 to 30 muffins.

# Chicken Bites with
# Apricot, Peanut & Sesame Sauce

*The sauce is a delicious glaze to brush on chicken. It is especially good with chicken wings. But as an hors d'oeuvre, chicken breasts are less messy. Unused sauce can be stored in the refrigerator for weeks. Crumbs can be stored in freezer indefinitely.*

2   chicken breasts, boned, skinned and cut into 1-inch pieces.
      Sprinkle with salt and pepper.

1/2   cup bread crumbs
1/2   cup flour
  1   tablespoon paprika
1/2   teaspoon garlic powder

In a jar with a tight-fitting lid, shake together crumbs, flour, paprika and garlic powder. Roll chicken pieces in crumb mixture and saute in a little margarine until browned on both sides. Place chicken pieces in a chafing dish to keep warm and serve the Apricot, Peanut & Sesame Sauce close by for dipping. Or sauce can be brushed on the chicken before serving. Serve with picks or cocktail forks. Serves 8.

Apricot, Peanut & Sesame Sauce:
  1   cup apricot jam, sieved
1/4   cup peanut butter, smooth or nutty grind
  2   tablespoons lemon juice
  2   tablespoons ketchup
  2   tablespoons toasted sesame seeds

In a saucepan, stir together all the ingredients and heat through until blended. Yields 1 1/2 cups sauce.

# Shrimp with Red Hot Cocktail Sauce

1/2   cup chili sauce
1/2   cup ketchup
  2   tablespoons prepared horseradish
  4   tablespoons lemon juice
  3   tablespoons minced green onions

  2   pounds cooked medium shrimp, shelled and deveined

In a jar with a tight-fitting lid, stir together first group of ingredients, and store in the refrigerator. When ready to serve, place sauce in a pretty serving bowl and surround with cooked shrimp for dipping, Serves 12.

# Clams Romano Stuffed with Garlic & Herbs

3   cans minced clams (7 ounces each) drained.  Reserve juice.
1   package, (8 ounces) herbed stuffing
1/4   pound butter, melted
2   cloves garlic, minced
1   teaspoon Italian Herb Seasoning
1   tablespoon chopped parsley
3   tablespoons finely minced onion
6   tablespoons grated Parmesan cheese
    salt and pepper to taste

Combine all the ingredients and toss until well mixed.  Now, slowly add the reserved clam broth until the stuffing holds together and is moist.  Do not let filling get soggy or stay too dry.  Divide mixture between 12 clam shells.  Sprinkle with a little extra Parmesan cheese, paprika and a pinch of oregano.

Place clam shells on a cookie sheet and heat in a 350° oven until piping hot.  Brown under the broiler for a few seconds until golden.  Serves 12 as a first course.

# Spinach Dumplings with Lemon Dill Yogurt

1   package (10 ounces) frozen chopped spinach, defrosted and
       pressed in a strainer to drain
1/3   cup bread crumbs
1   egg, beaten
1/2   cup grated Parmesan cheese
1/4   cup chopped chives

In a large bowl, stir together all the ingredients until mixture is blended. Divide mixture into 12 parts and shape into patties.  Saute patties in a little margarine until browned on both sides.  Or place patties on a parchment-lined cookie sheet and bake at 400° for about 20 minutes or until tops are browned.  Serve with Lemon Dill Yogurt for dipping. Yields 12 dumplings

Lemon Dill Yogurt:
1/2   cup non-fat plain yogurt
1   tablespoon lemon juice
2   tablespoons chopped chives
1/4   teaspoon dried dill weed

In a bowl, stir together all the ingredients until blended.  Store in the refrigerator until serving time.

# Layered Mexican Dip with Chiles & Cheese

- 1 onion, chopped
- 2 cloves garlic, minced
- 1 tablespoon oil

- 1 pound lean ground beef or turkey
- 1 envelope prepared Taco Mix (about 1.25 ounces)
  salt and pepper to taste

- 1 can (1 pound) refried beans
- 1 cup sharp Cheddar cheese, grated
- 1 can (4 ounces) diced green chiles

- 1 cup low-fat sour cream
- 2 tomatoes, peeled, seeded and chopped
- 1/2 cup chopped green onions

Saute together first 3 ingredients until onion is transparent. Add the next 4 ingredients and saute until meat loses its pinkness. Drain beef and place in a 9x9-inch baking pan. Spread refried beans over the top and sprinkle cheese and chiles evenly over all. Bake at 350° for 15 to 20 minutes, or until heated through and cheese is melted. Stir together the remaining ingredients and spoon on top of casserole. Serve at once with tortilla chips for dipping. Delicious. Serves 8 as a hefty hors d'oeuvre.

# Easiest & Best Guacamole with Tomatoes, Onions & Chiles

- 2 large avocados, mashed
- 1 small onion, finely chopped
- 1 can (4 ounces) diced green chiles
- 1 tomato, seeded and chopped
- 4 tablespoons lemon juice
- 1 cup low-fat sour cream

Combine all the ingredients in a large bowl and stir until blended. Serve with crisp tortilla chips for dipping. Yields about 2 cups.

# Cold Vegetable Platter with Sauce Verte

Arrange a large platter of sliced carrots, celery, cucumbers, zucchini, mushrooms, cherry tomatoes, jicama, etc. in any combination you desire. Slice the vegetables straight, on the diagonal, into circles, sticks, curls, etc. Arrange on a bed of lettuce. Dip the ends of the lettuce leaves in paprika for an attractive effect. Place the Imperial Sauce Verte in the center and place an abundant quantity of vegetables decoratively around.

## Imperial Sauce Verte

| | |
|---|---|
| 1/2 | cup frozen chopped spinach, defrosted and drained |
| 3 | sprigs parsley, stems removed, use only the leaves |
| 2 | green onions, use the green tops and the white bulbs |
| 3/4 | cup low-fat mayonnaise |
| 3/4 | cup low-fat sour cream |
| 1 1/2 | tablespoons lemon juice or more to taste |
| | salt to taste |

Place spinach in strainer and drain liquid. Set aside. Place remaining ingredients in food processor or blender and blend at high speed until smooth. Stir together spinach and blended ingredients and mix well. Refrigerate until ready to use. Makes 2 cups.

# Emerald Sauce Dip with Raw Vegetables

*This sauce is delicious with raw vegetables and is also a fine salad dressing.*

| | |
|---|---|
| 1/2 | cup low-fat mayonnaise |
| 1/2 | cup low-fat sour cream |
| 2 | medium green onions, (green and white part) |
| 6 | sprigs of parsley leaves (no twigs) |
| 1/4 | teaspoon garlic powder |
| 4 | tablespoons lemon juice |
| 1/4 | teaspoon dried dill weed |
| | assorted sliced raw vegetables, carrots, zucchini, cucumbers, celery, jicama, etc. |

Place first group of ingredients in a food processor or blender container and process until mixture is pureed. Place sauce in a lovely serving bowl and surround with vegetables. Sauce can be made earlier in the day and stored in the refrigerator. Yields 1 1/2 cups sauce.

# Soups & Garnitures

Mexican Corn Chowder, 76
Mexican Chili Soup with Orzo & Garbanzos, 76
Hungarian Chicken Goulash Soup, 77
Honey Pumpernickel Raisin Bread, 77
Farmhouse Cabbage & Tomato Soup, 78
Black Bread & Raisin Butter, 78
Stracciatella with Spinach & Cheese, 78
Best Old-Fashioned Lentil Soup, 79
Best Old-Fashioned Split Pea Soup, 79
Country Cabbage & Apple Soup, 80
Zucchini Soup Darling, 80
Cauliflower Soup with Light Creme Fraiche, 81
Broccoli Soup with Light Creme Fraiche, 81
Asparagus Soup with Light Creme Fraiche, 81
Tomato Soup with Light Creme Fraiche, 81
Classic French Onion Soup, 82
Moroccan Lamb Dumpling Soup with Cicis, 83
Curried Lamb & Vegetable Soup, 84
Cabbage & Tomato Soup with Meatballs, 84
Italian-Style Bean & Pasta Soup, 85
The Best Leek & Potato Soup with Creme Fraiche & Chives, 86
Roulades of Chives & Cheese, 86
Classic Country French Vegetable Soup, 87
Croustades of Garlic & Cheese, 87
Shrimp Soup Mediterranean, 88
Croustades of French Bread with Cheese, 88
The Best Mushroom & Onion Soup, 89
Crispettes of Cheese & Chives, 89
Honey Carrot Soup with Apples & Cinnamon, 90
Chicken with Instant Noodles, 90
Italian Bean Soup with Cicis & Orzo, 91
Beef & Barley Mushroom Soup, 91
Clam Chowder Darling, 92
Clam Chowder, Manhattan Style, 92

# Mexican Corn Chowder

*This delicious soup is assembled in minutes with ingredients from your pantry. Add some leftover chicken and it serves nicely for a light supper.*

| | |
|---|---|
| 1 | quart rich chicken broth, or 3 cans (10 1/2 ounces, each) chicken broth |
| 1 | can (1 pound) stewed tomatoes, chopped. Do not drain |
| 1 | large onion, minced |
| 3 | cloves garlic, minced |
| 3 | carrots, grated |
| 1 | tablespoon Chili con Carne Seasoning (Spice Islands) |
| 1 | teaspoon turmeric |
| 1/2 | teaspoon ground cumin |
| | |
| 1 | jar (2 ounces) slivered pimientos |
| 1 | can (4 ounces) diced green chiles |
| 2 | packages (10 ounces, each) frozen corn kernels |
| 1 | shake cayenne pepper |

In a Dutch oven casserole, with lid slightly ajar, simmer together first group of ingredients until vegetables are tender, about 15 minutes. Add the remaining ingredients and simmer soup for an additional 15 minutes. Serve with Pita Crisps with Parmesan Cheese. Serves 6.

# Mexican Chili Soup with Orzo & Garbanzos

| | |
|---|---|
| 4 | cups chicken broth |
| 2 | large onions, chopped |
| 8 | cloves garlic, minced |
| 1 | can (1 pound) garbanzos, rinsed and drained |
| 1/2 | cup large-sized orzo |
| 1 | can (1 pound) stewed tomatoes, chopped. Do not drain. |
| 1 | can (8 ounces) tomato sauce |
| 1 | can (7 ounces) diced green chiles |
| 1 | tablespoon Chili con Carne Seasoning (Spice Islands) |
| 1 | teaspoon ground turmeric |
| 1/4 | teaspoon ground cumin |
| | salt and pepper to taste |

In a covered Dutch oven casserole, stir together all the ingredients, and simmer mixture for 30 minutes or until orzo is tender. Serve in deep bowls with cornbread or corn tortillas. Serves 6.

# Hungarian Chicken Goulash Soup
## with Honey Pumpernickel Raisin Bread

*The classic Hungarian Goulash is given a new dimension when prepared as a soup. I substituted chicken for the beef and took a few more liberties as well. This is a very sturdy soup that can serve well as a main course. Please cook the noodles separately and add them after the soup is cooked. In this manner, you will have better control of the timing and will avoid soggy noodles. The Honey Pumpernickel Bread adds a touch of sweetness which balances the spicy paprika.*

| | |
|---|---|
| 3 | onions, chopped |
| 3 | cloves garlic, minced |
| 2 | cups chicken broth |
| 2 | cans (10 1/2 ounces, each) beef broth |
| 1/2 | cup dry white wine |
| 2 | tablespoons paprika (Spice Islands) |
| 1 | tablespoon brown sugar |
| | salt and pepper to taste |
| | |
| 2 | pounds chicken wings, tips removed and cut at the joint |
| 1/4 | pound medium egg noodles, cooked tender and drained |
| 6 | tablespoons low-fat sour cream or non-fat unflavored yogurt |

In a covered Dutch oven casserole, bring first group of ingredients to a boil. Add chicken, cover pan, and simmer soup for 1 hour, or until chicken is tender. Remove any trace of fat. Stir in cooked noodles and simmer soup for another 10 minutes. Serve soup with a dollup of sour cream or yogurt on top. Honey Pumpernickel Raisin Bread is a must! Serves 6.

Honey Pumpernickel Raisin Bread:
| | |
|---|---|
| 6 | thin slices pumpernickel raisin bread |
| 6 | teaspoons butter |
| 6 | teaspoons honey |

Spread each slice of bread with a little butter and honey. Broil for a few seconds to warm bread. Do not bake or bread will get too crisped.

# Farmhouse Cabbage & Tomato Soup with Black Bread & Raisin Butter

*When the weather is raging outside, this is a comforting soup to serve. It is filled with all manner of good things that will nurture your spirit.*

1   head cabbage (about 1 1/4 pounds), shredded or coarsely chopped
2   onions, chopped
4   cloves garlic, minced
2   carrots, grated (not sliced)
1   can (1 pound) stewed tomatoes, chopped. Do not drain.
1   cup fresh (not canned) sauerkraut, undrained
3   cups chicken broth
1   can (10 1/2 ounces) beef broth
2   tablespoons lemon juice
1   teaspoon sugar

In a Dutch oven casserole, with cover slightly ajar, simmer together all the ingredients for about 45 minutes, or until cabbage is tender. Serve with Black Bread & Raisin Butter as a hearty accompaniment. Serves 8.

**Black Bread & Raisin Butter:**
8   thin slices pumpernickel bread
8   teaspoons butter
4   tablespoons finely chopped raisins

On each slice of bread, spread 1 teaspoon butter and 1/2 tablespoon chopped raisins. Place bread on a cookie sheet and broil for a few seconds to melt butter and to crisp the bread. Serves 8.

# Stracciatella with Spinach & Cheese

*This soup cooks up in minutes and is very much like an egg-drop soup. The difference is, that in this soup, the egg is studded with spinach, chives and cheese.*

1     quart rich chicken broth
2     eggs
3     tablespoons grated Parmesan cheese
1/3   cup frozen chopped spinach, defrosted and drained in a strainer
        (about 1/2 of a 10-ounce package)
1/4   cup chopped chives
        salt and pepper to taste

In a Dutch oven casserole, bring chicken broth to a boil. Beat together the remaining ingredients, and slowly, drizzle it into the boiling broth. Simmer soup for 2 minutes and serve with Pita Crisps with Honey & Sesame Seeds. Serves 4.

# The Best Old-Fashioned Lentil Soup

2    large onions, finely chopped
3    large carrots, peeled and grated
3    shallots, minced
3    cloves garlic, minced
1    tablespoon butter

1    can (1 pound) stewed tomatoes, chopped.  Do not drain.
3    cans (10 1/2 ounces, each) chicken broth
1    can (10 1/2 ounces) beef broth
1/2  pound ham steak, cut into 1/2-inch cubes
1    package (1 pound) lentils, rinsed and picked over for foreign
      particles
      salt and pepper to taste

In a Dutch oven casserole, saute together first 5 ingredients, until onions are softened.  Add the remaining ingredients, and simmer soup, with cover slightly ajar, for about 1 hour 15 minutes, or until lentils are very tender.  (Add a little chicken broth if soup is too thick.)  Serve with Honey Pumpernickel with Raisins.  Serves 8.

Honey Pumpernickel with Raisins:
8    thin slices pumpernickel raisin bread
8    teaspoons honey
8    sprinkles sesame seeds

Place bread on a 10x15-inch cookie sheet.  Spread each top with 1 teaspoon honey and a sprinkle of sesame seeds.  Broil for 1 minute, or until seeds just begin to take on color.  (Watch carefully, because there are only a few seconds between brown and burnt.)  Serves 8.

# The Best Old-Fashioned Split Pea Soup

Substitute the lentils with 1 pound dried split peas, rinsed and picked over for any foreign particles.

# Country Cabbage & Apple Soup

*This is a thick soup, almost a stew. If you like it thinner, add 1 extra cup of beef broth. A good soup to serve around a fire, on a cold wintry night, when the wind is howling outside. The black bread is the perfect accompaniment.*

2　pounds lean boneless chuck, cut into 1/2-inch cubes
3　cloves garlic, minced
2　onions, finely chopped
3　carrots, grated
1　can (1 pound) stewed tomatoes, chopped
1　cup sauerkraut, with juice
1　small head cabbage (1 pound) grated or chopped
2　apples, peeled, cored and grated
1　tablespoon sugar
2　tablespoons lemon juice
4　cups beef broth
　　salt and pepper to taste

In a Dutch oven casserole, bring all the ingredients to a boil. Lower heat and simmer mixture, with cover slightly ajar, for about 1 1/2 hours, or until meat is very tender. Remove any fat that settles on top. Serve with warm black raisin pumpernickel bread and a little creamy butter. Serves 8.

# Zucchini Soup Darling

*I have served this soup numerous times over the years and it never fails to bring raves. It is a thick soup, but delicate. Add a little broth, if necessary.*

6　medium zucchini. Do not peel. Cut into 1/4-inch slices.
2　large onions, sliced
6　shallots, minced
6　cloves garlic, minced
1/4　cup parsley leaves
2　tablespoons butter

2　cans (10 1/2 ounces) concentrated chicken broth, undiluted
1　cup half and half
1/2　teaspoon dried dill weed
1/4　teaspoon ground poultry seasoning
　　salt and pepper to taste

In a Dutch oven casserole, combine first 6 ingredients and saute over low heat until vegetables are tender and liquid rendered is evaporated. Do not let vegetables brown. Place vegetables in a food processor container and blend with some of the chicken broth until vegetables are pureed and smooth. Pour mixture back into the pan, and stir in the remaining chicken broth with the remaining ingredients. Simmer soup for 5 minutes, uncovered. Serves 6.

# Cauliflower Soup with Light Creme Fraiche

*This very elegant soup is a great starter for a dinner party. It can be prepared earlier in the day and heated before serving. It is also delicious served cold. If you are planning to serve this cold, there are a few points to consider. First, omit the butter, for it makes unsightly lumps when chilled. Instead, simmer together the second and third group of ingredients until vegetables are soft and continue as described below. This is a good basic recipe. Variations are listed below.*

| | |
|---|---|
| 1/2 | cup low-fat sour cream |
| 1/2 | cup half and half |
| | |
| 2 | packages (10 ounces, each) frozen cauliflower |
| 2 | onions, chopped |
| 6 | shallots, minced |
| 4 | cloves garlic, minced |
| 3 | tablespoons lemon juice |
| 1/4 | cup butter |
| | |
| 4 | cups chicken broth |
| 1/4 | teaspoon dried dill weed |
| | salt and white pepper to taste |
| | |
| 2 | tablespoons chopped chives |

Stir together sour cream and half and half and set aside at room temperature. In a Dutch oven casserole, saute together next 6 ingredients until vegetables are soft, but not browned. In a food processor, puree vegetable mixture with some of the broth and return to pan. Stir in remaining chicken broth, dill and seasonings. Stir in cream mixture until blended. Simmer soup for 5 minutes to blend flavors. Serve with a spoonful of chopped chives. Serves 6.

**To Make Broccoli Soup with Light Creme Fraiche:**
Substitute chopped broccoli for the cauliflower.

**To Make Asparagus Soup with Light Creme Fraiche:**
Substitute asparagus for the cauliflower.

**To Make Tomato Soup with Light Creme Fraiche:**
Substitute 1 1/2 pound tomatoes, peeled, seeded and chopped, instead of the cauliflower. Add 1/2 teaspoon sugar to offset the acid in the tomatoes.

# Classic French Onion Soup

| | |
|---|---|
| 4 | large onions, remove stems and skins. Slice in half lengthwise and cut into 1/8-inch slices |
| 6 | shallots, minced |
| 4 | cloves garlic, minced |
| 2 | teaspoons brown sugar |
| 4 | tablespoons butter (1/2 stick) |
| | |
| 2 | tablespoons flour |
| 2 1/2 | cups chicken broth |
| 2 | cans (10 1/2 ounces each) beef broth, undiluted |
| 1/4 | cup dry white wine |
| | |
| 1 | cup grated Gruyere or Swiss cheese (4 ounces) |
| | salt and pepper to taste |
| | |
| 8 | slices French bread, toasted |
| 8 | tablespoons grated Parmesan cheese |

In a Dutch oven casserole, over low heat, cook together first 5 ingredients, until onions are very soft but not browned, about 30 minutes. Add flour and continue cooking and stirring for a minute or two. Add broths and wine and simmer for 10 minutes.

In 8 soup bowls, divide the grated Gruyere. Place a slice of toasted French bread in each soup bowl. Sprinkle with 1 tablespoon Parmesan cheese and pour boiling soup over all. Serves 8.

Note: ♥ *If you have ovenproof soup bowls, divide the soup and the Gruyere cheese into the individual bowls and heat in a 350° oven until soup is hot and cheese is melted. Sprinkle bread with grated cheese and broil for a few seconds to brown top. Float bread on top of soup.*

# Moroccan Lamb Dumpling Soup with Cicis

*This is an adaptation of my Moroccan Lamb made into an exotic soup. It is very rich and flavorful. Cooking the lamb dumplings separately eliminates all the fat. Serve with Pita with Honey & Sesame Seeds or Flatbread with Green Onions & Parsley.*

| | |
|---|---|
| 2 | onions, chopped |
| 4 | shallots, minced |
| 6 | cloves garlic, minced |
| 1 | tablespoon oil |
| | |
| 6 | carrots, peeled and sliced |
| 2 | apples, peeled, cored and sliced |
| 2 | cans (1 pound, each) cici peas, rinsed and drained |
| 3 | cups chicken broth |
| 1 | cans (10 1/2 ounces) beef broth |
| 1/3 | cup dried currants |
| 1 | teaspoon ground turmeric |
| 1/2 | teaspoon ground cumin |
| | salt and pepper to taste |

In a Dutch oven casserole, saute together first 4 ingredients until onion is transparent. Add the remaining ingredients and simmer soup for 30 minutes. Add the Moroccan Lamb Dumplings and simmer soup for 20 minutes. Serves 6.

**Moroccan Lamb Dumplings:**

| | |
|---|---|
| 1 | pound ground lamb |
| 1 | small onion, grated |
| 2 | slices egg bread, crusts removed, dipped in water and squeezed dry |
| 1 | egg, beaten |
| 3 | tablespoons dried currants |
| | salt and pepper to taste |

In a bowl, mix together all the ingredients until blended. Shape mixture into 1-inch balls and flatten slightly. Saute in a little oil until browned on both sides. Alternatively, bake at 350° for 10 minutes. Dumplings will continue cooking in the soup.

# Curried Lamb & Vegetable Soup

| | |
|---|---|
| 1 1/2 | pounds boneless lamb, cut from the leg into 3/4-inch cubes |
| 2 | tablespoons olive oil |
| 2 | onions, chopped |
| 2 | cloves garlic, minced |
| 1 | can (10 1/2 ounces) beef broth |
| | |
| 1 | can (1 pound) stewed tomatoes, chopped.  Do not drain. |
| 2 | tablespoons tomato paste |
| 4 | carrots, sliced |
| 1 | stalk celery, thinly sliced |
| 2 | cans (10 1/2 ounces, each) beef broth |
| 1 | can (1 pound) garbanzos |
| 1/4 | cup rice |
| 2 | teaspoons curry powder, or more to taste |
| 1/2 | teaspoon ground cumin |
| | salt and pepper to taste |

In a Dutch oven casserole, over high heat, saute together first 4 ingredients for 5 minutes, tossing and turning, to lightly brown meat.  Add the first can of broth, cover pan, lower heat, and simmer lamb for 30 minutes.  Now, stir in the remaining ingredients, cover pan and bring soup to a boil.  Lower heat and simmer soup for about 1 hour, or until lamb is tender.  Remove any trace of fat.  Serve with Flatbread with Onions & Poppy Seeds.  Serves 8.

# Cabbage & Tomato Soup with Meatballs

*Here's an easy stuffed cabbage soup where the stuffing is made into little meat balls.  This is easy to prepare and very satisfying.*

| | |
|---|---|
| 1 | head cabbage, 1 pound, cored and shredded |
| 2 | cans (1 pound, each) stewed tomatoes, chopped.  Do not drain. |
| 1 | can (16 ounces) tomato sauce |
| 2 | cups chicken broth |
| 1 | can (10 1/2 ounces) beef broth |
| 4 | tablespoons lemon juice |
| 1 | tablespoon sugar |
| | salt and pepper to taste |

In a Dutch oven casserole, place all the ingredients and simmer soup for 45 minutes.  Add the meatballs and simmer soup for 30 minutes.   Serves 6 to 8.

**To Make Meatballs:**
In a bowl, stir together until blended, 1 pound ground beef, 2 cups cooked rice, 1 grated onion, 1 clove minced garlic, 1 egg,  1/4 cup water, salt and pepper to taste.  Shape mixture into 1-inch balls.

# Italian-Style Bean & Pasta Soup

*This recipe is an adaptation of the traditional Pasta Fagiole Soup. It is one of my husband's favorites. Please notice that the pasta is cooked separately and added to the soup at the end. This avoids a soggy pasta.*

2    onions, chopped
6    shallots, minced
6    cloves garlic, minced
2    tablespoons olive oil

1    can (1 pound) red kidney beans, rinsed and drained
1    can (1 pound) cannellini beans, rinsed and drained
1    can (1 pound) stewed tomatoes, chopped. Do not drain.
1    tablespoon tomato paste
3    cans (10 1/2 ounces, each) beef broth
2    tablespoons chopped parsley leaves or flat Italian parsley
1/2    teaspoon, each, sweet basil flakes and Italian Herb Seasoning
      pinch of red pepper flakes
      salt and pepper to taste

1/4    pound (4 ounces) short tube pasta (tubettini),
      cooked in boiling water until tender and drained

In a Dutch oven casserole, saute together first 4 ingredients until onions are tender. Add the next group of ingredients and simmer soup, with cover slightly ajar, for 30 minutes. Add the drained, cooked pasta and heat through. Serve with a little grated Parmesan on top. Serves 8.

# The Best Leek & Potato Soup with Creme Fraiche & Chives

*This is a delicious soup served hot or cold. It is very elegant with the Creme Fraiche, but is also delicious made with buttermilk. Substitute 1 cup buttermilk for the sour cream and half and half for a low-calorie version of this classic Vichyssoise.*

**Soup Base:**
- 1 pound leeks, white part and about 1-inch of the tender green part only. Cut into thin slices and wash thoroughly to remove every trace of sand.
- 1 pound potatoes, peeled and sliced
- 4 cups chicken broth
  salt and white pepper to taste

**Creme Fraiche with Chives:**
- 1/2 cup low-fat sour cream
- 1/2 cup half and half
- 4 tablespoons chopped chives
- 1 tablespoon chopped parsley
- 2 tablespoons lemon juice

In a Dutch oven casserole, with cover slightly ajar, simmer first group of ingredients for about 45 minutes, or until vegetables are very soft. Meanwhile, in a glass bowl, stir together remaining ingredients until blended. Cover bowl and allow to stand at room temperature while soup is simmering.

Blend vegetables in a food processor until very finely chopped, but not pureed. (Leave a little texture.) Return to pan and stir in Creme Fraiche with Chives. Serve with Roulades of Chives & Cheese. Serves 6.

**Roulades of Chives & Cheese:**
- 6 slices egg bread, crusts removed and rolled flat with a rolling pin
- 6 teaspoons melted butter
- 6 teaspoons grated Parmesan cheese
- 6 teaspoons chopped chives

  melted butter
  grated Parmesan cheese

Spread 1 teaspoon butter on each slice of egg bread. Sprinkle each with 1 teaspoon grated cheese and chopped chives. Roll each slice up jelly-roll fashion and spear with a toothpick. Brush roulades with additional melted butter and sprinkle with a little grated Parmesan. Bake at 400° for about 15 minutes or until lightly browned and crisped. Remove toothpicks and serve warm. Serves 6.

# Classic Country French Vegetable Soup

*This is a low-calorie very tasty soup that I prepare often. In fact, it is a staple at our table. Garbanzos can be substituted with rice or orzo or 1 can (1 pound) white beans (Cannellini or White Northern).*

2   onions, finely chopped
4   shallots, minced
6   cloves garlic, minced
3   carrots, thinly sliced
1   stalk celery, thinly sliced
1   teaspoon dried thyme flakes
1   can (1 pound) stewed tomatoes, chopped. Do not drain.
1   can (1 pound) garbanzos (cici peas), rinsed and drained
3   cups chicken broth
1   teaspoon grated orange zest (the orange part of the peel only)
   salt and pepper to taste

In a Dutch oven casserole, simmer together all the ingredients, with cover slightly ajar, for 30 minutes, or until vegetables are tender. Serve with Croustades of Garlic & Cheese as a delicious accompaniment. Serves 6.

Croustades of Garlic & Cheese:
12   slices French bread (cut into 1/2-inch slices or 1/2-ounce, each)
6   teaspoons butter
3   tablespoons grated Parmesan cheese
12   sprinkles coarse grind garlic powder

On each slice of French bread, spread 1/2-teaspoon butter, 3/4 teaspoon grated cheese and a sprinkling of coarse grind garlic powder. Place bread on a cookie sheet and wrap securely with plastic wrap. Just before serving, broil bread for a few minutes, or until cheese is bubbly and top is golden. Careful not to burn, so watch carefully. Serves 6.

# Shrimp Soup Mediterranean

*Serving shrimp in a light broth is a grand first course...and very low in calories, too. Croustades of French Bread with Cheese is a deliciously simple, yet ultimate accompaniment.*

**Soup Base:**

| | |
|---|---|
| 1 | can (1 pound stewed tomatoes) chopped.  Do not drain. |
| 1 | leek, white part and tender green part only, rinsed of all sand, and cut into very thin slices |
| 6 | cloves garlic, minced |
| 4 | shallots, minced |
| 1/2 | cup dry white wine |
| 1 1/2 | cups clam broth |
| 1 | bay leaf |
| 1/2 | teaspoon sweet basil flakes |
| 2 | teaspoons olive oil |
| | |
| 1 | pound medium shrimp, shelled and deveined, tails left on (about 20 to the pound) |

In a covered Dutch oven casserole, simmer together soup base ingredients for 20 minutes, or until leek is soft.  Bring soup to a rolling boil and add the shrimp.  Cook shrimp just until they become opaque and turn pink, about 4 minutes.  Do not overcook.  Remove bay leaf and serve at once in shallow soup bowls, with some crusty French bread.  Serves 4.

**Croustades of French Bread with Cheese:**

| | |
|---|---|
| 8 | 1/2-inch slices French bread (1/2-ounce, each) |
| 8 | teaspoons butter |
| 8 | teaspoons grated Parmesan cheese |

Spread each slice of bread with 1 teaspoon butter and sprinkle with 1 teaspoon grated cheese.  Place on a broiling pan and broil for a few seconds to brown tops.  Watch carefully to avoid burning the cheese.  Serves 4.

# The Best Mushroom & Onion Soup

- 1   pound mushrooms, cleaned and thinly sliced
- 2   large onions, finely chopped
- 6   shallots, minced
- 6   cloves garlic, minced
- 1/2  teaspoon dried thyme flakes
- 1/4  teaspoon ground poultry seasoning
- 3   tablespoons butter
- 1/3  cup dry white wine
       salt and pepper to taste

- 2   tablespoons flour

- 4   cups chicken broth
- 1   cup half and half

In a Dutch oven casserole, cook together first group of ingredients until vegetables are soft and liquid rendered is evaporated.  Stir in the flour and cook and stir for 2 minutes, turning all the while.  Stir in the broth and half and half and simmer soup, uncovered, for 5 minutes.  Serve with Crispettes of Cheese and Chives as a delicious accompaniment.  Serves 8.

Crispettes of Cheese and Chives:
- 16  thin slices French bread (1/2 ounce, each)
- 8   teaspoons butter
- 16  teaspoons grated Parmesan cheese
- 16  teaspoons chopped chives

Spread each slice of bread with 1/2 teaspoon butter and sprinkle with 1 teaspoon grated Parmesan and chives.  Place on a cookie sheet and broil for 2 to 3 minutes, or until cheese is melted and edges of bread are lightly browned.  Watch carefully...there are only a few seconds between toasted and burnt.  Serves 8.

# Honey Carrot Soup
## with Apples, Raisins & Cinnamon

*This is a great soup to serve at Thanksgiving. All the flavors match well with the usual accompaniments. Buttermilk can be substituted with half and half if you are feeling wreckless.*

| | |
|---|---|
| 1 | pound carrots, peeled and sliced |
| 2 | apples, peeled, cored and sliced |
| 1 | onion, chopped |
| 3 | shallots, chopped |
| 2 | cloves garlic, sliced |
| 2 | cups apple juice |
| 2 | cups chicken broth |
| 2 | tablespoons honey |
| | salt to taste |
| | |
| 1 | cup buttermilk |
| 1/2 | cup low-fat sour cream, at room temperature |
| 1/3 | cup chopped yellow raisins |
| | |
| | cinnamon |

In a Dutch oven casserole, simmer together first group of ingredients for 30 to 40 minutes or until vegetables are very soft. Transfer vegetables to a food processor container and blend until mixture is pureed. Return vegetables to the pot and stir in next 3 ingredients until blended. Heat through, but do not boil. Serve with a dollup of low-fat sour cream (optional) and a sprinkling of cinnamon. Serves 8.

# Chicken Soup with Instant Noodles

| | |
|---|---|
| 4 | cups rich chicken broth |
| 3 | eggs |
| 3 | tablespoons flour, sifted |
| | pinch of salt and white pepper |
| | |
| 6 | tablespoons chopped chives |
| | salt and pepper to taste |

Bring chicken broth to boil. Beat together the eggs, flour and pinch of salt and pepper until the mixture is blended.

Slowly and in a steady stream, trickle the egg mixture into the boiling broth. Spaezle-like noodles will have formed. Add chives and seasonings. Lower heat and simmer soup for 5 minutes. Serve with Croustades of Garlic & Cheese (page 87.) Serves 6.

# Italian Bean Soup with Cicis & Orzo

*Without a doubt, this is the heartiest soup in this chapter. High in complex carbohydrates, without added fat, this is the soup that memories are made of. Using the canned beans saves hours of preparation time and is recommended. Soup can be prepared earlier in the day or 1 day earlier and stored in the refrigerator. It is also delicious the second day.*

1   can (1 pound,) red kidney beans, rinsed and drained
1   can (1 pound) white beans (cannellini), rinsed and drained
1   can (1 pound) cici peas, rinsed and drained
1   can (1 pound) stewed tomatoes, chopped. Do not drain.
2   onions, finely chopped
4   shallots, minced
6   cloves garlic, minced
3   carrots, peeled and grated
1/4   cup large-sized orzo
4   cups chicken broth
1   teaspoon sweet basil flakes
1/2   teaspoon Italian Herb Seasoning
    salt and pepper to taste

In a Dutch oven casserole, stir together all the ingredients and with cover slightly ajar, simmer soup for 45 minutes. Serve in deep bowls with a spoonful of grated cheese on top and thin slices of crusty Italian bread. Serves 8 to 10.

# Beef & Barley Mushroom Soup

2   cans (10 1/2 ounces each) beef broth
1   cup chicken broth
1   teaspoon beef seasoned stock base (Spice Islands)
1   onion, finely chopped
1   carrot, grated
1/2   cup pearl barley
1/2   pound boneless chuck, cut into 1/2-inch cubes

1/2   pound mushrooms
2   teaspoons butter

1   tablespoon chopped parsley
    pinch of salt and pepper to taste

In a Dutch oven casserole, place first group of ingredients and simmer mixture until barley and beef are tender, about 1 hour. Meanwhile, saute mushrooms in butter until they are tender, and add to soup. Stir in the remaining ingredients and heat through. Serve with crusty pumpernickel and raisin bread and a little whipped butter. Serves 6.

# Clam Chowder Darling

8    shallots, minced
2    tablespoons butter
1    teaspoon flour

8    strips of bacon, cooked, drained and crumbled
1    can minced clams (8 ounces)
1    cup bottled clam juice
1/2  teaspoon basil
     pinch of thyme
1    small potato, peeled, boiled and very finely chopped
1/2  cup half and half stirred with 1/2 cup low-fat sour cream
     salt and white pepper to taste

In a Dutch oven casserole, saute shallots in butter until shallots are soft. Add flour and cook for a minute or two, stirring. Add the remaining ingredients and simmer soup for about 10 minutes. Serves 4.

# Clam Chowder, Manhattan Style

1    large onion, finely chopped
2    tablespoons butter

1    large potato, peeled and diced
1/2  cup diced celery
3/4  cup diced carrots
1    can (1 pound) stewed tomatoes, chopped.  Do not drain.

2    cans (8 ounces) minced clams, drained.  Reserve broth.
     Bottled clam juice

     salt and white pepper to taste
1    teaspoon thyme flakes
     pinch of curry powder
1    tablespoon minced parsley

In a Dutch oven casserole, saute onion in butter until onion is soft. Add potato, celery, carrots and tomatoes and cook for 10 minutes. Combine clam broth and bottled clam juice to measure 2 cups. Add seasonings. Simmer soup, with cover ajar, for about 20 minutes or until vegetables are tender. Add reserved clams and heat through. Serve with hot crusty French bread. Serves 4

# Salads & Dressings

# Kasha (Cracked Wheat) Salad with Tomatoes, Cucumbers & Lemon Vinaigrette

*Looking for a healthy salad, that is also delicious? Well, here's one to consider. This can also be prepared with cooked vegetables. You can use any number of cooked vegetables, carrots, peas, broccoli florets, cauliflower florets, etc. Kasha has a way of soaking up the dressing, so, add dressing to taste.*

| | |
|---|---|
| 1 1/2 | cups kasha (cracked wheat) |
| 3 | cups boiling water |
| | |
| 2 | cucumbers, peeled and chopped |
| 2 | tomatoes, peeled, seeded and chopped |
| 1/2 | cup chopped green onions |
| 1/4 | cup chopped parsley leaves (no stems) |
| 1/2 | cup lemon juice |
| 2 | tablespoons olive oil |
| | salt and pepper to taste |

In a large bowl, soak cracked wheat in boiling water for about 1 1/2 hours. Line a collander with double thicknesses of cheese cloth and thoroughly drain cracked wheat. In a large bowl, combine the cracked wheat with the remaining ingredients and toss until mixture is nicely blended. Cover bowl and refrigerate until ready to serve. Adjust seasonings. Serves 6.

# Artichoke, Potato & Red Pepper Salad

*If you find yourself in need of a great, colorful salad for a buffet or antipasto, this one is made from cupboard ingredients and is assembled in, literally, minutes. This salad can be made from scratch, but not worth the extra work. It is exceedingly attractive, white and red and shades of green. Can be prepared 1 day earlier and stored in the refrigerator.*

| | |
|---|---|
| 1 | jar (6 to 7 ounces) marinated artichoke hearts, cut into chunks. Do not drain. |
| 1 | can (1 pound) sliced potatoes, rinsed and drained |
| 2 | marinated red peppers, cut into slivers |
| 1/4 | cup chopped green onions |
| 4 | tablespoons lemon juice |
| | salt and pepper to taste |

In a bowl, stir together all the ingredients until nicely blended. Cover and refrigerate until serving time. Serves 6.

# Chicken & Cous Cous Salad with Raisins & Almonds

*I love cous cous with any number of additions. Fruits, nuts, vegetables are all good. Outside of the fact that this is a delicious dish, with its abundance of flavors, it is also attractive, served in a large shallow bowl, with its myriad of colors. Great choice for a ladies lunch. Be certain to purchase the "precooked" cous cous as it cooks in minutes. Plump the dried fruit in boiling water and drain. For my taste, to prevent almonds from getting soggy, I add them just before serving. Cous Cous has a way of soaking up the dressing, so add dressing to taste.*

| | |
|---|---|
| 1 | cup pre-cooked cous cous |
| 1 1/4 | cups boiling water |
| | |
| 1 | bag (1 pound) frozen cut carrots |
| 4 | chicken breast halves, skinned and boned (about 1 pound) or 3 cups leftover chicken or turkey (white meat only) |
| 1/2 | cup chicken broth |
| | |
| 1/2 | cup chopped green onions |
| 1/4 | cup yellow raisins or dried apricots, plumped |
| 1/4 | cup black currants, plumped |
| 3 | tablespoons oil |
| 1/3 | cup red wine vinegar |
| 3 | tablespoons lemon juice |
| | salt and pepper to taste |
| | |
| 1/3 | cup chopped toasted almonds |

In a saucepan, bring water to a boil. Stir in cous cous, cover pan, lower heat and cook for about 3 minutes. Remove from heat and continue stirring to help separate the grains. Cook the carrots in boiling water until tender, but firm, drain and chop coarsely in a food processor. Poach chicken breasts in chicken broth until they are opaque, about 4 to 5 minutes. Drain and cut chicken into bite-size pieces.

In a large bowl, place all the ingredients (except the almonds), and toss until nicely blended. Taste and adjust seasonings. Cover bowl and refrigerate until serving time. Before serving sprinkle in chopped almonds. Serves 6.

# Broiled Vegetables with Yogurt Dressings

*The basic difference between broiling and grilling is the source of heat. When broiling, the heat comes from above...when grilling, the heat comes from below. Broiling or grilling vegetables has become a passion of mine. Served with a low-calorie dressing, it is a deeply satisfying and filling dish. Brushing the vegetables with the lightest coat of olive oil and sprinkling with lemon juice is perhaps the simplest of dressings. For a nice alternative, the following dressings are delicious and low-calorie, too. Broil or grill vegetables about 6 to 8 minutes on each side or until they are tender and flecked with brown.*

Note: To make broiling and turning the vegetables easier, purchase a long-handled grill that sandwiches the vegetables firmly in place. It is a handy tool that can be used in the oven or on the barbecue and takes the fuss out of broiling or grilling small-sized vegetables.

**Vegetables for Broiling or Grilling:**
The following vegetables are marvelous for broiling:  eggplant, zucchini, bell peppers (red, green or yellow are wonderful), asparagus, yellow squash, onions, cooked baby potatoes (not often included, but very good, too.)

**Yogurt Dressing with Lemon, Garlic & Basil:**

| | |
|---|---|
| 1 | cup low-fat or non-fat plain yogurt |
| 2 | tablespoons lemon juice |
| 1 | teaspoon vinegar |
| 2 | cloves garlic, minced |
| 1/4 | cup minced chives |
| 1/2 | teaspoon dried sweet basil flakes |
| | white pepper to taste |

Stir together all the ingredients until blended.  Yields 1 1/3 cups dressing.

**Honey Dill Yogurt Dressing:**

| | |
|---|---|
| 1 | cup low-fat or non-fat plain yogurt |
| 2 | teaspoons oil |
| 4 | tablespoons lemon juice |
| 1 | tablespoon Dijon mustard |
| 2 | tablespoons honey |
| 1/2 | teaspoon dried dill weed |
| | white pepper to taste |

Stir together all the ingredients until blended.  Yields 1 1/2 cups dressing.

**Tomato Salsa with Yogurt & Chives:**

| | |
|---|---|
| 1 | cup low-fat or non-fat yogurt |
| 2 | tomatoes, finely chopped |
| 4 | tablespoons chopped chives |
| 2 | tablespoons vinegar |
| 2 | tablespoons diced green chiles (from a 3-ounce can) |

Stir together all the ingredients until blended.  Yields 1 3/4 cups dressing.

# Cucumber Salad with Chives & Dill

*This is an old-fashioned cucumber salad, made without oil, in a sweet vinaigrette. The dressing is quite good and stores indefinitely in the refrigerator. Paper-thin sliced onions can be added to taste. The following is the basic salad. Please note that the cucumbers will render a great deal of liquid and dilute the dressing. A little extra vinegar can be added.*

- 3   large cucumbers, very thinly sliced
- 1/3   cup chopped chives
- 1   teaspoon dried dill weed

In a large bowl, toss together all the ingredients. Add Sweet Vinaigrette to taste. Cover bowl and refrigerate. To serve, taste, add a little vinegar if necessary and drain. Serves 6 to 8.

**Sweet Vinaigrette:**
- 1/2   cup white vinegar
- 1/3   cup water
- 1/3   cup sugar

In a jar with a tight-fitting lid, stir together vinegar, water and sugar until sugar is dissolved.

# The Incomparable Salad Caesar

**Caesar Dressing:**
- 6   tablespoons olive oil
- 1   tablespoon wine vinegar
- 4   tablespoons fresh lemon juice
- 1/2   cup grated Romano cheese
- 1/4   teaspoon salt or to taste
-   freshly ground pepper to taste
- 1   clove garlic, put through a garlic press
- 6   fillets of anchovies, minced. (Optional as original salad does not include anchovies.)

- 2   heads romaine lettuce, washed, dried and torn into bite-size pieces

- 1   cup prepared garlic croutons. (You can make croutons by cutting 6 slices of French or Italian bread into 1/2-inch squares. Saute bread cubes in olive oil or butter with 1 clove crushed garlic until they are crisp and golden.)

Beat oil with a wire whisk. Continue beating, adding the vinegar, lemon juice, grated cheese, salt, pepper, garlic and anchovies. Add lettuce, and toss carefully until the lettuce leaves are completely coated. Toss in croutons and serve at once so that the croutons do not get soggy. Serves 6.

# Chicken Salad in Honey Lemon Dressing

*Low-cholesterol mayonnaise and low-fat sour cream can be used, reducing the calories and cholesterol. This is a lovely salad to serve for a luncheon. It is also attractive on a buffet, mounded on a platter and surrounded by curly-leaf lettuce.*

1 1/2   pounds boneless chicken breasts, cut into cubes. Sprinkle lightly with garlic and onion powder and poach in 1 cup chicken broth until just cooked through and opaque. Do not overcook. Drain.
1/2   cup chopped chives
1/3   cup yellow raisins
1/2   cup slivered toasted almonds

Honey Lemon Dressing:
1/2   cup mayonnaise
1/2   cup sour cream
1/4   cup honey
3   tablespoons lemon juice

In a large bowl, toss together first 4 ingredients. Stir together dressing ingredients until blended and pour over the chicken mixture. Toss until everything is nicely coated. Serves 6.

# Broiled Marinated Vegetable Salad

*This is an interesting colorful salad, very delicious, and very filling. It is glamorous served warm and delicious when served cold. The large cuts are beautiful if you are arranging vegetables on individual plates. If you plan to serve this on a buffet, then cut the vegetables into smaller pieces.*

4   zucchini, cut in half lengthwise. Do not peel.
4   yellow zucchini, cut in half lengthwise. Do not peel.
1   red bell pepper, cut into 8 wedges
1   green bell pepper, cut into 8 wedges
1   small onion, cut into rings
3   cloves garlic, minced
1/4   cup lemon juice
1   tablespoon red wine vinegar
1   tablespoon water
2   tablespoons olive oil
   pinch of salt
   black pepper to taste

In a 9x13-inch baking pan, toss together all the ingredients, until everything is nicely mixed. Allow mixture to stand in the refrigerator for several hours. Broil vegetables, about 4-inches from the heat, for about 8 minutes. Toss and turn the vegetables and continue broiling for another 6 to 8 minutes, or until vegetables are tender and flecked with brown. Serve hot or cold. Serves 8.

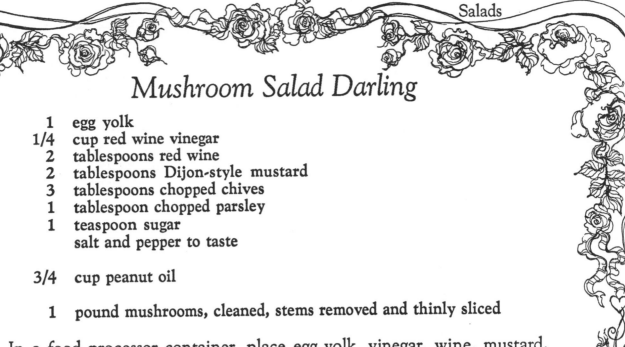

# Mushroom Salad Darling

- **1** egg yolk
- **1/4** cup red wine vinegar
- **2** tablespoons red wine
- **2** tablespoons Dijon-style mustard
- **3** tablespoons chopped chives
- **1** tablespoon chopped parsley
- **1** teaspoon sugar
  salt and pepper to taste

- **3/4** cup peanut oil

- **1** pound mushrooms, cleaned, stems removed and thinly sliced

In a food processor container, place egg yolk, vinegar, wine, mustard, chives, parsley, sugar, salt and pepper. Blend for 30 seconds.

Now add oil in a steady trickle, with the motor running, until dressing is creamy and oil is thoroughly incorporated. Pour 3/4 cup dressing over the mushrooms and toss until the mushrooms are completely coated. Sprinkle with some chopped chives and serve at once. Yields 1 1/2 cups.

*Note: -Unused dressing can be stored in the refrigerator for 1 week.*

# Homey Cole Slaw with Apples & Raisins

*Apples and raisins add a delicious sweetness to this cole slaw. This recipe is a nice change from the more-often-used crushed pineapple.*

- **1/2** cup low-fat mayonnaise
- **1/2** cup low-fat sour cream
- **1** teaspoon sugar

- **2** apples, peeled, cored, grated and tossed with 1/4 cup lemon juice

- **1** small head of cabbage, about 1 pound, shredded
- **2** carrots, peeled and grated
- **1/3** cup yellow raisins
- **1/2** teaspoon celery seed
  salt to taste

Stir together first 3 ingredients until blended. Toss apples in lemon juice until nicely coated. In a large bowl, toss together all the ingredients until well mixed. Serves 6 to 8.

# Grandma Stella's Treasured Potato Salad

*This salad is the best...and should be made just as described. It is important to follow the instructions. The vinegar and sugar should mix with the potatoes for 10 minutes before adding the mayonnaise. Why? Because this flavors the potatoes just a little stronger than if you mixed it all at once. Potato Salad can be prepared 1 day earlier and stored in the refrigerator.*

- 8 medium-sized potatoes, scrubbed and tubbed
- 3 carrots, grated
- 6 green onions, finely chopped. (Use the whole onion.)
- 2 tablespoons sugar
- 3 tablespoons cider vinegar
  salt to taste
  pepper, optional
- 3/4 cup mayonnaise

Cook the potatoes, unpeeled, in boiling water until they are tender. Do not overcook. Peel and cut them into small slices. (I find slicing more satisfactory than cubing.)

Combine potatoes, carrots and green onions. Sprinkle with sugar, vinegar and salt and toss to coat evenly. (Important!) Let mixture rest for 10 minutes. Now add sufficient mayonnaise to coat potatoes. Mix well and refrigerate. Garnish with some finely chopped green onions and carrot curls. Serves 8.

# Cucumbers with Chives & Dill Dressing

- 1/2 cup low-fat sour cream
- 1/4 cup low-fat mayonnasie
- 3 tablespoons fresh lemon juice
- 2 tablespoons chopped chives
- 1 tablespoon fresh dill weed or 1 teaspoon dried dill weed
  salt and white pepper to taste

- 3 cucumbers, thinly sliced

Combine all the ingredients except the cucumbers. Place dressing in a covered glass jar and refrigerate. Pour dressing over the cucumbers when ready to serve. Makes about 2 cups.

*Note: ♥ Do not mix cucumbers with dressing too much earlier, as cucumbers can render a good deal of liquid.*

## Red & Yellow Pepper, Artichoke, Onion Salad

- 2 red bell peppers, cut into 1-inch strips
- 2 yellow bell peppers, cut into 1-inch strips
- 1 large onion, cut into thin rings
- 1 jar (6 ounces) marinated artichoke hearts, cut into fourths. Do not drain.
- 2 tablespoons lemon juice
- 2 tablespoons red wine vinegar
- pinch of red pepper flakes
- salt and pepper to taste

In a covered Dutch oven casserole, simmer together all the ingredients for 25 minutes, or until peppers are tender. Place in a glass bowl and refrigerate. When ready to serve, add a little lemon juice, if necessary. Serves 8.

## Green Pea, Pimiento & Onion Salad

- 1 package (1 pound) frozen baby sweet peas
- 1/3 cup chopped green onions
- 1 tablespoon oil
- 4 tablespoons seasoned rice vinegar or red wine vinegar
- 1 jar (2 ounces) slivered pimiento
- 1 tablespoon grated Parmesan cheese
- salt and pepper to taste

Defrost peas and cook in boiling water for 2 minutes and drain. In a bowl, stir together all the ingredients until nicely blended. Cover and refrigerate until serving time. This is delicious served warm or cold. Serves 6.

## Cucumbers in Sour Cream

- 3 large cucumbers, peeled and thinly sliced

- 1 teaspoon sugar
- 1/8 teaspoon pepper
- 1 tablespoon lemon juice
- 2 tablespoons vinegar
- 3/4 cup low-fat sour cream
- 4 tablespoons chopped chives

Mix the cucumbers with the remaining ingredients and serve at once. Do not allow to stand too long or cucumbers will render their liquid and dressing will become watery. Serves 6.

# Carrot & Parsley Salad

*This is a nice little salad to serve on a buffet or antipasto. Using the whole baby carrots is a change from the usual slices or curls. Can be prepared 1 day earlier and stored in the refrigerator.*

   1    package (1 pound) frozen baby carrots
   2    tablespoons minced parsley
   2    tablespoons minced chives
   1    tablespoon oil
1/4    cup red wine vinegar
   1    teaspoon Dijon mustard
1/2    teaspoon sugar
       salt and pepper to taste

Cook carrots in boiling water for 4 minutes, or until tender but firm. In a bowl, stir together all the ingredients until nicely blended. Cover bowl and refrigerate until serving time. Serves 6.

# White Bean Salad
# with Red Peppers & Scallions

*Here is a nice salad with the colors of the Italian flag and just right for an antipasto. Using the canned beans saves hours of preparation and is recommended.*

   1    can (15 ounces) Cannellini or Great Northern beans,
           rinsed and drained
   2    marinated red peppers, cut into slivers
1/3    cup minced green onion
   4    tablespoons minced red onions
   1    clove garlic, minced
1/3    cup red wine vinegar
   2    tablespoons oil
   1    teaspoon Italian Herb Seasoning
       salt and pepper to taste

In a large bowl, toss together all the ingredients until nicely blended. Cover bowl and refrigerate until serving time. Serves 6.

# Mixed Bean Salad with Garlic Vinaigrette

*Using the canned beans saves you hours of preparation time, and the results are very good, indeed. This is a good choice for a dinner in a Mexican or Spanish mood. Italian is good, too. Can be prepared 1 day earlier and stored in the refrigerator.*

    1    can (1 pound) red kidney beans, rinsed and drained
    1    can (1 pound) garbanzos (chick peas), rinsed and drained
    1/3  cup chopped green onions
    2    cloves garlic, minced
    2    tablespoons chopped parsley
    3    tablespoons oil
    6    tablespoons red wine vinegar
    1    tablespoon Parmesan cheese
         salt and pepper to taste

In a bowl, stir together all the ingredients, until blended. Cover bowl and refrigerate until serving time. Serves 6 to 8.

# Vegetable & Pasta Pesto Salad

*This is an interesting pasta salad as it is filled with vegetables. The number of vegetables can be doubled for a very low-calorie dinner. If you are pressed for time, using the frozen vegetables is recommended in this recipe, as they are cut to perfect size, do not contain stalks or stems, and include only the florets of the vegetables.*

    1    package (8 ounces) corkscrew pasta or any small-sized pasta,
             cooked until tender and drained
    2    jars (6 ounces, each) marinated artichoke hearts, undrained
    4    tablespoons lemon juice
    1/2  cup chopped chives
    2    teaspoons sweet basil flakes
    1    package (1 pound) frozen Del Sol vegetables ( a combination of
             carrot sticks, broccoli florets and cauliflower florets in perfect
             cut sizes), parboiled and drained

In a large bowl, toss together all the ingredients and taste if more lemon juice is needed. Refrigerate until serving time. Taste again, as pasta has a way of soaking up all the flavor. Serves 8.

# Salad Dressing Joseph

*This is a marvellous little dressing. It is delicate and delicious. Serve it on salad greens, tomatoes or cucumbers.*

3/4 cup low-fat mayonnaise
3/4 cup low-fat sour cream
3 sprigs parsley (remove stems)
2 green onions, (use the whole onion...white and green parts)
2 tablespoons fresh lemon juice
salt and pepper to taste

Blend all the ingredients in the container of a food processor until onions and parsley are pureed, about 1 minute. Makes 2 cups dressing.

# Cucumber Garlic Yogurt Dressing or Dip for Raw Vegetables

1/2 cup non-fat unflavored yogurt
1/2 cup low-fat sour cream
2 cloves garlic, minced
1/3 cup chopped chives
2 tablespoons chopped parsley leaves
3 tablespoons lemon juice
1/3 teaspoon dried dill weed

2 large cucumbers, peeled, seeded and grated

In a large bowl, stir together first group of ingredients, cover bowl and refrigerate. Place cucumbers in a dish towel and squeeze to extract some of the liquid. When ready to serve, stir cucumbers into the dressing and serve as a dressing on salad or as a dip for raw vegetables. Yields about 3 1/2 cups.

# Pickled Beets with Onions

1 can (1 pound) sliced beets, drained. Reserve 1/2 cup beet juice.
1 onion, thinly sliced in rings

4 tablespoons wine vinegar
1 teaspoon sugar
1 tablespoon olive oil
1 clove garlic, cut in half
salt and pepper to taste

In a glass jar with a tight-fitting lid, combine all the ingredients with reserved 1/2 cup beet juice. Refrigerate for at least 2 days. Serve chilled. Serves 6.

# Mexican Salsa for Dipping with Raw Vegetables

| | |
|---|---|
| 1 | can (1 pound) stewed tomatoes, finely chopped.  Do not drain. |
| 1/3 | cup chopped green onions |
| 2 | tablespoons minced red onions |
| 1 | can (4 ounces) diced green chiles |
| 1 | clove garlic, minced |
| 2 | tablespoons chopped parsley |
| 2 | tablespoons red wine vinegar |
| 2 | tablespoons lemon juice |
| 1 | tablespoon oil |
| 2 | tablespoons chopped cilantro |
| 1/4 | teaspoon ground cumin |
| | pinch of sugar |
| | salt and pepper to taste |

In a quart-jar with a tight-fitting lid, shake together all the ingredients until mixture is nicely blended.  Refrigerate salsa for several hours. Overnight is good, too.  Serve with raw vegetables, cut on the diagonal, to make more room for the sauce.  You probably should have a few corn chips close by, and they are ideal, but higher in calories.  Yields 2 1/2 cups sauce.

# Green Goddess Dressing Darling

*This salad dressing is also exceptionally good as a dip for a cold vegetable platter.*

| | |
|---|---|
| 1 | cup mayonnaise |
| 1/4 | cup half and half |
| 1/4 | teaspoon garlic powder |
| 1/4 | cup parsley leaves |
| 3 | green onions, medium-sized, use the whole onion |
| | pinch of salt |

Combine all the ingredients in food processor container and blend at high speed until mixture is smooth.  Pour dressing into a glass jar, cover and refrigerate.  Makes 1 1/2 cups.

*Note:  -Dressing will keep for a week in the refrigerator.*

## The Best Dilled Pickles

        4   pounds pickling cucumbers, scrubbed, rubbed and tubbed
      1/3   cup salt
        2   cups water
       16   garlic cloves, sliced
        4   tablespoons pickling spice
      1/2   cup white vinegar
            water
    1 1/2   stalks fresh dill.  (Use the dill that has become twiggy.)
        1   slice rye bread with seeds

Boil together the salt and water until the salt is completely dissolved.  In a gallon wide-mouthed glass jar, place alternate layers of cucumbers, garlic, and pickling spice.  Add salted water, vinegar and enough extra water to cover the cucumbers.

Fold the dill and lay it across the top.  Place rye bread over the dill.  Cover and leave in a cool place for 3 days.  Test pickles for desired strength.  Give them an extra day or so if you desire more pickling.  Remove dill and rye bread and refrigerate pickles in the jar with the pickling juices.

## Tomatoes Deborah

*Years and years ago, this was a favorite salad with our friends.  And yet, to this day, when I serve it, everyone still loves it.*

        3   large tomatoes, cut into 1/2-inch slices
        2   tablespoons dried toasted onion flakes
        1   tablespoon chopped parsley leaves
        6   tablespoons salad oil
        3   tablespoons white wine vinegar
      3/4   teaspoon salt
        1   clove garlic, minced
        4   tablespoons grated Parmesan cheese

Place the tomatoes in a lovely glass serving bowl.  Combine the remaining ingredients and mix well.  Pour dressing over the tomatoes and marinate for at least 4 to 6 hours.  Serves 4.

# Fish & Shellfish

Baked Sea Bass with Eggplant & Tomatoes, 108
Sea Bass with Salsa Espagñol, 109
Red Snapper with Walnut Pesto Sauce, 109
Sea Bass with Tomatoes & Chiles, 110
Sea Bass with Sun-Dried Tomatoes & Peppers, 110
Sea Bass with Garlic & Rosemary, 111
Halibut with Garlic & Feta Cheese, 111
Halibut Vera Cruz with Hot Spanish Salsa, 112
Halibut with Tomato & Leek Sauce, 112
Fillets of Sole with Mushrooms & Wine Sauce, 113
Fillets of Sole with Mushrooms & Artichokes, 113
Red Snapper in Spicy Artichoke Sauce, 114
Swordfish with Sun-Dried Tomatoes & Red Peppers, 114
Swordfish with Tomatoes & Artichokes, 115
Fillets of Sole with Mustard Butter, 115
Fillets of Sole with Tomato Cheese Sauce, 116
Baked Tuna in Sauce Espagñol with Currants & Pine Nuts, 117
Whitefish with Lemon, Dill & Garlic Crumbs, 118
Shrimps in Lemon Garlic Sauce, 119
Tartar Sauce for Fish & Shellfish, 119
Shrimp Stuffed with Red Pepper & Chives, 120
Curried Shrimp with Yogurt Lemon Sauce, 120
Shrimp Jambalaya, 121
Pink Mayonnaise for Fish & Shellfish, 121
Shrimp with Mushroom & Sorrel Sauce, 122
Scallops Creole with Garlic & Herb Sauce, 123
Scallops in Mexican Salsa, 123
Shrimps with Mushroom & Shallot Sauce, 124
Lobster with Garlic Pesto & Parmesan Sauce, 125
Lobster in Mushroom & Shrimp Sauce, 125
Scallops with Caviar, Dill & Chive Sauce, 126
Crabmeat with Basil Shrimp Sauce, 126

# Baked Sea Bass with Eggplant & Tomatoes

*This is a really delicious sauce to serve over fish. It also serves well with sole or red snapper. Baking times will vary with the thickness of the fish. When fish flakes easily with a fork, remove it from the oven. Fish does not fare well with overcooking.*

1 eggplant (about 1 pound) peeled, quartered and thinly sliced
1 tablespoon olive oil

1 onion, chopped
2 cloves garlic, minced
1 can (1 pound) stewed tomatoes, chopped. Do not drain.
4 tablespoons lemon juice
1 teaspoon sugar
1 teaspoon olive oil

1 1/2 pounds sea bass fillets, sprinkled with garlic powder

In a 9x13-inch pan, lay the eggplant slices and drizzle with oil. Cover the pan tightly with foil and bake at 350° for 30 minutes, or until eggplant is soft. Remove eggplant and rinse pan. (Juices rendered can be bitter.)

Meanwhile in an uncovered Dutch oven casserole, simmer together next 6 ingredients until onion is soft, about 20 minutes. Add the eggplant and simmer uncovered for 10 minutes longer, or until sauce is slightly thickened. In the rinsed 9x13-inch baking pan, place fish in 1 layer and spread sauce evenly over the top. Bake at 350° for about 20 minutes, or until fish flakes easily with a fork. Yields 4 generous servings.

# Sea Bass Valencia with Salsa Espagñol

*This Spanish Sauce is delicious with any number of fish and shellfish. Sauce can be prepared earlier in the day and spooned over the fish before baking.*

Salsa Espagñol:
- 1 can (1 pound) stewed tomatoes, chopped. Do not drain.
- 2 tablespoons tomato paste
- 2 medium onions, chopped
- 1/2 green bell pepper, cut into strips
- 1/2 sweet red bell pepper, cut into strips
- 1 stalk celery, cut into very thin slices
- 3 cloves garlic, minced
- 4 tablespoons lemon juice
- 4 tablespoons dry white wine
- 1 teaspoon turmeric
- 1/2 teaspoon ground cumin
- 1/4 teaspoon hot red pepper flakes
  salt and pepper to taste

- 2 pounds sea bass fillets

In an uncovered Dutch oven casserole, simmer together first group of ingredients until vegetables are soft, and sauce has thickened slightly, about 25 minutes. Place fish in a 9x13-inch baking pan and spread sauce evenly on top. Bake at 350° for about 20 minutes, or until fish flakes easily with a fork. Do not overbake. Broil for a few seconds to brown the vegetables. Serves 6.

# Red Snapper with Walnut Pesto Sauce

- 1 1/2 pounds fillets of red snapper, cut into 4 ounce portions

Walnut Pesto Sauce:
- 1/4 cup minced fresh parsley
- 1/4 cup minced fresh basil
- 1 tablespoon melted butter
- 2 tablespoons grated Parmesan cheese
- 2 tablespoons lemon juice
- 4 tablespoons bottled clam broth
- 2 cloves garlic, minced
- 1/4 cup chopped walnuts

Place fish in one layer in a 9x13-inch baking pan. In a food processor, puree the remaining ingredients. Spread pesto mixture over the fish and bake in a 350° oven for 15 to 20 minutes or until fish is opaque and flakes easily with a fork. Brown tops for a few seconds under the broiler. Serves 6.

# Sea Bass with Tomatoes & Chiles

*Mildly hot and spicy, this sauce is also good with sole or red snapper. Cooking time will depend on the thickness of the fish. Reduce cooking time with sole. Do not overcook fish as it will become tough and rubbery.*

- 1/3 cup minced green onions
- 1 clove garlic, minced
- 4 canned tomatoes, drained and chopped
- 3 tablespoons lemon juice
- 1 can (7 ounces) diced green chiles
- 3 shakes cayenne pepper
- 2 tablespoons chopped cilantro
- salt to taste

- 1 1/2 pounds sea bass fillets, cut into 4-ounce portions

In a bowl, stir together first group of ingredients. Place fish in 1-layer in a 9x13-inch baking pan and spread sauce evenly on top. Bake in a 350° oven for about 20 minutes, or until fish flakes easily with a fork. Do not overbake. Place under a broiler for a few seconds to brown the vegetables. Serve with pink rice, pink orzo, or bulgur. Serves 6.

# Sea Bass with Sun-Dried Tomatoes & Peppers

*As a general rule, buy sun-dried tomatoes that are packed in oil. They are far more flavorful and the little bit of oil can easily be drained. Sun-dried tomatoes packed in salt, must be rinsed and then stored in oil. They are too salty for my taste.*

- 1 sweet red bell pepper, chopped
- 1/3 cup chopped sun-dried tomatoes
- 1 tablespoon oil
- 4 shallots, minced
- 2 cloves garlic, minced
- 2 tablespoons lemon juice
- 1 teaspoon Italian Herb Seasoning
- 1/3 cup, each, bottled clam broth and white wine

- 1 1/2 pounds fillets of sea bass, cut into 4-ounce portions

In a covered saucepan, simmer together first group of ingredients and simmer mixture for 30 minutes, or until pepper is tender. In a 9x13-inch baking pan, place fish in one layer and place sauce on top. Bake fish for 20 minutes, or until fish becomes opaque and flakes easily with a fork. Do not overbake. Serve with Pink Orzo. Serves 6.

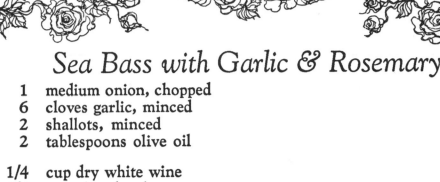

# Sea Bass with Garlic & Rosemary

| | |
|---|---|
| 1 | medium onion, chopped |
| 6 | cloves garlic, minced |
| 2 | shallots, minced |
| 2 | tablespoons olive oil |
| 1/4 | cup dry white wine |
| 1/4 | cup clam broth |
| 1/4 | cup half and half |
| 1 | teaspoon dried rosemary |
| 1/4 | teaspoon hot red pepper flakes |
| | salt and pepper to taste |
| 2 | pounds sea bass fillets |

In a large uncovered skillet, saute together first 4 ingredients until onion is soft. Add the wine and clam broth and simmer mixture for 3 minutes or until sauce is reduced by half. Add the next 5 ingredients and simmer another 5 minutes or until sauce is slightly thickened.

In a 9x13-inch baking pan, place fillets in one layer and pour sauce on top. Bake at 350° for 20 minutes or until fish flakes easily with a fork. Do not overbake. If fish has rendered too much liquid, remove the fish from the pan, return the pan to the oven, and continue baking until sauce is reduced to the consistency of heavy cream. Spoon sauce on top of fish and serve 6.

# Halibut with Tomatoes, Garlic & Feta Cheese

*This is a delicious dish in a Spanish mood. It is very low in fat and cholesterol. Cheese can be omitted, but it adds a good deal of taste for the small amount used.*

| | |
|---|---|
| 1 | medium onion, finely chopped |
| 2 | cloves garlic, minced |
| 2 | tablespoons lemon juice |
| 1 | can (1 pound) stewed tomatoes, chopped |
| 1/4 | teaspoon sweet basil flakes |
| 1 1/2 | pounds halibut fillets, cut into 6 serving pieces |
| 2 | tablespoons chopped black olives |
| 1/4 | cup (1 ounce) crumbled Feta cheese |

In an uncovered saucepan, cook together first 5 ingredients until onion is soft, about 15 minutes. In an 8x12-inch baking pan, spread half the sauce. Place fish on top in one layer, and top with the remaining sauce. Sprinkle top with olives and Feta cheese. Bake at 350° for 25 minutes, or until fish flakes easily with a fork. Serve with wild rice or brown rice. Serves 6.

# Halibut Vera Cruz with Hot Spanish Salsa

*This is a good sauce to use over sole, red snapper, bass or shrimp. If you like it really hot, increase the amount of cayenne.*

1 onion, chopped
4 shallots, minced
2 cloves garlic, minced
1 carrot, grated
1 tablespoon olive oil

1 can (1 pound) stewed tomatoes, drained and chopped. Reserve
   juice for another use.
1 can (3 ounces) diced green chiles
3 tablespoons lemon juice
2 tablespoons chopped cilantro
2 shakes cayenne pepper (or more to taste)
  salt and pepper to taste

2 pounds halibut fillets

In a saucepan, cook together first 5 ingredients until onion is soft. Add the next group of ingredients and simmer sauce for 5 minutes. Place fish in a 9x13-inch baking pan and pour the sauce over the top. Bake at 350° for about 20 minutes or until fish is opaque and flakes easily. Do not overbake. Broil for a few seconds to brown the vegetables. Serve with hot tortillas. Serves 8.

# Halibut with Tomato & Leek Sauce

Tomato & Leek Sauce:
2 leeks, chopped. (Use only the white and soft green parts.) Rinse
   every trace of sand.
3 shallots, minced
3 cloves garlic, minced
1 tablespoon oil
2 tomatoes, peeled, seeded and chopped
1/4 cup dry white wine
2 tablespoons lemon juice

6 halibut steaks (about 6 ounces, each)

In a saucepan, cook together first group of ingredients, until leeks are soft. Place fish in a 9x13-inch baking pan and spoon sauce on top. Bake at 350° for about 25 minutes, or until fish flakes easily with a fork. Serve with Pink Orzo. Serves 6.

## Fillets of Sole with Mushrooms & Wine Sauce

*Sauce can be prepared earlier in the day and spooned over the fish before baking. Sauce can be frozen. This sauce serves nicely with red snapper or sea bass.*

Mushroom & Wine Sauce:
- 1 pound mushrooms, thinly sliced
- 4 shallots, minced
- 2 cloves garlic, minced
- 1/2 teaspoon dried thyme flakes
- 1 tablespoon butter
- 1/4 cup dry white wine
- 1/4 cup clam broth

- 4 tablespoons lemon juice
- 2 pounds fillets of sole

In an uncovered Dutch oven casserole, over low heat, simmer together first group of ingredients, stirring from time to time, until mushrooms are tender and most of the liquid is absorbed. Stir in the lemon juice. Place fish in one layer, in a 12x16-inch baking pan and spoon sauce on top. Bake at 350° for 12 minutes, or until fish flakes easily with a fork. Serves 6.

## Fillets of Sole with Mushrooms and Artichokes

- 1 pound fillets of sole. Sprinkle with salt, pepper, garlic powder and paprika to taste

- 1/2 pound mushrooms, thinly sliced
- 1 jar (6 1/2 ounces) marinated artichokes, drained and chopped. Reserve 2 tablespoons marinade.
- 2 teaspoons lemon juice
- 1 can (1 pound) stewed tomatoes, drained and chopped
- 2 green onions, sliced thin

- 1/4 cup bread crumbs
- 1/4 cup grated Parmesan cheese

Place fillets in one layer in a 9x13-inch baking pan. Combine the next 5 ingredients and place evenly over the fish. Bake in a 350° oven for about 15 minutes or until fish flakes easily with a fork. Do not overcook. Combine bread crumbs and Parmesan cheese and sprinkle evenly over the top. Brown under the broiler for a few seconds. Serve with Paprika Parsley Potatoes. Serves 4.

## Red Snapper in Spicy Artichoke Sauce

*The Artichoke Sauce is also a fine accompaniment to fillets of sole or sea bass.*

| | |
|---|---|
| 1 | onion, chopped |
| 4 | shallots, minced |
| 6 | cloves garlic, minced |
| 1 | jar (6 1/2 ounces) marinated artichoke hearts, coarsely chopped |
| 1/4 | cup dry white wine |
| 1/4 | cup clam broth |
| 4 | canned tomatoes, drained and chopped |
| 1 | tablespoon tomato paste |
| 1 | teaspoon turmeric |
| 1/2 | teaspoon ground cumin |
| 3 | shakes cayenne pepper |
| | |
| 2 | pounds red snapper fillets, cut into 2-inch pieces |

In a Dutch oven casserole, simmer together first group of ingredients until onion is soft and sauce is slightly thickened. Place fish in one layer in a 9x13-inch baking pan and spread sauce on top. Bake in a 350° oven for 20 minutes or until fish is opaque and flakes easily with a fork. Do not overbake. Serve with Pink Rice with Tomato & Chives. Serves 8.

## Swordfish with Sun-Dried Tomatoes, Garlic & Red Peppers

| | |
|---|---|
| 8 | 1-inch thick swordfish steaks (about 6 ounces, each) |
| | |
| 2 | tablespoons olive oil |
| 4 | tablespoons lemon juice |
| 3 | sun-dried tomatoes packed in oil, drained and finely chopped |
| 2 | marinated red peppers, cut into thin strips |
| 1/4 | cup chopped green onions |
| 2 | cloves garlic, minced |
| 1/2 | tablespoon minced fresh, sweet basil or 1/2 teaspoon dried pepper to taste |

Place fish in one layer in a 9x13-inch baking pan. Combine the remaining ingredients and spread evenly over the fish. Bake fish at 350° for 20 minutes, or until it flakes easily with a fork. Broil for a few seconds to brown vegetables. Serves 8.

# Swordfish with Tomatoes & Artichokes

6   swordfish steaks, about 1-inch thick (about 6 ounces, each)
2   cloves garlic, minced
4   tablespoons lemon juice
1   can (1 pound) stewed tomatoes, drained and chopped
1   jar (7 ounces) marinated artichoke hearts, chopped
1/3  cup minced green onions
1/2  teaspoon sweet basil flakes
1   tablespoon chopped parsley
    pinch of cayenne pepper
2   tablespoons grated Parmesan cheese

In a 9x13-inch pan, place the swordfish in one layer. Stir together the remaining ingredients and place evenly over the fish. Bake at 350° for about 20 minutes, or until fish is opaque and flakes easily with a fork. Broil for a few seconds to lightly brown vegetables (optional). Serve with brown rice or bulgur. Serves 6.

# Fillets of Sole with Mustard Butter

2   pounds fillets of sole, sprinkled with salt, pepper and paprika

1   tablespoon butter
1   tablespoon olive oil
2   cloves garlic, minced or put through a press
2   tablespoons lemon juice

Spread fillets in one layer in a 12x16-inch baking pan. Heat together next 4 ingredients and brush butter mixture over the fillets. Place fish under a preheated broiler and broil for about 4 minutes or until the fish flakes easily. Not necessary to turn the fish and do not overcook. Transfer fillets to a serving dish. Garnish with lemon wedges and sprigs of parsley. Serve with a teaspoon of Mustard Butter on top. Serves 6.

Mustard Butter:
2   tablespoons butter (1/4 stick) softened
1   teaspoon Grey Poupon Dijon Mustard
1   tablespoon lemon juice
1/2  teaspoon grated lemon peel
    pinch of salt and pepper to taste

Beat butter with remaining ingredients until blended. Place mixture in a small glass serving bowl and refrigerate. Remove from the refrigerator about 15 minutes before serving. Yields 1/4 cup.

# Fillets of Sole with Tomato Cheese Sauce

2    pounds fillets of sole, sprinkled lightly with salt

1    tablespoon olive oil
1    tablespoon melted butter
2    cloves garlic, finely minced

2    cups Tomato Cheese Sauce
1/4  pound grated low-fat Mozzarella cheese

In a 12x16-inch pan, lay the fillets flat in one layer. Heat together the oil, butter and garlic and drizzle this mixture evenly over the fillets. Broil the fillets for about 3 to 4 minutes or until fish is opaque. Do not overcook.

Ladle Tomato Cheese Sauce over the fillets and then sprinkle the grated Mozzarella evenly over all. Broil for another minute or so until sauce is hot and cheese is melted and browned. Serves 6 to 8.

Tomato Cheese Sauce:
1    can (1 pound) Italian plum tomatoes, finely chopped.
        Do not drain.
3    ounces tomato paste (1/2 of a 6-ounce can)
1    teaspoon sugar
1    teaspoon olive oil
1/2  teaspoon Italian Herb Seasoning
1/2  teaspoon sweet basil flakes
1    tablespoon dried onion flakes
        pinch of salt and pepper to taste
2    tablespoons grated Parmesan cheese

Combine all the ingredients except the Parmesan cheese and simmer sauce for about 15 minutes. Stir in the cheese. Makes about 2 cups sauce.

# Baked Tuna in Spicy Sauce Espagñol with Currants & Pine Nuts

*This is a delicious change from broiled or grilled tuna. The sauce can be prepared earlier in the day and stored in the refrigerator. Spoon sauce over the fish just before baking.*

Sauce Espagñol:

| | |
|---|---|
| 1 | tablespoon olive oil |
| 3 | cloves garlic, minced |
| 2 | small onions, minced |

| | |
|---|---|
| 1 | can (1 pound) stewed tomatoes, drained and chopped |
| 1 | teaspoon sugar |
| 4 | tablespoons dried black currants |
| 2 | tablespoons lemon juice |
| 3 | shakes cayenne pepper |
| | salt and pepper to taste |

| | |
|---|---|
| 6 | tuna steaks, about 1-inch thick, about 2 pounds |
| 1/4 | cup toasted pine nuts |

In a saucepan, simmer together first group of ingredients until onions are softened. Add the next group of ingredients and simmer sauce for 10 minutes, uncovered, until sauce thickens slightly. Place fish in a 9x13-inch baking pan and spoon sauce over the top. Bake at 325° for about 30 minutes, or until fish flakes easily with a fork. Sprinkle top with pine nuts before serving. Serves 6.

# Whitefish with Lemon, Dill & Garlic Crumbs

*These savory crumbs made with lemon, chives, garlic and dill are lovely over sole, red snapper, sea bass or shrimp.*

Lemon, Dill & Garlic Crumbs:
| | |
|---|---|
| 1/4 | cup butter |
| 6 | cloves garlic, minced |
| 4 | shallots, minced |
| | |
| 1/4 | cup dry white wine |
| | |
| 1/2 | cup chopped chives |
| 2 | tablespoons chopped parsley leaves |
| 1/2 | teaspoon dried dill weed |
| 2 | tablespoons lemon juice |
| 1/2 | cup fresh bread crumbs |
| | |
| 2 | pounds whitefish fillets, brushed with a little butter and sprinkled with salt and white pepper |

In a skillet, saute together first 3 ingredients until shallots are softened. Add the wine and cook briskly for 3 or 4 minutes, or until wine has almost evaporated. Place mixture in a bowl and toss in the next 5 ingredients until blended. Place fish in one layer in a baking pan and sprinkle tops with crumb mixture. Pat crumbs down lightly. Bake at 350° for 15 minutes, or until fish flakes easily with a fork. Broil for a few seconds to brown crumbs. Sprinkle top with a little more lemon juice when serving. Serves 6.

# Shrimps in Lemon Garlic Sauce

2    pounds raw shrimp, peeled and deveined. Sprinkle with salt,
       white pepper and dust lightly with flour.
2    tablespoons olive oil
2    tablespoons butter, melted
4    tablespoons lemon juice
6    cloves garlic, minced

In a round or oval copper baker, combine all the ingredients. Turn and toss to coat shrimp evenly. Broil shrimp about 6-inches from the heat for about 3 minutes on each side, or until they just turn pink. Do not overcook. Remove shrimp from oven and sprinkle top with Garlic Crumbs. Broil for another minute or until crumbs are lightly browned. Serves 6.

Garlic Crumbs:
1    clove garlic, minced
1    tablespoon melted butter
1/8    cup cracker crumbs
1/8    cup grated Parmesan cheese
1    tablespoon minced parsley

Saute garlic in butter for 1 minute. Toss in the remaining ingredients until mixture is thoroughly blended.

# Tartar Sauce for Fish & Shellfish

3/4    cup mayonnaise
3/4    cup low-fat sour cream
1    tablespoon chopped parsley
1    green onion (Use the whole onion.)
2    tablespoons fresh lemon juice
    salt to taste

3    tablespoons sweet relish

In a food processor, blend first 6 ingredients. Stir in relish. Place mixture in a covered jar and refrigerate. Serve with fried fish or shellfish. Makes about 1 1/2 cups.

# Shrimp Stuffed with Red Pepper & Chives

*This savory herbed stuffing can be used with fillets of sole, sea bass or red snapper.*

- 1 carrot, grated
- 2 cloves garlic, minced
- 1/2 cup sweet red bell pepper, minced
- 1/2 teaspoon paprika
- 1/2 teaspoon sweet basil flakes
- 2 tablespoons butter

- 1/2 cup chopped chives
- 2 cups herb-seasoned stuffing mix
- 3/4 cup clam broth
- 1/2 cup water (use only enough to hold stuffing together)

- 2 pounds medium-size shrimp, shelled and deveined. Butterfly the shrimp by cutting a deep slit along the back. Brush shrimp with melted butter and sprinkle generously with garlic powder.

In a skillet, saute together first 6 ingredients until pepper is soft. Place mixture in a large mixing bowl and toss in the chives, stuffing mix and clam broth. Add only enough water to hold stuffing together. Divide the stuffing in the cut edge of each shrimp, pressing up the sides to hold stuffing in. Place shrimp in one layer in a 9x13-inch baking pan and bake at 400° for about 8 minutes, or until shrimp turn pink. Do not overbake. Serves 6.

# Curried Shrimp with Yogurt Lemon Sauce

- 1 egg
- 2 tablespoons half and half cream
- 4 tablespoons lemon juice
- 1/2 teaspoon finely grated lemon peel
- 1 teaspoon curry powder, or more to taste
- 1 cup unflavored low-fat yogurt
- 1/4 cup chopped chives
- white pepper to taste

- 1 1/2 pounds cooked shrimp

In your electric mixer, beat together all the ingredients, except the shrimp, until blended. Place mixture on the top of a double boiler over hot water and heat, stirring until mixture is warm. Do not boil.

Place shrimp in a shallow, oval baker. Spread sauce evenly over the shrimp and heat in a 350° oven until heated through. Do not overcook. Serve with Curry Rice with Raisins and Almonds. Serves 6.

# Shrimp Jambalaya

*This is a nice, easy shrimp dish that is bursting with flavor. The calories can be lowered by using firm-fleshed white fish like sole or halibut. This can be added to the soup base just before serving and cooked for 5 minutes, or until fish is opaque. Do not overcook. Soup base can be prepared earlier in the day and heated before serving. Add the shrimp or the fish just before serving.*

Soup Base:

| | |
|---|---|
| 2 | tomatoes, peeled, seeded and chopped, fresh or canned |
| 1 | small sweet red bell pepper, finely chopped |
| 1 | small green bell pepper, finely chopped |
| 1/2 | pound mushrooms, sliced |
| 1 | medium onion, finely chopped |
| 4 | cloves garlic, thinly sliced |
| 2 | teaspoons paprika |
| 1 | cup bottled clam broth |
| 1 | teaspoon turmeric, or more to taste |
| 2 | shakes cayenne pepper |
| | salt to taste |

| | |
|---|---|
| 1 | pound small raw shrimp, shelled and deveined |
| 2 | tablespoons butter |

In a covered Dutch oven casserole, simmer together first group of ingredients until vegetables are softened, about 20 minutes.

In a large skillet, over medium high heat, saute shrimp in butter until shrimp are opaque. Do not overcook. Add shrimp to the Dutch oven and heat through. Serve on a bed of rice. Serves 4.

# Pink Mayonnaise for Fish & Shellfish

| | |
|---|---|
| 1/2 | cup low-fat sour cream |
| 1/2 | cup low-fat non-cholesterol mayonnaise |
| 1/4 | cup chili sauce |
| 1/4 | cup chopped chives |
| 2 | tablespoons chopped parsley leaves |
| 2 | tablespoons lemon juice |
| | salt and pepper to taste |
| 1/2 | teaspoon dried dill weed (optional, but nice) |

Beat together all the ingredients until blended. Place dressing in a covered jar and refrigerate. Serve with cold fish or shellfish. Yields about 1 1/2 cups.

# Shrimp with Mushroom & Sorrel Sauce

*This is a simple little dish that can be assembled and cooked in literally a few minutes. The Mushroom Sauce can be made earlier in the day. Entire dish can be assembled earlier in the day, but should be heated just before serving. Do not overcook this dish. It should simply be heated through and served.*

*Sorrel puree is getting easier and easier to find in the gourmet section of most markets. The one I particularly like is packed in water and imported from Belgium. A teaspoon goes a long way to flavor a sauce. See note below on how to make sorrel puree in your kitchen.*

Mushroom & Sorrel Sauce:
- 1/2 pound mushrooms, sliced
- 1 tablespoon butter
- 1 tablespoon flour

- 1/2 cup half and half
- 2 tablespoons lemon juice
- 1/2 teaspoon sorrel puree
  pinch of salt and white pepper to taste

- 1 pound cooked shrimp

- 2 ounces Swiss or Gruyere cheese, grated (optional)
- 4 teaspoons chopped chives

Saute mushrooms in butter for about 5 minutes. Add flour and cook for a minute or two, stirring. Add next 4 ingredients and cook sauce for a few minutes until sauce thickens, stirring to keep sauce smooth.

Place shrimp in a 10-inch round baking pan and spoon sauce evenly over the shrimp. Top with Swiss cheese (optional) and chopped chives. Heat in a 350° oven until heated through. Do not overcook. Serve with baby roasted potatoes. Serves 4.

**To make sorrel puree:**
Remove the stems and drop the sorrel leaves in boiling water for just under one minute. Drain, lightly salt, puree and freeze the sorrel in small quantities in plastic bags.

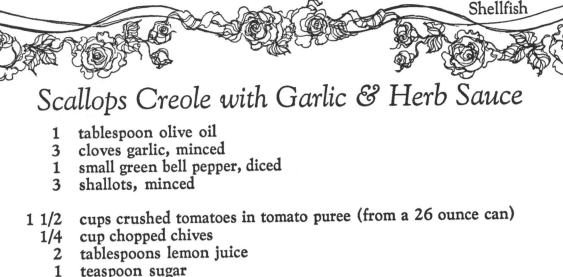

## Scallops Creole with Garlic & Herb Sauce

1   tablespoon olive oil
3   cloves garlic, minced
1   small green bell pepper, diced
3   shallots, minced

1 1/2   cups crushed tomatoes in tomato puree (from a 26 ounce can)
1/4   cup chopped chives
2   tablespoons lemon juice
1   teaspoon sugar
1/4   cup clam broth
3   shakes cayenne pepper or more to taste
1/2   teaspoon dried thyme flakes
1   bay leaf
    salt and pepper to taste

1   tablespoon olive oil
1 1/2   pounds bay scallops, sprinkled with salt and white pepper

In a Dutch oven casserole, saute together first 4 ingredients until vegetables are softened. Add the next group of ingredients and simmer sauce, uncovered, for 10 minutes. Meanwhile heat oil in a skillet, add the scallops, and saute, over high heat, stirring, until scallops are opaque. Do not overcook. Place scallops into the sauce and heat through. Serves 6.

## Scallops in Mexican Salsa

4   large stewed tomatoes (canned), seeded and chopped
1/3   cup chopped green onions
2   tablespoons vinegar
1   teaspoon oil
2   tablespoons chopped cilantro
1   teaspoon turmeric
1/2   teaspoon ground cumin
    salt and white pepper to taste

2   tablespoons oil
3   cloves garlic, minced
1   pound bay scallops, sprinkled lightly with salt and white pepper

In a Dutch oven casserole, heat first group of ingredients for 5 minutes. In a skillet, heat the oil and saute the garlic until softened. Raise the heat and saute the scallops, turning, until scallops are opaque. Place scallops in sauce and heat through. Serve on a bed of Pink Rice. Serves 4.

# Shrimps with Mushroom & Shallot Sauce

2     pounds raw shrimp, peeled and deveined

1     tablespoon butter
1     tablespoon olive oil
4     cloves garlic, finely minced
      salt and pepper to taste

In a 12-inch oval or 10-inch round copper baking pan (or any pan that will safely go under a broiler), heat together the butter, olive oil, garlic, salt and pepper for 1 minute. When butter mixture is hot, add shrimp. Cook shrimp, on the stove, over medium heat, tossing and turning, for about 5 minutes, or just until shrimp turn pink. Do not overcook or shrimp will toughen.

Spoon Mushroom and Shallot Sauce over the cooked shrimp and top with Seasoned Bread Crumbs. Broil for a minute or so until top is lightly browned. Serves 8.

Mushroom & Shallot Sauce:
      2     tablespoons butter
      6     shallots, minced
      1     onion, finely chopped
   1/2    red bell pepper, finely chopped
      1     pound mushrooms, cleaned and sliced

   1/2    cup low-fat sour cream
   1/2    cup half and half cream
   1/4    cup grated Parmesan cheese
   1/4    teaspoon thyme flakes
       pinch of salt and pepper to taste

In a large skillet, melt butter. Add shallots, onion and red pepper and saute until vegetables are soft. Add mushrooms and cook, over high heat, for another 5 minutes, or until mushrooms are tender and liquid is almost absorbed. Stir in remaining ingredients and heat through.

Seasoned Bread Crumbs:
   1/8    cup bread crumbs
   1/8    cup Parmesan cheese
      1     tablespoon chopped chives

Combine all the ingredients and mix thoroughly.

# Lobster with Garlic Pesto & Parmesan Sauce

*Using yogurt, instead of oil, in this delicious pesto sauce, reduces the calories markedly. It is not a rich sauce, but quite tasty. This pesto sauce can be used with any number of fish and shellfish.*

Garlic Pesto & Parmesan Sauce:
- 1/2    cup basil leaves, packed
- 1/2    cup pine nuts
- 4    cloves garlic
- 1    cup unflavored low-fat yogurt
- 3    tablespoons lemon juice
- 1/4    cup grated Parmesan cheese

- 6    halved, cooked lobster tails, about 6 ounces, each. Remove meat and cut it into large pieces. Reserve shells

- 6    teaspoons, each, bread crumbs and grated Parmesan cheese, mixed

In a food processor, puree together first 6 ingredients. Place sauce in a large bowl and toss with lobster meat. Fill reserved shells with lobster mixture and sprinkle tops with crumbs and cheese. Bake at 350° for 15 to 20 minutes, or until heated through. Broil for a few seconds to brown the tops. Serves 6.

# Lobster in Mushroom & Shrimp Sauce

- 6    halved, cooked lobster tails in shells, about 6 ounces each. Remove meat and cut into large pieces. Reserve shells.

Mushroom & Shrimp Sauce:
- 1/2    pound mushrooms, thinly sliced
- 6    shallots, minced
- 1    tablespoon butter

- 1    cup half and half cream
- 1/2    cup clam juice
- 2    tablespoons white wine

- 1/4    pound cooked tiny baby shrimp
- 1    cup grated Swiss cheese (3 ounces)

- 1/4    cup chopped chives

Saute mushrooms and shallots in butter for about 5 minutes. Add cream, clam juice and white wine and simmer over low heat for 10 minutes, or until sauce is reduced to about 1 cup. Add cooked baby shrimp, cheese and lobster.

Spoon mixture into reserved lobster shells and sprinkle tops generously with chopped chives. Heat through in a 350° oven and place under the broiler for a few seconds to lightly brown the tops. Serves 6.

# Scallops with Caviar, Dill & Chive Sauce

*This is a wonderful sauce to serve with any poached fish or shellfish. Using low-fat sour cream helps keep the calories low. Served in scallop shells makes a lovely presentation. Prepare earlier in the day and store in the refrigerator.*

1 1/2    pounds bay scallops, poached, just until opaque, about 2 or 3
         minutes in 1/2 cup white wine and 1 tablespoon lemon juice.

Caviar, Dill & Chive Sauce:
- 1    cup low-fat sour cream
- 1    clove garlic, very finely minced
- 2    tablespoons lemon juice
- 3    tablespoons minced chives
- 1/4   teaspoon dried dill weed
- 1    jar (2 ounces) red or golden caviar

Prepare scallops and drain. Place in a covered bowl and refrigerate. Stir together sauce ingredients until blended and refrigerate. When ready to serve, toss together scallops and sauce and serve in scallop shells. Serves 6.

# Crabmeat with Basil Shrimp Sauce

*The sauce is a Hollandaise, enhanced with baby shrimp and basil. Eliminate the egg and the butter and add 1 cup of low-fat yogurt for a less rich sauce.*

- 1    egg
- 4    tablespoons lemon juice
-     pinch of salt and white pepper

- 1/2   cup butter (1 stick)

- 1/4   cup sweet basil leaves
- 1/4   pound cooked baby shrimp

- 2    pounds cooked crabmeat, picked over for bones

Place first 4 ingredients in a blender or food processor container and blend for 10 seconds at high speed. Heat butter until it is sizzling hot and bubbly, but be careful not to brown it. Add the hot, sizzling butter very slowly, in a steady stream, while the motor continues running at high speed. When the butter is completely incorporated, add the basil and blend until it is pureed. Stir in the baby shrimp.

Place cooked crabmeat in 10-inch round baking pan and drizzle the sauce evenly on top. Broil until top is lightly browned, about 1 minute. Serves 8.

# Poultry & Dressing

Orange Honey Chicken with Sesame Topping, 128
Chicken in Mushroom Champagne Sauce, 128
Moroccan Chicken with Honey Lemon Glaze, 129
Bulgur with Apricots, Raisins & Pine Nuts, 129
Chicken Breasts with Herbed Stuffing & Mushroom Sauce, 130
Old-Fashioned Rosemary & Garlic Chicken, 131
Chicken Paella with Pine Nuts & Cheese, 131
Chicken with Hot Honey Plums, 132
Chicken in Raisin & Currant Sauce, 132
Old-Fashioned Stuffed Chicken with Herbs & Butter, 133
Chicken Breasts Stuffed with Apples & Pecans, 134
Golden Plum-Glazed Chicken Teriyaki, 135
Dark Currant Glazed Chicken Francaise, 135
Sesame Winglets in Honey Barbecue Sauce, 136
Honey & Orange Glazed Chicken, 136
Chicken with Sweet Potatoes, Figs & Apricots, 137
Chicken with Tomatoes & Mushrooms, 138
Buttermilk & Corn Flake Oven-Fried Chicken, 138
Chicken in an Elegant Lemon Dill Sauce, 139
Chicken Breasts with Tomatoes & Mozzarella, 139
Chicken Normandy with Apples & Raisins, 140
Southern Fried Chicken Epicurean, 141
Crispy Chicken Oven-Fried, 141
Cherry Glazed Chicken Breasts Stuffed with Wild Rice, 142
Chicken in Spanish Rice with Garbanzos, 143
Chicken & Vegetables with Garlic & Wine, 143
Cherry Orange Glazed Rock Cornish Hens, 144
Turkey Curry with Apples & Raisins, 145
Traditional Thanksgiving Turkey, 146
Old-Fashioned Bread Stuffing, 147
Chicken with Apples & Sauerkraut, 148
Garlic Puddings with Lemon & Cheese, 148

## Orange Honey Chicken with Sesame Topping

2   fryer chickens (about 3 pounds, each), cut into serving pieces.
      Sprinkle with pepper and garlic powder and dust with flour.
4   tablespoons butter (1/2 stick) melted

1/2   cup orange juice
1/2   cup honey

      sesame seeds

Place prepared chicken in roasting pan and drizzle with melted butter. Roast chicken in a 350° oven for 45 minutes. Meanwhile, heat together the honey and orange juice until the mixture is blended. Baste the chicken with the honey mixture and sprinkle with sesame seeds. Continue baking and basting for another 15 or 20  minutes, or until chicken is tender. Serves 6.

## Chicken in Mushroom Champagne Sauce

*The apple lends a delightful sweetness to the sauce. Baking the chicken first replaces the old way of browning it in fat. This is a very simple sauce but very delicate and delicious. If you use the sauce with chicken breasts, it would serve well for a dinner party.*

1   fryer chicken (2 1/2 to 3 pounds) cut into serving pieces
      Sprinkle with white pepper to taste.

1   onion, minced
4   shallots, minced
1/2   pound mushrooms, sliced
3/4   cup Champagne or dry white wine
1   apple, peeled, cored and grated

1/2   cup half and half

In a 9x13-inch roasting pan, bake chicken at 350° for 30 minutes. In a Dutch oven casserole, simmer together next 5 ingredients for 20 minutes. Add the half and half and simmer sauce for another 10 minutes. Place chicken in Dutch oven, cover pan, and simmer chicken for 25 minutes, or until chicken is tender. Serve chicken and sauce on a bed of noodles. Serves 4.

# Moroccan Chicken with Honey Lemon Glaze

*This is a really simple way to prepare chicken, but the bulgur is a little more work...but worth it.*

2     fryer chickens (2 1/2 pounds, each) cut into serving pieces. Sprinkle with garlic and onion powders.

1/4     cup honey
1/4     cup lemon juice
2     teaspoons curry powder

In a 12x16-inch pan, place chicken in 1 layer. Bake at 350° for 40 minutes. Stir together the remaining ingredients and baste chicken, every 10 minutes, until chicken is tender and glazed, about 30 minutes. Serve with Bulgur with Apricots, Raisins & Pine Nuts. Serves 8.

# Bulgur with Apricots, Raisins & Pine Nuts

1     large onion, chopped
6     cloves garlic, coarsely chopped
1     tablespoon olive oil

2     cups bulgur (cracked wheat)
4     cups chicken broth
1     teaspoon turmeric
    pepper to taste

1/4     cup chopped dried apricots
1/4     cup yellow raisins
1/4     cup dark raisins
2     cups boiling water

1/4     cup toasted pine nuts

In a Dutch oven casserole, saute together first 3 ingredients until onions are soft. Add the next 4 ingredients, cover pan, and a simmer mixture for 20 minutes or until bulgur is tender and liquid is absorbed. Meanwhile, soak dried fruit in boiling water for 20 minutes, or until plumped. Drain thoroughly, and pat dry with paper towelling. Add dried fruit to cooked bulgur and fluff it with a fork. Sprinkle with pine nuts before serving. Serves 8.

# Chicken Breasts with Herbed Stuffing
## & Sour Cream Mushroom Sauce

    4    chicken breast halves (about 4 ounces each), skinned, boned and
         slightly flattened.  Sprinkle with paprika, white pepper and
         garlic powder.

Herbed Stuffing:
    2    cups fresh white bread, remove crusts and cube, (about 6 slices)
    1/4  teaspoon paprika
    1/4  teaspoon poultry seasoning
         salt and white pepper to taste
    1/4  cup water
    1    teaspoon chicken seasoned stock base
    1    tablespoon finely chopped onion
    3    tablespoons melted butter

Mash all the stuffing ingredients together until they are thoroughly
blended.  Divide stuffing into 4 parts.  Place 1 part stuffing in center of
chicken breast, roll and secure with toothpicks.  Roll breasts in flour.

In an 8x8-inch baking pan, melt 2 tablespoons butter.  Roll stuffed breasts in
butter and bake at 325° for about 40 minutes or until breasts are opaque.  Do
not overbake.  Baste frequently during baking with juices in the pan.

Serve with a spoonful of Sour Cream and Mushroom Sauce ladled on top.
Decorate with parsley and whole spiced peaches.  Serves 4.

Sour Cream Mushroom Sauce:
    1/4  cup finely minced onion
    2    tablespoons butter
    1/4  pound mushrooms, thinly sliced
    1    tablespoon flour
    1/2  cup light cream
    1/2  cup sour cream
         salt and white pepper to taste
    1    tablespoon sauterne or sherry

Saute onion in butter until it is soft.  Add mushrooms and continue
sauteing until mushrooms are tender.  Add flour and cook for a minute or
two, stirring.  Add cream and cook over low heat, stirring, until sauce
thickens.  Add sour cream, seasonings and wine and heat through.  Do not
boil. Serve warm.

# Old-Fashioned Rosemary & Garlic Chicken

*Baking the chicken with the vegetables, gives this old-fashioned stew a totally different character.*

2 fryer chickens, (about 2 1/2 pounds, each), cut into
    serving pieces
1 onion, minced
6 cloves garlic, minced
6 carrots, thinly sliced
4 potatoes, peeled and cut into 1/2-inch slices
1 apple, peeled and sliced
1 stalk celery, very thinly sliced
1 teaspoon dried rosemary
2 cups chicken broth
    salt and pepper to taste

In a 12x16-inch pan, place chicken and all the ingredients. Cover pan tightly with foil and bake in a 350° oven for 30 to 40 minutes. Uncover pan and continue baking until chicken and vegetables are tender and browned, about another 30 minutes. Serves 8.

# Chicken Paella with Pine Nuts & Cheese

1 tablespoon oil
1 1/2 cups rice
3 cups rich chicken broth
1 teaspoon turmeric
1/2 teaspoon ground cumin
    salt and pepper to taste

1 clove garlic
4 shallots minced
3 sun-dried tomatoes, packed in oil, drained and chopped
1/4 cup chicken broth
4 cups left-over cooked and diced chicken or turkey

1/4 cup toasted pine nuts
1/4 cup grated Parmesan cheese

In a covered Dutch oven casserole, simmer together first group of ingredients for 30 minutes, or until rice is tender and liquid is absorbed. Meanwhile in a saucepan, cook together next 4 ingredients until shallots are soft. Stir in the chicken and heat through. Stir tomato mixture into rice until blended. Place paella in a large shallow bowl and serve sprinkled with pine nuts and cheese. Delicious! Serves 6.

# Chicken with Hot Honey Plums

*This is a lovely dish to serve for an informal dinner with family and friends. This is an adaptation of a chicken dish I used to make with prunes. Fresh plums are delicious when in season.*

2 fryer chickens (about 2 1/2 pounds each) cut into serving pieces. Sprinkle with garlic powder, onion powder and paprika and baste lightly with a little oil.

Hot Honey Plums:
- 3/4 cup plum jam
- 4 tablespoons honey
- 1/4 cup ketchup
- 3 tablespoons grated orange (1/2 medium orange, grated)
  pinch of cayenne
- 12 Italian purple plums, pitted and sliced

Place chicken in a 12x16-inch baking pan, and bake at 350° for 30 minutes. In a saucepan, heat together the sauce ingredients for 5 minutes. Pour sauce over the chicken and baste to cover the tops. Continue baking, basting now and again, for about 40 minutes, or until chicken is tender. Serve with brown rice. Serves 8.

# Chicken in Raisin & Currant Sauce

2 fryer chickens (about 3 pounds, each), cut into serving pieces. Sprinkle with pepper, paprika and garlic powder.
2 tablespoons butter, melted

- 1/2 cup dry red wine
- 1/2 cup beef broth
- 1 cup golden raisins
- 1/2 cup currants
- 1/2 cup currant jelly
- 1/4 cup ketchup
- 1 package dry onion soup
  salt and pepper to taste

Place chicken in a 12x16-inch roasting pan and drizzle with melted butter. Roast chicken in a 325° oven for 30 minutes, basting 2 or 3 times with the juices in the pan.

Meanwhile, heat together the remaining ingredients until the jelly is melted and the mixture is blended. Pour this sauce evenly over the chicken and continue baking for 45 minutes. Serve with Sweet and Sour Red Cabbage and Potato Pancakes. Serves 8.

# Old-Fashioned Stuffed Chicken, Roasted & Seasoned with Herbs & Butter

- 1 large roaster chicken (about 5 pounds)
- 1 package (12 ounces) Herb Seasoned Stuffing Mix

- 1 onion, finely chopped
- 1/2 cup celery, finely chopped
- 1/4 cup butter (1/2 stick)
- 1/4 pound mushrooms, thinly sliced

- 1 egg, beaten
- 3 tablespoons chopped parsley
- 1 teaspoon chicken seasoned stock base
- 1 teaspoon poultry seasoning
  salt and pepper to taste
- 3 cups chicken broth. (Use only enough to hold stuffing together.)

Place stuffing mix in a large bowl and set aside. Saute onion and celery in butter until soft. Add mushrooms and saute until mushrooms are tender. Add vegetables to stuffing mix. Add remaining ingredients using only enough chicken broth to hold stuffing together. Set aside.

Baste entire chicken, inside and out with Basting Mixture. Stuff and skewer chicken (see below) and baste again. Roast in a 350° oven for about 2 hours, basting every 15 or 20 minutes. Remove from oven, cut string and remove pins and string. Serve with hot biscuits and gravy. Serves 6 .

**Basting Mixture:**
- 1/3 cup melted butter
- 1/8 teaspoon salt
- 1/8 teaspoon pepper
- 1 teaspoon paprika
- 1 clove garlic, finely minced
- 1/4 teaspoon onion powder
- 2 tablespoons white wine

In a bowl, stir together all the ingredients.

**To Stuff and Skewer Chicken:**
Place stuffing loosely into neck and body of chicken. Pull neck skin over to back and skewer it down. Skewer body opening with 2 or 3 poultry pins. Lace strings around pins, back and forth. At the last turn, bring the string under the legs and tie them together. Tuck wings under.

*Note:* ♥ *To make gravy, use 1 cup of drippings from which all the fat has been removed. Cook it with 1 tablespoon flour until slightly thickened.*

# Chicken Breasts Stuffed with Apples & Pecans

*This is a nice dish to consider for a dinner party. It is very elegant and delicious. The stuffing is flavored with apples and raisins and the Brandy Cream Sauce is a perfect blend.*

6     chicken breast halves (about 4 ounces each), skinned, boned and slightly flattened. Sprinkle with paprika, white pepper and garlic powder.

Apple & Pecan Stuffing:
- 1 1/2   cups herb seasoned stuffing mix
- 1/2    cup coarsely chopped pecans
- 1     apple, peeled and grated
- 1/2    cup golden raisins
- 3     tablespoons melted butter
- 1     teaspoon chicken seasoned stock base
-      salt and pepper to taste
- 1     cup apple juice. (Use only enough to hold stuffing together.)

Combine all the ingredients, adding only enough apple juice to hold stuffing together. Divide stuffing into 6 parts. Place 1 part stuffing in the center of each chicken breast, roll and secure with toothpicks. Roll stuffed breasts lightly in flour.

In an 8x12-inch baking pan, melt 3 tablespoons butter. Roll stuffed breasts in butter and bake at 325° for about 30 minutes. Baste at least twice more during baking with the juices in the pan.

Serve with a spoonful of Brandy Cream Sauce ladled on top. Decorate with parsley and crab apples. Serves 6.

Brandy Cream Sauce:
- 1     onion, finely chopped
- 2     tablespoons butter (1/4 stick)
- 1/2    pound mushrooms, thinly sliced
- 1/4    cup brandy
- 1     tablespoon flour
- 1     cup half and half cream

Saute onion in butter until onion is soft. Add mushrooms and continue sauteing until mushrooms are tender. In a brandy warmer, warm brandy, ignite and carefully pour over the mushrooms. When flames are out, add flour and cook for a minute or two. Add cream and continue cooking over low heat until sauce has thickened. Serve warm.

# Golden Plum-Glazed Chicken Teriyaki

*This recipe has become a favorite and standard Friday night dinner with more people than I can recount. Perhaps because it is exceedingly simple to prepare and the glaze is beautiful and delicious.*

> 2 fryer chickens (about 2 1/2 pounds, each), cut into serving pieces. Baste generously with Teriyaki Marinade (page 162). Sprinkle with pepper and garlic powder.

Bake chicken in a preheated 325° oven for about 40 minutes. Baste with Plum Glaze 2 or 3 times during the remainder of the cooking time, about 40 minutes more. Excellent with Fried Rice. Serves 8.

**Plum Glaze:**
- 1 cup plum preserves
- 2 tablespoons ketchup
- 1 tablespoon vinegar
- 2 tablespoons brown sugar
- pinch of ginger

Combine all the ingredients and heat through until well blended.

# Dark Currant Glazed Chicken Francaise

> 2 fryer chickens (about 2 1/2 pounds, each), cut into serving pieces. Sprinkle with pepper and garlic powder and dust with flour.

> 2 tablespoons butter, melted

In a 12x16-inch pan, place chicken pieces and drizzle with butter. Bake chicken in a 325° oven for 45 minutes. Now baste with Francaise Sauce every 10 minutes until chicken is tender and glazed, about 30 minutes longer. Serves 8.

**Francaise Sauce:**
- 1 cup currant jelly
- 1 tablespoon ketchup
- 2 tablespoons lemon juice
- 2 tablespoons water

Combine all the ingredients and heat through until currant jelly is melted and mixture is well blended. (Unused glaze can be stored in the refrigerator for 1 week.)

## Sesame Winglets in Honey Barbecue Sauce

*This is a nice messy dish, so have lots of paper napkins close by. The glaze is sticky but yummy, so no one will mind.*

24  chicken wings, remove wing tips and then separate each into 2 pieces at the joint. Sprinkle with salt, pepper and garlic powder and brush with soy sauce.

Honey Barbecue Sauce:
- 3/4  cup honey
- 3/4  cup barbecue sauce
- 2  tablespoons lemon juice
- 1/4  teaspoon dried mustard
- smallest pinch of cayenne pepper

3  tablespoons sesame seeds

In a 9x13-inch baking pan, place chicken wings in 1 layer. Stir together next 5 ingredients until blended and baste chicken wings with sauce. Bake at 350° for 40 minutes, basting now and again with the sauce. Sprinkle chicken with sesame seeds and bake for another 20 minutes, or until seeds are just beginning to take on color. Careful not to burn. Serves 4.

## Honey & Orange Glazed Chicken

2  fryer chickens (about 2 1/2 pounds, each) cut into serving pieces. Sprinkle with salt, pepper and garlic powder.
1/4  cup butter (1/2 stick), melted

Place chicken in a 12x16-inch baking pan and drizzle melted butter over it. Bake in a 325° oven for about 30 minutes.

Now baste frequently with Honey & Orange Glaze until chicken is tender and a rich golden color, about another 30 or 40 minutes. Serve with brown rice. Serves 8.

Honey & Orange Glaze:
- 1  medium orange, grated (about 6 tablespoons fruit, juice and peel)
- 3/4  cup honey
- 1/4  teaspoon Dijon-style mustard

Combine all the ingredients and simmer over low heat for a few minutes until well blended.

# Chicken with Sweet Potatoes, Figs & Apricots

*This is a variation of a homey, family dish, made exotic with the addition of figs instead of prunes. If prunes are not your favorite dried fruit, you might enjoy this combination. It is basically a rich stew, flavored with dried fruits and cinnamon. Sweet potatoes are traditional, but can be omitted as the fruits stand alone quite well. Plain Cous Cous is a great accompaniment.*

- 2 fryer chickens (about 2 1/2 pounds, each) cut into serving pieces. Sprinkle with garlic powder, white pepper and paprika.
- 1/2 cup chicken broth

- 8 dried figs
- 8 dried apricots
- 2 pounds sweet potatoes, peeled and cut into 1/2-inch slices
- 1/2 cup orange juice
- 2 tablespoons brown sugar
- 2 tablespoons butter
- 1/2 teaspoon cinnamon

In a 12x16-inch roasting pan, place chicken in 1 layer and drizzle with broth. Set remaining ingredients evenly around the chicken. Cover pan with foil and bake at 350° for 35 minutes. Remove foil and continue baking for 35 minutes, or until chicken and potatoes are tender. Serve on a bed of Cous Cous as a perfect accompaniment. Serves 8.

**Plain Cous Cous:**
- 1 tablespoon oil
- 2 cups chicken broth
  pinch of salt
- 2 cups pre-cooked cous cous

Bring chicken broth, oil and salt to a boil. Stir in cous cous, lower heat, cover pan and cook cous cous for 2 or 3 minutes or until it is tender. Fluff with a fork to serve. Serves 8.

# Chicken with Tomatoes & Mushrooms

*Chicken in a mixed vegetable sauce is another great comfort food. The sauce is in an Italian mood...great with rice and delicious over pasta. This can be prepared a day earlier and stored in the refrigerator. Reheat before serving.*

- 2 fryer chickens (about 3 pounds, each) cut into serving pieces. Sprinkle with pepper, garlic powder and paprika. Dust lightly with flour.

- 1 onion, cut in half lengthwise and thinly sliced
- 1/2 pound mushrooms, remove stems and leave caps whole
- 1 green bell pepper, seeded and cut into thin strips
- 2 carrots, grated
- 1 can (1 pound 12 ounces) crushed tomatoes in puree
- 1 teaspoon sugar
- 1 teaspoon chicken seasoned stock base
- 1/2 cup dry red wine
- 1 bay leaf
  salt and pepper to taste
- 1 teaspoon Italian Herb Seasoning

In a 12x16-inch roasting pan, bake chicken at 350° for 30 minutes. In a Dutch oven casserole, cook together the remaining ingredients for 30 minutes. Pour sauce over the chicken and continue baking for 45 minutes, or until chicken is tender. Remove bay leaf. Serve with Rice with Tomatoes and Chives. Serves 6.

# Buttermilk & Corn Flake Oven-Fried Chicken

*This is a nice homey dish for a Sunday night dinner with the family. Crumbs can be additionally seasoned with onion powder, paprika or 1/4 cup grated Parmesan. Chicken can stick to the pan, and greasing the pan doesn't really help that much. If you do not own a non-stick baking pan, then line the pan with parchment paper.*

- 1 egg
- 1/4 cup buttermilk

- 1 cup prepared cornflake crumbs
- 1/2 teaspoon garlic powder
  salt and pepper to taste

- 1 fryer chicken (3 pounds) cut into serving pieces
- 3 tablespoons melted butter or margarine

In a shallow bowl, beat together egg and buttermilk. Stir together crumbs and seasonings and place in another shallow bowl. Dip chicken pieces into egg mixture and then coat with crumbs. Place in a non-stick 9x13-inch baking pan and drizzle with melted butter. Bake at 350°, without turning, for 1 hour 10 minutes or until chicken is tender. Serves 4 to 6.

# Chicken in an Elegant Lemon Dill Sauce

*This is another very subtle sauce that is light and very flavorful. If you are planning a dinner party on a night when time is really tight, this is a good dish to consider. Sauce can be prepared earlier in the day and stored in the refrigerator. Chicken should be baked before serving.*

8    chicken breast halves, sprinkled with garlic powder and flour. Brush lightly with 3 tablespoons melted butter.

Bake chicken at 350° for 20 to 25 minutes or until just cooked through.

Lemon Dill Sauce:
- 1/2   pound mushrooms, thinly sliced
- 4    shallots, minced
- 2    garlic cloves, minced
- 2    tablespoons butter

- 1/4   cup dry white wine
- 1/2   cup rich chicken broth
- 1/2   teaspoon dried dill weed
- 2    tablespoons lemon juice
- 1    cup half and half
-    salt to taste

In a saucepan, saute together first 4 ingredients until mushrooms are tender. Add the remaining ingredients and simmer the sauce, uncovered, for 10 minutes or until slightly thickened. Place the chicken on a serving platter and spoon a little sauce on top. Pass the remaining sauce at the table. Serves 8.

# Chicken Breasts with Tomatoes & Mozzarella

*This is a great family dish and good for informal dinners. Young and old seem to love it. Serve it with a side of pasta and zucchini.*

8    chicken breast halves (about 4 ounces each), skinned, boned and slightly flattened. Sprinkle with paprika and garlic powder.

   5-Minute Tomato Sauce
4    ounces low-fat Mozzarella cheese, grated
1/3   cup grated Parmesan cheese

Place chicken, in one layer, in a 9x13-inch baking pan and bake at 350° for 15 minutes, or until chicken is just cooked through. Do not overbake. Spoon 5-Minute Tomato Sauce over the top and sprinkle with Mozzarella and Parmesan cheese. Bake chicken at 350° for 10 minutes or until cheese is melted. Serves 8.

More →

Seasoned Flour:
- 1   cup flour
- 1/4  cup grated Parmesan cheese
- 1/2  teaspoon garlic powder
- 1/2  teaspoon onion powder
- 2   tablespoons paprika
-    pinch of cayenne pepper

In a plastic bag, shake together all the ingredients until blended. Unused flour can be stored in the freezer for an indefinite period.

5-Minute Tomato Sauce:
- 1   can (1 pound 12 ounces) crushed tomatoes in tomato puree
- 1/4  teaspoon coarse grind garlic powder
- 1   teaspoon sugar
- 1   teaspoon oil
- 1   teaspoon sweet basil flakes
- 1   teaspoon Italian Herb Seasoning
-    salt and pepper to taste
-    pinch of cayenne pepper

In a saucepan, heat together all the ingredients for 5 minutes.

# Chicken Normandy with Apples & Raisins

- 1   fryer chicken (2 1/2 to 3 pounds) cut into serving pieces.
  Sprinkle with white pepper to taste.

- 1   onion, minced
- 4   shallots, minced
- 2   cloves garlic, minced
- 1/2  cup apple cider
- 2   apples, peeled, cored and grated

- 1/3  cup yellow raisins
- 1/2  cup Low-Calorie Creme Fraiche

In a 9x13-inch roasting pan, bake chicken at 350° for 30 minutes. In a Dutch oven casserole, simmer together next 5 ingredients for 20 minutes. Place chicken in Dutch oven, cover pan, and simmer chicken for 25 minutes. Add the Creme Fraiche and raisins and simmer for another 10 minutes, or until chicken is tender. Serve chicken and sauce on a bed of noodles. Serves 4.

Low-Calorie Creme Fraiche:
- 1/4  cup low-fat sour cream
- 1/4  cup half and half

In a glass jar with a tight-fitting lid, stir together sour cream and half and half and allow to stand at room temperature for 1 hour. Cover jar and refrigerate for several hours until thickened. Yields 1/2 cup.

# Southern Fried Chicken Epicurean

*Hardly anyone fries chicken nowadays. And it's not because we avoid the oil because there are no end of convenient take-out places. This recipe is very tasty, can be lightly fried on the stove, and continued baking in the oven.*

2    fryer chickens (about 2 1/2 pounds, each) cut into serving pieces.
      Sprinkle with salt and pepper and dust lightly with flour.

2    eggs, beaten
2    tablespoons water
2    tablespoons grated Parmesan cheese

1    cup bread crumbs
1/2   teaspoon garlic powder
1    tablespoon paprika
1/2   cup grated Parmesan cheese
      salt and pepper to taste

Beat together the eggs, water and 2 tablespoons grated Parmesan and set aside. Combine crumbs, garlic powder, paprika, grated Parmesan and salt and pepper and mix together. (Unused crumb mixture can be stored indefinitely in the freezer.)

Dip prepared chicken pieces into the egg mixture and then into the crumb mixture and set chicken on waxed paper.

In a large skillet, heat 1/4-inch of oil. Over high heat, quickly fry and turn chicken pieces until golden brown on all sides. When brown, place chicken in a 12x16-inch baking pan and bake at 350° for 30 minutes or until chicken is tender. Serve with biscuits and honey. Serves 8.

# Crispy Chicken Oven-Fried

*Oven-fried chicken, sparkled with mustard and crunchy with crumbs and cheese is a good choice for Sunday night dinners with family and friends. This is also a good choice for a backyard picnic.*

2    fryer chickens (about 3 pounds, each), cut into serving pieces.
      Sprinkle with pepper and garlic powder and dust with flour.

1/4   cup Grey Poupon Dijon-style Mustard
1/4   cup mayonnaise

1/4   cup finely crushed Ritz cracker crumbs
1/4   cup Parmesan cheese, grated

2    tablespoons oil

More →

(Crispy Chicken Oven-Fried, Cont.)

Combine mustard and mayonnaise and mix together. Coat chicken with mustard mixture. Combine cracker crumbs and Parmesan cheese. Sprinkle cracker crumb mixture lightly over the chicken. Place chicken in one layer in a 12x16-inch baking pan.

Bake in a 325° oven for 30 minutes. Drizzle oil over the chicken and continue baking for 1 hour or until chicken is tender. Serves 6.

# Cherry Glazed Chicken Breasts Stuffed with Wild Rice

8   chicken breast halves (about 4 ounces each), skinned, boned and
    slightly flattened. Sprinkle with paprika and garlic powder.

     Wild Rice Stuffing
1/4  cup butter
     Cherry Glaze

Place 1 part stuffing in center of each chicken breast. Roll and secure with toothpicks or skewers. Roll stuffed breasts lightly in flour. Melt 1/4 cup butter in a 9x13-inch baking pan. Roll stuffed breasts in butter and bake in a 325° oven for 40 minutes. Continue baking for 20 minutes, basting with Cherry Glaze 2 or 3 times .

Wild Rice Stuffing:
Cook 1 package Herb Seasoned Wild and Long Grain Rice according to directions on the package. When rice is cooked, add 1/2 cup toasted slivered almonds. Divide stuffing into 8 parts.

Cherry Glaze:
1    cup black cherry preserves
1/3  cup frozen orange juice concentrate. Do not dilute.
1    teaspoon grated orange zest

Stir together all the ingredients and heat through.

Note:  ♥ Chicken breasts can be assembled in the morning and refrigerated.
          Bake before serving.
       ♥ I have not found it satisfactory to freeze.

## Chicken in Spanish Rice with Garbanzos & Sun-Dried Tomatoes

1   fryer chicken, about 3 pounds, cut into serving pieces.  Sprinkle with garlic and onion powder, turmeric and ground cumin.

1/2  cup chicken broth

1   cup rice
2   cups chicken broth
1   teaspoon turmeric
1/2  teaspoon ground cumin
2   teaspoons oil
1   can (1 pound) garbanzos, rinsed and drained
1   small onion, chopped
2   cloves garlic, minced
3   sun-dried tomatoes, chopped
    pepper to taste

Place chicken in a 9x13-inch baking pan and baste with broth.  Bake at 350° for 1 hour, basting now and again with the juices in the pan.  Meanwhile, in a Dutch oven casserole, stir in the remaining ingredients, cover pan and simmer mixture for 30 minutes, or until rice is tender and liquid is absorbed.  Serve rice on a large serving platter with chicken on top.  Serves 6.

## Chicken & Vegetables with Garlic & Wine

*Using a head of garlic sounds like a lot, but using the whole cloves renders a sweet and delicious flavor...not at all pungent or assertive.*

1   stalk celery, finely chopped
1   onion, finely chopped
2   carrots, finely chopped
2   tomatoes, peeled, seeded and chopped
1   head garlic, separated into cloves and peeled

1   fryer chicken (3 pounds) cut into serving pieces

2   tablespoons minced parsley
1/2  teaspoon dried thyme flakes
1   cup chicken broth
1/2  cup dry white wine
    salt and pepper to taste

In a 9x13-inch baking pan, scatter first 5 ingredients evenly.  Lay chicken chicken over the vegetables.  Stir together remaining ingredients and pour over the chicken.  Cover pan with foil and bake at 350° for 30 minutes.  Remove foil and continue baking for 30 minutes, or until chicken is tender.  Broil for a few seconds to brown top.  Serve with biscuits and honey.  Serves 6.

# Cherry Orange Glazed Rock Cornish Hens Stuffed with Fruits

*This is a good choice to serve for a dinner party. The stuffing, a medley of fruits that match the glaze, is unusual. The hens bake into a glorious golden color and present beautifully.*

6   Rock Cornish Hens (about 1 1/4 pounds, each).  Season with pepper, garlic powder, paprika and ginger.  Dust with flour.

1   onion, finely chopped
2   tablespoons butter
1   package (12 ounces) herb seasoned stuffing mix
1/8   teaspoon poultry seasoning
1/2   cup crushed pineapple, drained
1/2   cup orange sections, chopped
1/2   cup cherry pie filling
1/2   cup toasted, slivered almonds
    orange juice

Saute onion in butter until onion is soft.  Add remaining ingredients and mix well.  Add only enough orange juice to hold the stuffing together.  Stuff hen cavities about 3/4 full and skewer them with pins or toothpicks.

Brush the hens lightly with melted butter and bake them in a 325° oven for 45 minutes, basting them, every 15 minutes, with the juices in the pan.  Increase oven temperature to 350°.  Baste hens with Cherry Orange Glaze every 5 minutes for the next 15 to 20 minutes or until hens are tender and glaze is a golden color.  Serves 6.

**Cherry Orange Glaze:**
1   cup cherry pie filling
1/2   cup orange juice
1   teaspoon orange zest

Combine ingredients and heat through until they are blended.

# Turkey Curry with Apples & Raisins

*This is one of the most delicious ways to prepare leftover chicken or turkey. The apples and the raisins are a perfect counterpoint to the curry. Don't think for a minute that because it only contains humble ingredients, it is a dreary leftover dish. It is very, very good, indeed.*

3 cups cooked turkey or chicken, cut into large dice

1 onion, finely chopped
1 clove garlic, pressed or mashed
2 tablespoons butter

2 tablespoons flour
2 teaspoons curry powder or more to taste
   salt and pepper to taste

1 apple, peeled, cored and grated
1 tablespoon brown sugar
1/2 cup golden raisins, plumped in orange juice
1 cup turkey or chicken broth
1 cup low-fat sour cream

Saute onion and garlic in butter until onions are soft, but not brown. Add flour and cook and stir for a minute or so. Add curry powder, salt and pepper and mix well.

Add grated apple, brown sugar, raisins and broth. Cook over low heat, stirring until sauce thickens. (If the sauce is too thick, add a little more broth.) Taste and adjust seasonings. Add turkey and sour cream and heat through. Do not boil. Serves 6.

*Note:* ♥ *Entire dish can be made earlier in the day and refrigerated. Remove from the refrigerator about 1 hour before you are planning to heat it and let it come to room temperature. Reheat over low heat, stirring now and then, until heated through. Do not let the sauce boil.*

# Traditional Thanksgiving Turkey with Old-Fashioned Bread Stuffing

1   turkey (about 15 to 18 pounds), thoroughly cleaned

Baste turkey, inside and out, with Basting Mixture. Pack Old-Fashioned Bread Stuffing loosely into the neck and body of turkey. Pull neck skin over to the back and skewer it down. Skewer body opening with poultry pins. Lace string around pins, back and forth. At the last turn, bring the string under the legs and tie them together. Baste turkey again.

Place turkey on a rack in roasting pan, tent loosely with foil and baste often with Basting Mixture and juices in the pan. Continue baking and basting until turkey is done. (If special directions for roasting appear on the wrapper, follow them. If not, use the approximate roasting chart below.) Remove skewers and set turkey on a platter. Let it rest for 20 minutes, so that it will be easier to carve. Remove any fat from the gravy. Gravy is delicious and does not need to be thickened.

Basting Mixture:

 1   cup melted butter
1/2   teaspoon salt
 2   teaspoons onion powder
 2   teaspoons garlic powder
 2   tablespoons paprika

In a saucepan, heat together all the ingredients until blended. Use a 2-inch brush for basting turkey.

|  | Roasting Chart |  |
|---|---|---|
| Under 12 pounds | 325° | 25 minutes per pound |
| Over 12 pounds | 325° | 20 minutes per pound |

Roasting times are approximate. If you use a meat thermometer, insert it in the center of the inside thigh muscle. It should register 185° when turkey is cooked. You can test for doneness by moving the drumstick up and down. If it gives easily, turkey is done.

# Old-Fashioned Bread Stuffing

| | |
|---|---|
| 1/2 | cup butter |
| 2 | large onions, chopped (about 2 cups) |
| 1 | cup chopped celery |
| 1/2 | pound mushrooms, thinly sliced |
| | |
| 2 | eggs, beaten |
| 1/4 | cup chopped parsley leaves |
| 2 | teaspoons poultry seasoning |
| 1/2 | cup melted butter |
| | salt and pepper to taste |
| 2 | packages (8 ounces, each) herb seasoned stuffing mix |
| | |
| 2 | cans (10 1/2 ounces, each) chicken broth stirred with |
| | 2 teaspoons chicken seasoned stock base (Spice Islands) |

Saute onions and celery in butter until onions are soft. Add mushrooms and saute until mushrooms are tender. Place mixture in a large bowl and stir in the next 7 ingredients. Stir in only enough chicken broth to hold stuffing together.

*Note:* ♥ *Any leftover stuffing can be baked separately for 30 minutes before serving.*

Important:
1. Do not stuff turkey far in advance of roasting. Stuff shortly before roasting.
2. Remove stuffing before storing leftover turkey.
3. Improper handling of stuffing can lead to growth of harmful bacteria. So please take care to stuff turkey shortly before roasting and remove stuffing from turkey before storing.

## Chicken with Apples & Sauerkraut

*Here is a nice little chicken recipe in a German mood. Very easy to prepare and an interesting change from the usual. Partially baking the chicken in advance is a good way to brown it without fat.*

- 1 fryer chicken (about 3 pounds) cut into serving pieces. Sprinkle with garlic powder, onion powder and paprika.

- 1 large onion, chopped
- 3 cloves garlic, thinly sliced
- 1 tablespoon butter

- 1 apple, peeled, cored and grated
- 1/3 cup raisins
- 1 cup drained sauerkraut
- 1 large potato, peeled and diced
- 1 cup chicken broth

Place chicken in a 9x13-inch baking pan and bake at 350° for 40 minutes. Meanwhile, in a Dutch oven casserole, saute onion and garlic in butter until onion is softened. Add the remaining ingredients to the casserole, cover pan and simmer sauce for 30 minutes. Place the chicken into the sauce and continue cooking for about 30 minutes, or until chicken is tender. Serve with little Garlic Puddings. Serves 4.

## Garlic Puddings with Lemon & Cheese

*This is also a nice accompaniment to serve with roast lamb, veal or beef. Heady with garlic and flavored with lemon and cheese, this is an interesting alternative to potatoes or rice. Be certain to use a non-stick muffin pan and also, to grease it generously. These have a tendency to stick. Serve at once or they will settle down.*

- 6 cloves garlic, thinly sliced
- 1 tablespoon butter

- 3/4 cup milk
- 1/2 cup low-fat sour cream
- 2 eggs, beaten
- 6 slices fresh egg bread, crusts removed and cut into squares
- 1 tablespoon grated lemon
- 2 tablespoons grated Parmesan cheese
- salt to taste

In a skillet, saute garlic in butter for 1 minute. In the large bowl of an electric mixer, place the garlic and the remaining ingredients and beat until nicely blended. Divide mixture between 12 greased non-stick muffin cups and bake at 350° for 30 minutes, or until puffed and golden. Serve at once. Serves 6.

# Meats

Country Style Pot Roast, 150
Country Style Pot Roast II, 150
Easiest & Best Hungarian Goulash, 151
Tenderloin of Beef with Bearnaise Sauce, 152
Sour Cream Horseradish Sauce for Beef, 152
Easiest & Best Beef Stroganoff, 153
Mama's Meat Loaf in Herbed Tomato Sauce, 154
German Meat Loaf in Currant Sauce, 154
Hungarian Style Beef Paprikash, 155
Sauerbraten...German-Style Pot Roast, 155
Tenderloin of Beef with Mushroom & Chive Sauce, 156
Beef Burgundy...An Elegant Beef Stew, 157
Stuffed Leg of Lamb with Rosemary Gravy, 158
Rosemary Lamb with Tomatoes, Lemon & Garlic, 159
Lamb Shanks à la Grecque, 159
Lamb Dumplings with Currants in Spicy Sour Cherry Sauce, 160
Rice with Apricots, Raisins & Toasted Almonds, 160
Imperial Lamb Roast, 161
Curried Lamb with Yogurt & Garlic, 161
Roast Tenderloin of Pork with Apples & Honey Sauce, 162
Tenderloin of Pork with Orange Lemon Glaze, 163
Pork with Onions, 163
Apricot Glazed Pork Tenderloin with Sherry Creme Fraiche, 164
Stuffed Breast of Veal in Apricot Raisin Sauce, 165
Veal with Mushrooms & Dill Creme Fraiche, 166
Stuffed Veal Rolls in Herbed Tomato Sauce, 167
Veal Paprika in Cream, 168
Veal with Peppers, Tomatoes & Mushrooms, 169
Breaded Veal Scallops with Lemon & Green Onions, 169
Veal Scallops with Apples & Raisins, 170

*Good friends and informal dinners go together like love and marriage. What can smoothen a wrinkle in the spirit better than sitting around a table with some intimate friends, exchanging a few lively ideas and enjoying a country-style dinner with several hearty, robust dishes, a loaf of hot, crusty French bread and a flask of a full-bodied wine. Add a few fresh flowers, a candle or two and the pleasure will linger long after dinner is over. Country Style Pot Roast is a grand dish for just such occasions.*

# Country Style Pot Roast

4   pounds brisket of beef, lean and trimmed of all visible fat, and sprinkled with salt, pepper and garlic powder.

1   envelope dry Onion Soup Mix
1   can (12 ounces) beer
1/2   cup ketchup
1   cup (8 ounces) Whole Berry Cranberry Sauce

Place meat in a 9x13-inch roasting pan. Mix together the onion soup mix, beer, ketchup and cranberry sauce and pour mixture over the brisket. Cover pan tightly with foil and bake in a 350° oven until fork tender, about 2 1/2 hours. Remove from the oven and allow to cool in the refrigerator for several hours.

When cold, remove any fat that has congealed on top. Slice meat and return to pan with gravy. When ready to serve, heat in a 350° oven, covered with foil, for about 30 to 45 minutes or until meat is tender. Serves 8.

*Note:* ♥ *Gravy is delicious and does not need to be thickened.*
       ♥ *Entire dish can be prepared 1 day earlier and reheated at the time of serving with excellent results.*
       ♥ *Serve with Mushroom Rice and Cranberry Tangerine Mold as excellent accompaniments.*

Country-Style Pot Roast II:
1   envelope dry Onion Soup Mix
1   cup white wine
1/2   cup ketchup
1/2   cup brown sugar

Use this mixture instead of the one listed above. Everything else remains the same. This also produces a delicious gravy that does not need to be thickened.

# Easiest and Best Hungarian Goulash

*The beauty of this dish is that, by using sirloin steak, the meat can be cooked in 2 minutes, instead of 2 hours. In addition, the sirloin beef is tender and succulent, and the sauce is delicious. Using sour cream at room temperature allows it to blend easier into the sauce.*

2 pounds sirloin steak cut into 3x1x1/8-inch strips
2 tablespoons Dijon-style mustard
1 tablespoon butter

2 large onions, finely chopped
3 cloves garlic, minced
1 tablespoon butter
2 tablespoons brown sugar

1/4 cup ketchup
1 teaspoon Bovril, (concentrated Broth and Seasoning Base)
1/2 cup white wine
2 tablespoons paprika
pepper to taste

1 cup low-fat sour cream, at room temperature

Toss meat with mustard to coat evenly. In a Dutch oven casserole, saute meat in very hot butter for a few minutes until meat loses its pinkness. Meat is very tender. Do not overcook. Remove meat from pan and set aside. In same pan, saute together next 4 ingredients until onions are soft. Add next 5 ingredients and simmer sauce for 5 minutes.

Just before serving, stir in sour cream and heat through. Add beef and heat through. Do not allow to boil or sauce will curdle and meat will toughen. Serve on a bed of buttered noodles. Serves 8.

When the days turn warm suddenly, all at once, my thoughts gypsy to the sweet outdoors, to a picnic in the park, a banquet at the beach or a feast in a rolling meadow. Plain or fancy, dining outdoors on a glorious day is a time of wonder for me. For the children, it is a time to be free...a time to cast off their shoes and to feel the sun or the sand or the sea.

And, of course, sooner or later, (mostly sooner) all heads lightly turn to thoughts of food. For your next picnic, why not try a delectable tenderloin of beef, roasted to rare perfection and ladled with some exquisite Bearnaise Sauce. The Bearnaise Sauce is trouble-free, for it is kept ready and perfect in a Thermos-type jar. Wrap the roast in double thicknesses of plastic wrap and foil. And surely, the Tenderloin of Beef with Bearnaise Sauce is also marvellous for a very elegant dinner party.

## Tenderloin of Beef with Bearnaise Sauce

3    pound tenderloin of beef, rubbed with cut, fresh garlic, sprinkled with salt and pepper and brushed with 1 tablespoon melted butter

Insert meat thermometer in thickest part of roast. Roast meat in a preheated 400° oven until thermometer registers 140° for rare or 150° for medium-rare. Allow to stand for about 5 minutes, and then cut into slices. Serve with a spoonful of Bearnaise Sauce.

**Bearnaise Sauce:**

| | |
|---|---|
| 3 | egg yolks |
| 1 1/2 | tablespoons lemon juice |
| | pinch of salt and white pepper |
| 1 | tablespoon tarragon vinegar |
| 1 | teaspoon chopped parsley |
| 2 | tablespoons chopped chives |
| 1/4 | teaspoon dried tarragon or to taste |
| 3/4 | cup butter |

Place all the ingredients, except the butter, in the container of a food processor or blender. Blend for 10 seconds at high speed. Heat butter until it is sizzling hot and bubbly, but be careful not to brown it. Add the hot, sizzling butter very slowly, in a steady stream, while the processor or blender continues running at high speed. When the butter is completely incorporated, sauce will be thick and ready to serve. Yields about 1 cup.

**Sour Cream Horseradish Sauce for Beef:**
*This is one of the nicest sauces to serve with roast beef or boiled beef. I have often made horseradish sauce with whipped cream. This one is far lower in calories and very good, too.*

| | |
|---|---|
| 1 | cup low-fat sour cream |
| 2 | tablespoons prepared horseradish |
| 2 | tablespoons lemon juice |
| 3 | tablespoons chopped chives |

Stir together all the ingredients until blended. Place in a glass jar, cover and refrigerate until serving time. Yields about 1 1/4 cups sauce.

# Easiest & Best Beef Stroganoff

*In this very elegant Stroganoff, I again substitute sirloin steak for the usual round steak. As the sirloin cooks up in minutes, the beef is marvelously tender and delicious. And actually, it is not more expensive, as there is less shrinkage and a little more yield. But that is all "commentary". The important point is, Stroganoff, prepared this way, is simply more delicious...period.*

| | |
|---|---|
| 2 | pounds sirloin steak cut into 3x1x1/4-inch strips |
| 2 | tablespoons Grey Poupon Dijon-style Mustard |
| 1 | tablespoon butter |
| | |
| 4 | shallots, finely chopped |
| 1/2 | pound mushrooms, cleaned and sliced |
| 1 | tablespoon butter |
| | |
| 1/4 | cup white wine |
| 1 1/2 | teaspoons flour |
| | salt and pepper to taste |
| | |
| 1 | cup low-fat sour cream, at room temperature |

Toss the meat with the mustard to coat evenly. In a Dutch oven casserole, saute meat in very hot butter for a few minutes until meat loses its pinkness. Meat is very tender. Do not overcook. Remove meat and set aside.

In the same pan, saute shallots and mushrooms in butter until mushrooms are tender. Add the wine and cook for a few minutes until wine has evaporated. Add the flour and seasonings and cook for 1 minute, stirring. Add the meat to the pan, stir in the sour cream and heat through. Do not allow to boil. Serve on a bed of buttered noodles. Serves 6.

## Mama's Meat Loaf in Herbed Tomato Sauce

*This recipe is an oldie, but goodie. It is my Mom's meat loaf and I have found very few to improve on it. It is a very juicy and succulent meat loaf. You can substitute ground turkey for the beef and it will still be very good. To delicately flavor the meat, the important point to consider is that the onion be grated. If you do not grate the onion, it will not be the same. Onion can be grated in a food processor.*

**Meat Loaf:**
| | |
|---|---|
| 1 1/2 | pounds ground beef |
| 1 | small onion, grated |
| 4 | slices bread, crusts removed. Dip lightly in water and squeeze dry. |
| 1 | egg |
| 1/8 | teaspoon garlic powder |
| | salt and pepper to taste |
| 1 | tablespoon finely minced parsley |
| 1/2 | cup 5-Minute Tomato Sauce (page 140) |

**Tomato Sauce Topping:**
| | |
|---|---|
| 1 | cup 5-Minute Tomato Sauce (page 140) |

Combine all the meat loaf ingredients and mix lightly, until thoroughly blended. Place meat mixture into a 9x5-inch loaf pan. Pour Tomato Sauce Topping on the top. Bake in a 350° oven for about 1 hour. Serves 6.

## German Meat Loaf in Currant Sauce

*This is an unusual meat loaf in a German mood. Serve with potato pancakes or dumplings and Sweet and Sour Red Cabbage.*

| | |
|---|---|
| 1 1/2 | pounds ground beef |
| 1 | cup herbed stuffing mix, soaked in 1/2 cup milk |
| 2 | eggs, beaten |
| 1 | small onion, grated |
| 1 | tablespoon chopped parsley |
| | salt and pepper to taste |

In a large bowl, mix together all the ingredients and spread mixture evenly in a 9x5-inch loaf pan. Spread Currant Sauce over the top. Bake at 350° for about 1 hour. Serves 6.

**Currant Sauce:**
| | |
|---|---|
| 1/2 | cup currant jelly |
| 1/2 | cup chili sauce |
| 1 | tablespoon lemon juice |
| 2 | tablespoons black currants |
| 1/2 | teaspoon prepared mustard |

Stir together all the ingredients in a saucepan, and heat until jelly is melted and mixture is blended.

# Hungarian-Style Beef Paprikash

*This is another classic dish where I have used the sirloin steak instead of stewing beef. It saves hours of preparation time, but the extra bonus is, it is more delicious and tender.*

| | |
|---|---|
| 1 | tablespoon oil |
| 1 1/2 | pounds sirloin steak, cut into 3x1x1/4-inch strips |
| | |
| 1 | large onion, finely chopped (about 1 cup) |
| 2 | tablespoons paprika |
| 1/2 | cup half and half cream |
| 1/2 | cup low-fat sour cream |
| | salt and pepper to taste |

In a Dutch oven casserole, heat oil until it sizzles, but does not brown. Add meat and cook and toss until meat loses its pinkness. Do not overcook or meat will toughen up. Remove meat and set aside.

In same pan, add onion and cook over low heat until onion is soft. Stir together paprika, cream, sour cream and seasonings until well mixed. Add to the pan and simmer sauce for 3 minutes over low heat. Do not allow to boil. Add beef and heat through. Serve with Noodles with Poppy Seeds. Serves 6.

# Sauerbraten . . . German -Style Pot Roast

*Traditionally, Sauerbraten is marinated for several days. However, it is very delicate prepared this way. This can be prepared 1 day earlier and stored in the refrigerator. Be careful when reheating, as the ginger snaps can scorch.*

| | |
|---|---|
| 4 | pounds top round of beef, cubed, sprinkled with pepper and garlic powder. Dust lightly with flour. |
| | |
| 1/2 | cup brown sugar |
| 1/2 | cup vinegar |
| 1/2 | cup dry red wine |
| 2 | cloves garlic, minced |
| 2 | bay leaves |
| 8 | peppercorns |
| 5 | cloves |
| 1 | onion, grated |
| | salt to taste |
| | |
| 1/2 | cup crumbled ginger snaps, rolled into crumbs |

More →

(Sauerbraten...German-Style Pot Roast, Cont.)

In a large Dutch oven casserole, brown meat on all sides. Add all the ingredients except the ginger snaps, cover pan and simmer gently for about 1 1/2 hours or until meat is tender. Turn 2 or 3 times during cooking. Remove meat and strain gravy. Skim off any excess fat.

Heat gravy and add the ginger snap crumbs to thicken, stirring all the while. Be careful not to let the gravy scorch. Return meat to the gravy and heat through. Traditionally served with Sweet and Sour Red Cabbage and either dumplings or potato pancakes. Delicious! Serves 8.

# Tenderloin of Beef with Mushroom & Chive Sauce

*The Mushroom & Chive Sauce is an excellent, light natural sauce that is just lovely with beef. The Sauce Robert can be found in 2 styles...imported from France or domestic. Purchase the domestic, as the imported one is markedly higher in price, and the quality and taste are identical.*

3 pound tenderloin of beef, rubbed with cut fresh garlic, sprinkled with salt and pepper and brushed with 1 tablespoon melted butter

Insert meat thermometer in thickest part of roast. Roast meat in a preheated 400° oven until thermometer registers 140° for rare or 150° for medium-rare. Allow to stand for about 5 minutes, and then cut into slices and serve with a spoonful of Mushroom & Chive Sauce.

Mushroom & Chive Sauce:
- 1/2 pound mushrooms, sliced
- 1 tablespoon butter
- 1 cup beef broth
- 1 teaspoon Bovril, concentrated meat extract
- 1 tablespoon chives, finely chopped
- 1 tablespoon parsley, finely chopped
- 1 tablespoon Sauce Robert
- salt and pepper to taste

Saute mushrooms in butter until they are tender. Add the remaining ingredients and simmer sauce for 3 minutes.

# Beef Burgundy . . .
## an Elegant Beef Stew in Wine

*There was a time when Beef Bourguignon was a hallmark of French cuisine. Today, it is a great family dish, and while not considered grand cuisine, it still packs a lot of pleasure and enjoyment. Have some crusty French bread close by, to dip into the delicious gravy.*

| | |
|---|---|
| 2 | tablespoons olive oil |
| 2 | pounds beef chuck, cut into 3/4-inch cubes and dredged in flour |
| 3 | cloves garlic, minced |
| | |
| 3 | medium carrots, peeled and quartered |
| 1 | large onion, peeled and quartered |
| 1 | can (10 1/2 ounces) beef broth |
| | |
| 1/2 | cup Burgundy wine |
| | salt to taste |
| 1/4 | teaspoon pepper |
| 1 | bay leaf |
| | pinch thyme flakes |
| 1 | tablespoon tomato paste |

In a Dutch oven casserole, heat oil. Add beef and garlic and brown meat on all sides. Place meat in a 9x13-inch baking pan.

Place vegetables and broth in food processor container and blend vegetable mixture until it is finely chopped. Now, place vegetable mixture and remaining ingredients over the meat, cover pan tightly with foil and bake in a preheated 350° oven for about 2 hours or until meat is tender. Remove bay leaf. Serve over rice or noodles. Serves 8.

# Stuffed Leg of Lamb with Rosemary Gravy

*Try this marvellous dish for your next dinner party. Stuffing and Rosemary Gravy can be assembled the day before. Lamb can be stuffed earlier in the day you are planning to serve it, providing the stuffing is frosty cold and the stuffed lamb is kept refrigerated. I would prefer, however, that you stuff the lamb just before roasting.*

1   leg of lamb (5 to 6 pounds). **Ask the butcher to remove the bone. Sprinkle with salt and pepper. Rub with fresh cut garlic.**

Stuffing:
- 1   onion, finely chopped
- 2   cloves garlic, minced
- 1   teaspoon butter
- 1   cup herb seasoned stuffing mix
- 1/4   teaspoon ground rosemary
- 2   tablespoons chopped parsley
- 1   egg, beaten
- 3/4   cup beef broth. Use only enough to hold stuffing together.
-   salt and pepper to taste

In a skillet, over low heat, saute onion and garlic in butter until onion is soft but not browned. Place in a bowl and add all the stuffing ingredients, with only sufficient broth to hold stuffing together. Lay meat, cut side up and place stuffing in center of cavity. Bring the sides up to cover the stuffing. Fasten with metal skewers and tie the roast with string to reshape it.

Place roast in a 9x13-inch baking pan and pour Rosemary Gravy over the top. Place a meat thermometer in the thickest part of the meat, and bake at 350° for about 1 hour and 10 minutes, or until meat thermometer registers 150° for medium-rare or 160° for medium. Baste frequently with the gravy mixture in the pan.

When lamb is cooked, remove any excess fat from the gravy and adjust the seasonings. If necessary, thicken gravy with 1 tablespoon flour. Slice the lamb with a sharp knife and ladle with hot gravy at time of serving. Serves 6.

Rosemary Gravy:
- 2   tablespoons olive oil
- 6   cloves garlic, minced
- 2   teaspoons dried rosemary
- 1/3   cup red wine vinegar
- 1/2   cup beef broth
- 1/2   cup red wine

Stir together all the ingredients until blended.

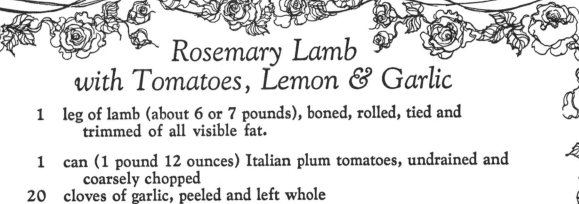

# Rosemary Lamb
## with Tomatoes, Lemon & Garlic

1   leg of lamb (about 6 or 7 pounds), boned, rolled, tied and
      trimmed of all visible fat.

1   can (1 pound 12 ounces) Italian plum tomatoes, undrained and
      coarsely chopped
20  cloves of garlic, peeled and left whole
1/4  cup lemon juice
1   teaspoon crumbled dried rosemary
      salt and pepper to taste

Insert meat thermometer in thickest part of lamb and place in roasting pan. Stir together the remaining ingredients and place around the lamb. Bake at 425° for 20 minutes, lower heat to 350° and continue roasting for about 1 1/2 hours or until thermometer registers 150° for medium rare. (During this time, baste lamb with the juices in the pan and keep garlic covered with the tomatoes to make certain the garlic does not burn.)

Remove meat from pan and place on a serving platter. Surround with the tomato/garlic mixture. Garlic is very sweet at this point. Slice at the table. Serves 8.

# Lamb Shanks à la Grecque

4   lamb shanks (about 12 ounces, each), trimmed of all visible fat
      and membranes. Sprinkle with salt and pepper to taste.
4   medium onions, cut into 1/4-inch slices and separated into rings
2   tablespoons olive oil

6   cloves garlic, minced
2   cans (1 pound, each) stewed tomatoes, chopped. Do not drain.
6   tablespoons tomato paste
1/2  cup dry white wine
1   carrot, grated
1   teaspoon sugar
1/2  teaspoon, each, oregano, sweet basil and thyme flakes
3   shakes cayenne pepper

In a 9x13-inch baking pan, place lamb shanks, scatter onions evenly on top and drizzle with oil. Bake at 400° for 30 minutes. In a bowl, stir together the remaining ingredients until blended and pour sauce evenly over the lamb. Cover the pan with foil and continue baking for 45 minutes, or until lamb is fork tender. Remove foil and continue baking for 15 minutes or until lamb is tender. Serve lamb and sauce with Pink Orzo as a delicious accompaniment. Generously serves 4.

# Lamb Dumplings with Currants in Spicy Sour Cherry Sauce

*These savory little meatballs make an interesting hors d'oeuvre or main course. Cherry glazes and sauces are becoming more and more popular lately. For the longest while they were on a back burner, so to speak. To make these as an hors d'oeuvre, shape meat into 3/4-inch balls and serve in a chafing dish with warm sauce close by for dipping. This recipe can be doubled.*

| | |
|---|---|
| 1 | pound lean ground lamb |
| 1 | small onion, grated |
| 2 | cloves garlic, minced |
| 3 | slices egg bread, crusts removed, soaked in water and squeezed dry |
| 1 | egg |
| 3 | tablespoons dried currants |
| 1/4 | teaspoon cinnamon |
| | salt to taste |

In a large bowl, stir together all the ingredients until blended. Form mixture into 1-inch balls. Flatten them slightly to make dumplings. Saute them in a little oil until browned on both sides and cooked through. Serve with a little Spicy Sour Cherry Sauce on top. Rice with Apricots, Raisins & Toasted Almonds is an exotic accompaniment. Makes 12 dumplings and serves 4.

Spicy Sour Cherry Sauce:

| | |
|---|---|
| 1 | cup sour cherry (or ruby red cherry) pie filling (from a 1 pound 5-ounce can) |
| 3 | tablespoons finely grated orange |
| 1/2 | teaspoon cinnamon |
| | pinch of ground cloves |

Heat together all the ingredients for 3 minutes or until orange peel is softened. Yields 1 1/4 cups sauce. (Extra sauce can be used to baste chicken.)

Rice with Apricots, Raisins & Toasted Almonds:

| | |
|---|---|
| 1 | small onion, minced |
| 1 | tablespoon butter |
| 1 | cup rice |
| 2 | cups chicken broth |
| 1/4 | cup minced dried apricots |
| 2 | tablespoons minced raisins |
| 2 | tablespoons toasted almonds |

In a saucepan, saute onion in butter until onion is transparent. Stir in rice and chicken broth, cover pan and simmer mixture for 30 minutes, or until rice is tender and liquid is absorbed. Stir in apricots and raisins. Place in a serving bowl and sprinkle almonds on top. Serves 4 to 6.

# Imperial Lamb Roast

*Although this is one of the simplest ways to prepare lamb it is still one of the best. You can use a lot more garlic but please keep in mind, garlic should be sliced, not minced.*

1    leg of lamb, about 7 pounds (Ask butcher to bone, roll and tie it.)

1/4   cup oil
1/3   cup vinegar
6    cloves garlic, sliced
     salt and pepper to taste

To thicken gravy (optional):
  2   teaspoons cornstarch
  1/2  cup beef broth

Place lamb in a large bowl. Combine oil, vinegar, garlic, salt and pepper and pour mixture over the lamb. Marinate the lamb in the refrigerator for several hours, turning now and again.

Insert meat thermometer in the thickest part of the lamb, and place lamb in a roasting pan with the marinade. Roast in a preheated 425° oven for 20 minutes. Lower temperature to 350° and continue roasting until meat thermometer registers 150° for medium-rare and 160° for medium. Baste frequently with the marinade.

Remove meat from pan and strain the gravy into a saucepan. Remove every trace of fat. Combine 2 teaspoons cornstarch with 1/2 cup beef broth and stir this into the strained meat juices. Heat it until gravy has thickened. Slice lamb and drizzle some sauce over the meat. Serves 8.

# Curried Lamb with Yogurt & Garlic

1   leg of lamb (about 6 or 7 pounds), boned, trimmed of all visible
     fat and cut into 1-inch squares
6   cloves garlic, chopped
2   tablespoons olive oil
1   cup unflavored yogurt
1   teaspoon ground cumin
1   tablespoon curry powder

In a glass bowl, combine all the ingredients, tossing and turning until lamb is nicely coated. Cover bowl with plastic wrap and allow to stand in the refrigerator for 2 to 6 hours, turning now and again.

More →

(Curried Lamb with Yogurt & Garlic, Cont.)

Thread the lamb on skewers and in a preheated broiler, broil lamb, 4-inches from the heat, for 5 minutes. Baste, now and again with the marinade. Turn skewers and continue broiling until lamb is medium rare, about 3 or 4 minutes. Serve with Vegetable Cous Cous. Serves 8.

# Roast Tenderloin of Pork with Apples & Honey Sauce

2   tenderloins of pork, (about 1 1/2 pounds each). Sprinkle with salt, pepper and garlic powder

**Teriyaki Marinade**

Place the tenderloins of pork in a shallow roasting pan and insert a meat thermometer in the thickest part of the meat. Roast in a preheated 350° oven for about 30 minutes, basting frequently with Teriyaki Marinade. Then baste every 15 minutes with Apples and Honey Sauce until meat is tender and meat thermometer registers 175°, about another 40 minutes. Serve with fried rice or with Oriental noodles. Serves 8.

Apple & Honey Sauce:
    1/2   cup apple juice
      1   apple, peeled, cored and grated
    1/4   cup honey
    1/2   teaspoon ground ginger
    1/4   cup apple jelly

Stir together all the ingredients and cook for a few minutes until heated through and honey and apple jelly are melted and well incorporated. Use to baste the pork.

Teriyaki Marinade:
    1/2   cup soy sauce
      3   tablespoons brown sugar

Stir together all the ingredients until blended. Unused marinade can be stored in the refrigerator for months.

## Tenderloin of Pork with Orange Lemon Glaze

1    tenderloin of pork (about 1 1/2 pounds).  Sprinkle with salt,
       pepper and garlic powder.

Place the tenderloin of pork in a shallow roasting pan and insert a meat
thermometer in the thickest part of the meat.  Roast in a preheated 350°
oven for about 30 minutes.  Now baste with Orange Lemon Glaze every 15
minutes until meat thermometer registers 170° and roast is nicely glazed,
about 1/2 hour longer.  Serve with Fried Rice.  Serves 6.

Orange Lemon Glaze:
       1/2    cup orange juice
         2    tablespoons lemon juice
       1/4    cup Port wine
       1/2    cup orange marmalade

Stir together all the ingredients and cook until heated through.  Use to baste
pork.    You may need to thin the glaze with a little orange juice.  Yields 1 1/4
cups sauce.

## Pork with Onions

1 1/2    pounds pork tenderloin, cut into 1/8-inch thick slices
     1    tablespoon oil
     2    cloves garlic, minced

     1    tablespoon oil
     2    pounds onions, peeled and stemmed.  Slice in half lengthwise
             and cut each half into 1/8-inch thick slices.
     2    teaspoons Beef Seasoned Stock Base
     1    teaspoon sugar
     2    tablespoons dark soy sauce
          salt and pepper to taste

Heat 1 tablespoon oil in a 12-inch skillet until it is very hot, but not
smoking.  Add meat and garlic and stir fry until meat loses its pinkness.
(Meat is very tender and should not be overcooked.)  Remove meat from pan
with a slotted spoon and set aside.

In same pan, over medium heat, heat additional oil until very hot, and add
remaining ingredients.  Lower heat and slowly cook onions until they are
tender and soft.  This will take about 30 minutes.  Add meat to onions and
heat through.  Serve with fried rice or Oriental noodles.  Serves 6.

# Apricot Glazed Pork Tenderloin
## Stuffed with Fruit in Sherry Creme Fraiche

2    pork tenderloins, about 1 1/2 pounds each. Ask your butcher to slice the tenderloins lengthwise, in half, about 3/4 the way through. Have him open them and pound them flat, but not too thin. Sprinkle meat with salt and pepper and garlic powder.

1/2    cup, each, golden raisins and dried apricots, plumped overnight in orange juice and drained
1    large apple, peeled, cored and grated
2    cups herb seasoned stuffing mix
1    egg, beaten
3    tablespoons melted butter
    salt and pepper to taste
1 1/4    cups chicken broth, or just enough to hold the stuffing together

1/2    cup apricot jam, heated

Combine raisins, apricots, apple, stuffing mix, egg, melted butter and seasonings. Add only enough chicken broth to hold the stuffing together.

Lay one tenderloin out flat, cut side up, and place stuffing mixture in the center. Pick up the sides. Lay the second tenderloin, cut side down, over the roll. Tuck it under the first tenderloin snugly and tie it in several places. Skewer the edges, shape it into a roll and place in an 8x12-inch baking pan. Bake in a 350° oven for 30 minutes. Baste with the melted apricot jam. Continue baking for 30 minutes, or until meat thermometer registers 170°, basting 2 or 3 times with the apricot jam.

Remove fat from pan or place meat and juices in an oval porcelain baker. Pour Sherry Creme Fraiche over the top. Bake for another 10 minutes, or until heated through. Decorate with parsley and apricot halves. Slice at the table and serve with kasha or brown rice. Serves 8.

### Sherry Creme Fraiche:
3/4    cup half and half cream
3/4    cup low-fat sour cream
2    teaspoons sugar
1    tablespoon sherry or sauterne

In a glass bowl, stir together all the ingredients, cover bowl and refrigerate for several hours or overnight. Yields 1 1/2 cups sauce.

*Note: -Cooking times are only approximate. Time will depend on the weight of the tenderloins and how thick they are. However, add the Sherry Creme Fraiche during the last 10 or 15 minutes of baking.*

# Stuffed Breast of Veal in Apricot Raisin Sauce

*This is the ultimate comfort food. To be assured of success, veal must be cold before slicing or the stuffing will not hold its shape. Also, be certain that the butcher removes the membranes on the veal. They can be tough. The dried fruit will practically dissolve in the sauce, so don't think anything went wrong. Gravy is rich and delicious and does not need to be thickened.*

**Stuffing:**

| | |
|---|---|
| 2 | onions, fincly chopped |
| 2 | carrots, grated |
| 6 | cloves garlic, minced |
| 1/2 | teaspoon sage flakes |
| 3 | tablespoons butter |
| | |
| 2 | cups herb seasoned stuffing mix |
| 1 1/4 | cups chicken broth or enough to hold stuffing together |
| | |
| 1 | whole breast of veal (about 6 pounds) boned and trimmed of all visible fat and membranes. Sprinkle with garlic powder over all. |

In a skillet, saute together first 5 ingredients until onions are soft. Place mixture in a bowl and add stuffing mix with enough broth to keep stuffing together. Lay veal flat, boned side up, and place stuffing across the center on the long side. Pick up the sides to enclose the stuffing, overlapping the ends about 1-inch. Close the seam with metal skewers and skewer the ends.

Place roast, seam side down in a 9x13-inch baking pan and pour Apricot Raisin Sauce over the top. Cover pan tightly with foil and bake in a 350° oven for about 2 to 2 1/2 hours or until veal is tender. Allow veal to cool and then refrigerate. Overnight is good, too. It's easier to cut the veal when cold.

Remove metal skewers and any trace of fat from the gravy. Cut the veal into 1-inch slices and return to the pan with the gravy. Cover pan with foil and heat at 350° for 25 minutes or until hot. Serves 8.

**Apricot Raisin Sauce:**

| | |
|---|---|
| 1 | cup dry white wine |
| 1 | medium onion, chopped |
| 6 | tablespoons ketchup |
| 1/3 | cup apricot jam |
| 1/2 | cup chopped dried apricots |
| 1/2 | cup yellow raisins |

Stir together all the ingredients until blended.

# Veal with Mushrooms & Dill Creme Fraiche

*This is another variation of a sauce made with Creme Fraiche. This one has half the calories of the original, as it uses low-fat sour cream and half and half. I hope you don't get tired of seeing "heat through" in so many of the meat recipes. "Heat through" means to STOP when the dish is hot. Using the most tender cuts of meat available, means cooking the meat in the least amount of time. Overcooking will toughen the meat.*

|        |                                                                                  |
|--------|----------------------------------------------------------------------------------|
| 1 1/2  | pounds veal scallops, (about 12 slices) sprinkle with salt, white pepper, garlic powder and flour |
| 2      | tablespoons butter                                                               |
| 1/4    | cup Cognac                                                                        |
|        |                                                                                  |
| 2      | onions, finely chopped                                                           |
| 1      | pound mushrooms, thinly sliced                                                   |
| 1      | tablespoon butter                                                                |

Dill Creme Fraiche Sauce (Low Fat):

|       |                             |
|-------|-----------------------------|
| 1/4   | teaspoon dried dill weed    |
|       | salt and pepper to taste    |
| 1/2   | cup low-fat sour cream      |
| 1/2   | cup half and half cream     |

In an aluminum skillet (not plastic-coated), cook the scallops in butter, a few at a time and a few minutes on each side until the meat loses its pinkness. In a brandy warmer, heat the Cognac, ignite it, and carefully pour it over the meat. When the flames are out, remove the meat and juices to an oval porcelain casserole.

In the same pan you cooked the veal, saute the onions and mushrooms in butter until onions are soft. Stir together the sauce ingredients, and stir into onion mixture. Pour sauce over the veal and place in a 350° oven to heat through. Serve on a bed of noodles, with spiced apricots and steamed broccoli. Serves 6.

# Stuffed Veal Rolls in Herbed Tomato Sauce

1 1/2   pounds veal scallops, (about 12 thin slices), sprinkle with salt, white pepper and garlic powder

Herbed Stuffing:
- 2   large onions, finely chopped
- 1   tablespoon butter

- 1   cup grated Gruyere cheese (4 ounces)
- 2   cups herb seasoned stuffing, rolled into crumbs
- 1/2   teaspoon poultry seasoning
- 1/2   teaspoon paprika
- salt and pepper to taste
- 1 1/4   cups chicken broth. Use only enough to hold the stuffing together

Herbed Tomato Sauce:
- 1   can (16 ounces) tomato sauce
- 1   teaspoon, each, oil and sugar
- 1/2   teaspoon, each, sweet basil, oregano and Italian Herb Seasoning
- 1/8   teaspoon coarse grind garlic powder

Saute onions in butter until onions are soft. In a mixing bowl, place onions, cheese, herbed crumbs and seasonings and mix together. Add only enough broth to hold stuffing together.

Divide stuffing between the 12 veal scallops. Roll each slice up and secure it with a toothpick. Roll veal in Herb Seasoned Bread Crumbs and saute them quickly in butter for about 5 minutes or until the meat loses its pinkness. Do not overcook.

Place veal rolls in a 9x13-inch porcelain baker. Sprinkle with a little extra grated Parmesan cheese. Cook together Herbed Tomato Sauce ingredients for 5 minutes and pour over the meat. Heat through in a 350° oven. Do not overcook. Serves 6.

Herb Seasoned Bread Crumbs:
- 1/2   cup bread crumbs
- 1/4   cup flour
- 1/2   cup grated Parmesan cheese
- 1/8   teaspoon garlic powder
- 1/2   teaspoon paprika
- 1/2   teaspoon Italian Herb Seasoning

Mix all the ingredients together until combined. Crumbs can be used on chicken or fish and stored in the freezer indefinitely. Yields 1 1/4 cups.

# Veal Paprika in Cream

*This is a wonderful little veal dish that I am certain you will enjoy. It is delicate and delicious too. If you are running late one evening, you will like the fact that this delightful dish can be assembled and cooked in less than fifteen minutes.*

| | |
|---|---|
| 1 1/2 | pounds veal scallops, cut into 1-inch pieces, seasoned with salt, white pepper and garlic powder |
| 2 | tablespoons butter |
| | |
| 1 | onion, chopped fine |
| 1/2 | pound mushrooms, sliced |
| | |
| 1/4 | cup white wine |
| 2 | tablespoons flour |
| | |
| 2 | tablespoons paprika |
| 1 | cup rich chicken broth |
| | |
| 1/2 | cup half and half cream |
| | salt and white pepper to taste |

Saute scallops in butter for a few minutes, until they lose their pinkness. They are very tender, so do not overcook. Remove veal from skillet and set aside.

In same pan, saute onion and mushrooms until onion is soft. Add wine and cook until wine has almost evaporated. Add flour and cook for a minute or two, stirring.

Add paprika and chicken broth and cook until sauce thickens. Add veal and cream. Taste for salt and pepper and heat through. Serve with Buttered Noodles with Onions and Poppy Seeds. Serves 6.

## Veal with Peppers, Tomatoes & Mushrooms

*Using the tender cut of veal, reduces preparation time by 90 minutes. But further, the veal is succulent and delicious.*

2 pounds veal scallops, cut into 1-inch strips. Sprinkle with salt, pepper and garlic powder and dredge in flour.
1 tablespoon olive oil

2 tablespoons butter
1 onion, cut in half and then cut into 1/8-inch slices
2 green bell peppers, cleaned, seeded and sliced into 1-inch strips
1 red bell pepper, cleaned, seeded and sliced into 1-inch strips
1/2 pound mushrooms, sliced

1/2 pound tomatoes (about 2 medium), cut into coarse dice
1 tablespoon chopped parsley
1/2 teaspoon Italian Herb Seasoning
1 1/4 cups rich chicken broth
2 tablespoons tomato paste
salt and pepper to taste

In a Dutch oven casserole, saute veal in hot oil, for a few minutes until meat loses its pinkness. Do not overcook. With a slotted spoon, remove meat and set aside.

In same pan, saute onion, peppers and mushrooms until vegetables are tender. (Add a little oil if necessary.) Add the remaining ingredients and cook and stir over low heat until sauce is slightly thickened, about 20 minutes. Add the meat and heat through. Serve with Rice with Tomatoes and Onions. Serves 6.

## Breaded Veal Scallops
## with Lemon Slices & Green Onions

*Veal flavored with a splash of lemon and butter and a sprinkling of chives is delicate and delicious. Unused crumbs can be stored in the freezer.*

2 pounds veal scallops, (12 slices), sprinkle with salt, pepper, garlic powder and dust with flour

1 egg, beaten
1 tablespoon water
1 tablespoon olive oil

More →

Seasoned Crumbs:
>    1    cup bread crumbs seasoned with 1/2 cup grated Parmesan cheese,
>            1/8 teaspoon garlic powder, 1/4 teaspoon paprika and
>            1/2 teaspoon Italian Herb Seasoning

Lemon Wash:
>    1/4    cup butter, melted
>    2    tablespoons lemon juice
>    1/4    cup chopped chives

Beat the egg with the water and the olive oil. Dip veal scallops into the egg mixture and then pat evenly with crumbs. Refrigerate breaded veal for about 1 hour.

Melt a little butter in a 12-inch skillet and saute about 4 slices of veal at a time, until meat loses its pinkness. Do not overcook. Continue with the remaining scallops, using a little more butter if needed. Remove meat to a lovely porcelain baker. Stir together butter, lemon juice and chives and sprinkle over the veal. Heat in a 350° oven for a few minutes to heat through. Serves 6.

# Veal Scallops with Apple and Raisins

*This simple way of preparing veal is fashioned after a popular French dish from Normandy. The sherry-flavored fruit and raisins add a delicious touch of sweetness to the sauce.*

>    1 1/2    pounds veal scallops, sprinkled with salt, white pepper and garlic
>                powder and dusted lightly with flour
>    2    tablespoons butter
>
>    2    apples, peeled, cored and grated
>    1    cup golden raisins
>    1/2    cup rich chicken broth
>    3    tablespoons sherry
>
>    1/3    cup low-fat sour cream
>    1/3    cup half and half cream
>    2    tablespoons currant jelly

In a Dutch oven casserole, brown veal quickly in butter, a few scallops at a time. Do not overcook. Remove veal from pan and set aside. In the same pan, cook together next 4 ingredients until apples are soft. Stir together sour cream, cream and currant jelly, and stir into the apple mixture. Heat through, over low heat, being careful not to let the sauce boil. Spoon sauce on veal and serve with buttered noodles. Serves 6.

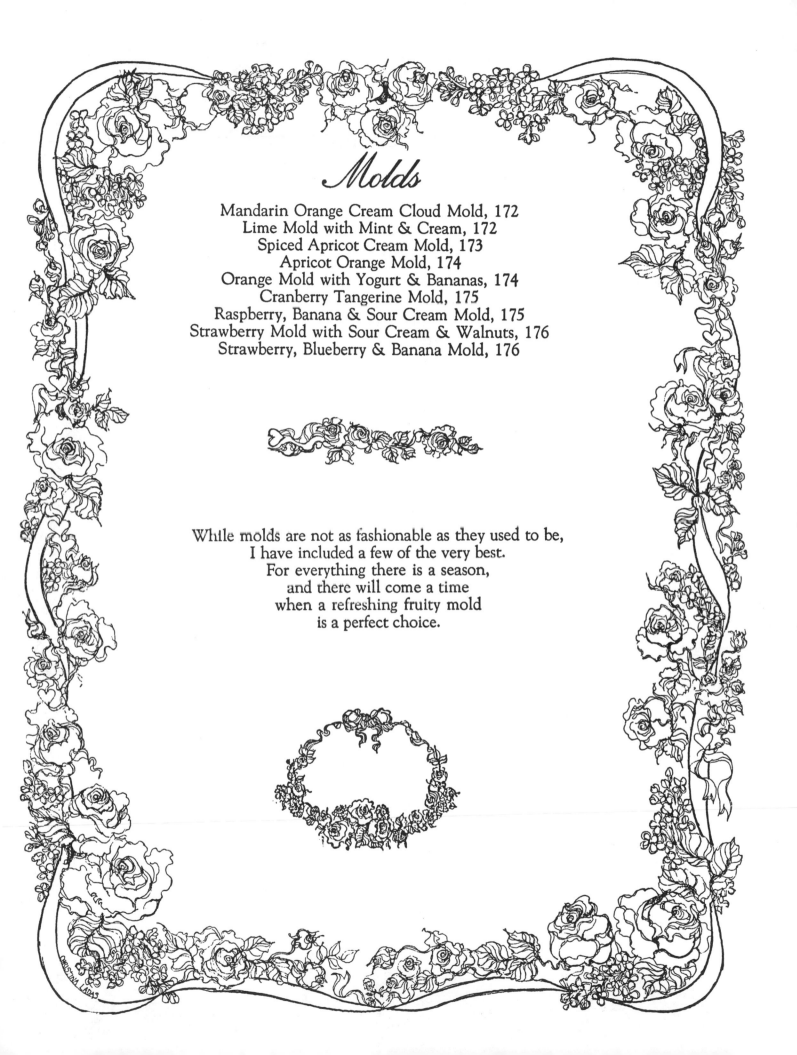

# Molds

Mandarin Orange Cream Cloud Mold, 172
Lime Mold with Mint & Cream, 172
Spiced Apricot Cream Mold, 173
Apricot Orange Mold, 174
Orange Mold with Yogurt & Bananas, 174
Cranberry Tangerine Mold, 175
Raspberry, Banana & Sour Cream Mold, 175
Strawberry Mold with Sour Cream & Walnuts, 176
Strawberry, Blueberry & Banana Mold, 176

While molds are not as fashionable as they used to be,
I have included a few of the very best.
For everything there is a season,
and there will come a time
when a refreshing fruity mold
is a perfect choice.

# Mandarin Orange Cream Cloud Mold

    1      package (6 ounces) orange gelatin
2 1/2      cups boiling water

    1      carton Dsertwhip (12 ounces) (non-dairy whipping cream)
    1      can (8 ounces) Mandarin orange sections, drained

In the large bowl of an electric mixer, stir together boiling water and orange gelatin until gelatin is dissolved.  Chill gelatin until it is partially congealed and not firm set.  Beat gelatin until it is light and frothy.  Beat Dsertwhip until it is the consistency of whipped cream.  On low setting of electric mixer, slowly beat together the gelatin and the whipped cream until the mixture is blended.  Gently fold in drained Mandarin orange sections.

Pour mixture into a 2-quart mold and refrigerate until firm.  When ready to serve, unmold and decorate with orange slices on green leaves. Serves 12.

# Lime Mold with Mint & Creme

    1      package, (6 ounces), lime gelatin
2 1/2      cups boiling water
    1      carton Dsertwhip (12 ounces) (non-dairy whipping cream)
    4      drops peppermint extract

In the large bowl of an electric mixer, stir together boiling water and lime gelatin until gelatin is dissolved.  Chill gelatin until partially congealed and not firm set.  Beat gelatin until it is light and frothy. Whip Dsertwhip until it is the consistency of whipped cream.  On low setting of electric mixer, slowly beat together the gelatin and the whipped *creme*.  Add a few drops of peppermint extract.  (If the mixture appears pale, add a drop or two of green food coloring.)

Pour mixture into a 2-quart mold and refrigerate until firm.  When ready to serve, unmold and fill center with dark purple grapes.  Decorate with green leaves and grape clusters and serve with pride.  Serves 12.

# Spiced Apricot Cream Mold

*Dsertwhip (yes, that is the correct spelling) is a sweetened non-dairy whipping cream. It is delicious with gelatins. In the event that it is not available at your markets, substitute 3 cups of non-dairy whipped topping, which is found in the freezer section of most markets.*

- 1 jar (1 pound 12 ounces) spiced apricots in syrup
  water
- 1 package (6 ounces) orange gelatin
- 1 carton Dsertwhip (12 ounces) (non-dairy whipping cream)

Drain apricots and reserve the juice. Slice the apricots and remove the stones. Set aside.

To the reserved juice, add water to make 2 1/2 cups liquid. Boil juice mixture with the orange gelatin until gelatin is dissolved. Place gelatin in the large bowl of an electric mixer, and refrigerate until it is partially congealed, but not firm set.

Whip gelatin at high speed until it is light and frothy. Beat Dsertwhip until it is stiff like whipped cream. Combine whipped gelatin and whipped Dsertwhip until well mixed. (You can do this in your mixer on low speed.) Carefully add the sliced apricots. Pour mixture into a 2-quart mold and refrigerate until firm.

Unmold by placing mold into warm water for a few seconds until it is loosened, and inverting it on a serving platter. Serves 12.

*Note: -This is a spectacular mold and deserves your prettiest serving platter.*
*   -The apricots can be substituted with spiced peaches.*
*   -Can be made the day before with excellent results. Unmold on the day you are planning to serve it.*

# Apricot Orange Mold

1    large can apricots (1 pound 12 ounces) drained.  Reserve juice.
       Boiling water and reserved apricot juice

1    package (6 ounces) orange gelatin

1    cup low-fat sour cream
1    cup low-fat vanilla ice cream

Drain apricots in a measuring cup.  Add water to drained apricot juice to measure 2 cups liquid.  Remove stones from apricots and puree fruit in food processor or blender and set aside.  Boil water and juice mixture. Add gelatin and stir to dissolve.

Add the sour cream and ice cream and beat until thoroughly mixed.  Add the pureed fruit and stir to mix well.  Pour mixture into a 2-quart mold and refrigerate until firm.

Unmold by placing mold in warm water for a few seconds until it is loosened and inverting it on a serving platter.  Serves 12.

Note:  -Can be prepared and unmolded the day before.  Decorate with orange
          slices and green leaves.

# Orange Mold with Yogurt & Bananas

1    package (6 ounces) orange gelatin
2 1/2    cups boiling water
1    cup unflavored yogurt
1    small orange, grated.  Remove any large pieces of membranes.
2    bananas, sliced

Add boiling water to orange gelatin and stir until it is dissolved.  Add yogurt and stir until blended.  Add orange and sliced bananas.

Pour mixture into a 2-quart mold and refrigerate it until it is firm. When ready to serve, unmold and decorate with orange slices and green leaves. Serves 10 to 12.

# Cranberry Tangerine Mold

*This is a great mold to serve around Thanksgiving. It is almost a relish, filled as it is, with all manner of good things. Orange can be substituted for tangerine with equally excellent results.*

- 1    package, (6 ounces), black cherry gelatin
- 2    cups boiling water

- 1    cup canned Whole Berry Cranberry Sauce (8 ounces)
- 1    tangerine, grated, use fruit, peel and juice. Remove any large pieces of membranes
- 1    can crushed pineapple (1 pound 4 ounces)
- 1/2   cup toasted walnuts, chopped

Combine gelatin and boiling water. Stir until gelatin is dissolved. Add the cranberry sauce and stir until the sauce is melted and the berries float loosely. Add remaining ingredients and stir to mix well. Pour mixture into a 2-quart mold and refrigerate until firm.

Unmold by placing mold in warm water for a few seconds until it is loosened and inverting it on a serving platter. Decorate mold with tangerine slices around the rim and some pretty green leaves that have been rubbed, tubbed and scrubbed. Serves 12.

# Raspberry, Banana & Sour Cream Mold

- 1    package, (6 ounces), raspberry gelatin
- 2    cups boiling water
- 1    cup low-fat sour cream, at room temperature
- 2    packages (10 ounces each) frozen raspberries in syrup, defrosted and sieved to remove seeds
- 2    bananas, thinly sliced

In the large bowl of an electric mixer, stir together gelatin and boiling water until gelatin is dissolved. Beat in the sour cream until smooth. Stir in the fruit. Pour mixture into a 6-cup ring mold and refrigerate until firm.

To unmold, place mold in warm water for a few seconds until it is loosened and invert it on a serving platter. Decorate mold with a ring of banana slices that were dipped in lemon juice and fresh raspberries (if in season.) Sprinkle with a few chopped walnuts over all. Serves 12.

## Strawberry Mold with Sour Cream & Walnuts

    1    package (6 ounces) strawberry gelatin
2 1/2    cups boiling water
    1    package (10 ounces) frozen sliced strawberries in syrup, drained.
            Reserve juice.
    1    pint low-fat sour cream
  1/4    cup coarsely chopped, toasted walnuts

Add boiling water to strawberry gelatin and stir until it is dissolved. Add the juice of the drained strawberries. Cool the gelatin until it is partially congealed and not firm set. Beat gelatin until it is light and frothy. Add sour cream and continue beating until sour cream is the size of small peas. Fold in the strawberries and the chopped walnuts.

Pour mixture into a 2-quart mold and refrigerate until firm. When ready to serve, unmold and decorate with green leaves and fresh strawberries. Serves 12.

## Strawberry, Blueberry & Banana Mold

    1    package (6 ounces) strawberry gelatin
    2    cups boiling water

    1    package (10 ounces) frozen strawberries in syrup
  1/2    cup fresh or frozen blueberries
    1    banana, thinly sliced

Combine gelatin and boiling water and stir until gelatin is dissolved. Add fruits and mix well. Pour mixture into a 2-quart mold and refrigerate until firm. Serves 8 to 10.

Note: -The amount of the fruits are flexible. You can add 1 cup of frozen
          blueberries, an extra banana, or fresh sliced strawberries.
      -Can be prepared the day before. Unmold on the day you are serving it.

# Noodles, Rice & Pastas

Green Noodles with Onions & Parsley, 178
Noodles with Orange & Raisins, 178
Lemon Noodles with Garlic & Cheese, 178
Best Velvet Noodle Pudding with Raisins, 179
Noodles Alfredo with Sour Cream & Almonds, 179
Winter Noodle Pudding with Dates & Raisins, 180
Noodle Pudding with Apples & Raisins, 180
Toasted Vermicelli with Toasted Almonds, 181
Fideos with Onions & Mushrooms, 181
Noodle Pudding with Apricots & Raisins, 182
Noodles with Poppy Seeds & Lemon Cream, 182
Toasted Pastina with Mushrooms & Onions, 183
Brown Rice with Carrots & Onions, 183
Brown Rice with Lentils, Mushrooms & Onions, 183
Yellow Chili Rice with Tomatoes & Chiles, 184
Fried Rice with Scallions & Water Chestnuts, 184
Curry Rice Indienne with Raisins & Almonds, 185
Golden Mexican Rice with Tomatoes & Chiles, 185
Rice with Pepper, Beef, Onion & Sun-Dried Tomatoes, 186
Pink Rice with Tomatoes & Chives, 186
Pink Rice with Artichokes & Cheese, 187
Mushroom Rice with Onion & Shallots, 187
Royal Rice Pudding with Apricots & Raisins, 188
Tomato Rice & Onions, 188
Kasha with Mushrooms & Onions, 189
Toasted Barley with Mushrooms & Onions, 189
Pink Orzo with Tomatoes, 190
Toasted Orzo with Mushrooms & Onions, 190
Cous Cous with Raisins & Pine Nuts, 191
Vegetable Cous Cous with Chick Peas, 191
Cheese Ravioli in Sun-Dried Tomato Sauce, 192
Spinach & Cheese Ravioli in Pesto Sauce, 193
Turkey Ravioli in Light Tomato Sauce, 194

## Green Noodles with Onions, Garlic & Parsley

1    package (8 ounces) spinach noodles, cooked and drained
6    tablespoons butter, (3/4 stick), melted with 2 cloves minced garlic
2    tablespoons lemon juice
1/3    cup minced parsley
1/3    cup minced green onions
     salt and pepper to taste

Combine all the ingredients and toss to mix well. Serve immediately and serves 6.

## Noodles with Orange, Raisins & Sesame Seeds

8    ounces wide noodles, cooked and drained
1/4    cup butter or margarine (1/2 stick), melted

1/2    cup low-fat sour cream
2    teaspoons finely grated orange peel
1/2    cup golden raisins plumped in orange juice and drained
3    tablespoons toasted sesame seeds

Toss drained noodles in butter until coated. Add the remaining ingredients and toss to combine. Place noodles in a casserole and heat in a 300° oven until heated through. Serves 6.

## Lemon Noodles with Garlic, Cheese & Chives

1/4    cup butter (1/2 stick)
1    clove garlic, minced (or more to taste)

8    ounces medium noodles, cooked al dente and drained
1/4    cup chopped chives
2    tablespoons lemon juice
1/4    cup cream or half and half
1/2    cup grated Parmesan cheese

In a saucepan, heat butter with garlic for 1 minute. Toss in drained noodles. Add the remaining ingredients and toss to combine. Serves 6.

# The Best Velvet Noodle Pudding
## with Sour Cream & Raisins

*This is one of the very best noodle puddings…the taste is divine, the texture creamy. I have received so many letters raving about its goodness. In fact, a world-famous party planner said it was the best he ever tasted. I have not altered the original recipe, but butter can be reduced to 6 tablespoons.*

|     |     |
| --- | --- |
| 8   | ounces (1/2 pound) medium noodles, cooked and drained |
| 1/2 | cup butter (1 stick) |
|     |     |
| 4   | eggs |
| 1   | pint (2 cups) sour cream |
| 1/2 | cup milk |
| 1   | teaspoon vanilla |
| 1   | cup sugar |
|     | salt to taste |
| 1   | cup yellow raisins, soaked overnight, in orange juice and drained |
|     |     |
| 2   | tablespoons cinnamon sugar |

In a 9x13-inch pan, melt the butter. Add the cooked and drained noodles and toss them in the butter until they are completely coated.

Beat together the eggs, sour cream, milk, vanilla, sugar and salt until the mixture is well blended. Stir in the yellow raisins.

Stir the egg mixture with the noodles and spread noodles evenly in the pan. Sprinkle top with cinnamon sugar. Bake in a 350° oven for 1 hour. Cut into squares and serve warm. Serves 8 to 10.

# Noodles Alfredo with Sour Cream & Almonds

*This is not the traditional Alfredo, as it is prepared with low-fat sour cream instead of cream. Low-fat sour cream imparts a little more flavor and fewer calories.*

|     |     |
| --- | --- |
| 1/2 | pound medium noodles, cooked al dente and drained |
|     |     |
| 1/4 | cup butter (1/2 stick), melted |
| 1/2 | cup low-fat sour cream |
| 1/4 | cup toasted slivered almonds |

Toss the noodles in the melted butter and then into the sour cream. Toss to coat evenly. Transfer noodles immediately to a serving dish, sprinkle with toasted almonds and serve hot. Serves 6.

# Winter Noodle Pudding with Dates & Raisins

*Prunes, figs or apricots can be substituted for the dates. Or mix a few dried fruits together. If the fruit is extra-dry, then, soak it in hot orange juice for a few minutes and drain. This is a great homey dish to serve with roast chicken for a family dinner on Sunday night.*

| | |
|---|---|
| 1 | package (12 ounces) wide noodles, cooked in boiling water until tender and drained |
| 4 | tablespoons margarine, melted |
| 1 | cup pitted dates, chopped |
| 1/2 | cup mixed yellow and dark raisins |
| | |
| 4 | eggs, beaten |
| 1/4 | cup sugar |
| 1/2 | cup milk |
| 1/2 | orange, grated. Use fruit, juice and peel. Remove any large pieces of membranes. |
| | |
| 2 | tablespoons cinnamon sugar |

In a 9x13-inch pan, toss together first 4 ingredients until nicely mixed. Combine the next 4 ingredients and mix with the noodles. Spread evenly in pan and sprinkle top with cinnamon sugar. Bake at 350° for about 45 minutes, or until eggs are set and top is golden brown. Serves 12.

# Noodle Pudding with Apples & Raisins

| | |
|---|---|
| 4 | large apples, peeled, cored and grated |
| 1/2 | cup yellow raisins |
| 1 | tablespoon grated orange peel |
| 4 | tablespoons cinnamon sugar |
| 1/4 | cup orange juice |
| | |
| 1 | package (8 ounces) medium noodles, cooked and drained |
| 1/4 | cup melted butter |
| | |
| 4 | eggs, beaten |
| 1/2 | cup sugar |
| 1 1/2 | cups low-fat sour cream |
| 1 | teaspoon vanilla |
| | salt to taste |

In a large bowl, toss together first 5 ingredients. In a 9x13-inch pan, toss together noodles and butter. Toss in apple mixture. Beat together the remaining ingredients until blended and pour evenly over the noodles. (Ease the noodles, here and there, so that the egg mixture is even.) Bake at 350° for about 1 hour or until top is golden and custard is set. Cut into squares to serve. Serve with roast chicken. Serves 12.

# Toasted Vermicelli with Toasted Almonds

*Vermicelli is a nice change from rice or potatoes and I do hope you make it soon. Instead of browning fideos in oil, I like to brown them in the oven. It is a lot easier, far less caloric and they brown more evenly this way.*

- 8 ounces vermicelli coils, also called "fideos"
- 1 can (10 1/2 ounces) beef broth
- 1 cup water
- 2 tablespoons butter
  salt and pepper to taste
- 1/4 cup toasted, chopped almonds (optional)

Toast vermicelli in a 350° oven for about 8 minutes or until it is golden brown. Careful not to burn it. Set aside.

Combine beef broth, water, butter and seasonings and bring mixture to a boil. Add toasted vermicelli, cover and reduce to low heat. Simmer mixture until vermicelli is tender and liquid is absorbed, about 10 minutes. Toss with toasted almonds (optional) before serving. Serves 6.

# Fideos with Onions & Mushrooms

- 8 ounces fideo or vermicelli coils
- 1 tablespoon butter or margarine
- 1/2 onion, finely minced
- 1/4 pound mushrooms, finely chopped

- 1 tablespoon butter
- 2 1/2 cups rich chicken broth
  salt and pepper to taste

Toast fideos in a 350° oven for about 8 minutes or until it is golden brown. Careful not to burn it. Set aside.

Saute onion in 1 tablespoon butter until onion is soft. Add mushrooms and continue sauteing until mushrooms are tender. Set aside.

In a saucepan melt 1 tablespoon butter and add chicken broth, salt and pepper. Bring mixture to a boil and add toasted fideos. Lower heat, cover pan and simmer until fideos are tender and liquid is absorbed, about 10 minutes. Add onion and mushroom mixture and toss to mix. Serves 6.

# Noodle Pudding with Apricots & Raisins

*Wonderful to serve with roast chicken or veal. Very tasty and fruity. Apricots can be substituted with grated fresh apples.*

| | |
|---|---|
| 1 | package (8 ounces) medium noodles, cooked and drained |
| 1/4 | cup butter or margarine (1/2 stick), melted |
| | |
| 4 | eggs |
| 1 1/2 | cups low-fat sour cream |
| 1/2 | cup sugar |
| 1 | teaspoon vanilla |
| | salt to taste |
| 1/2 | cup chopped apricots |
| 1/2 | cup yellow raisins |
| | |
| 2 | tablespoons cinnamon sugar |

In a 9x13-inch pan, toss together the noodles and melted butter. Beat together the next group of ingredients until blended. Pour egg mixture over the noodles and spread to even. (Press the apricots and raisins back into the filling if they have floated too high on top.) Sprinkle top with cinnamon sugar. Bake at 350° for 50 to 55 minutes or until top is browned and custard is set. Serves 10 to 12.

# Noodles with Poppy Seeds and Lemon Cream

| | |
|---|---|
| 1 | package (8 ounces) medium noodles, cooked al dente and drained |
| 1/2 | cup finely chopped onions, |
| 2 | ounces butter (1/2 stick) |
| 1 | tablespoon poppy seeds |
| 2 | tablespoons lemon juice |
| 1/2 | cup low-fat sour cream |
| | salt and pepper to taste |

Saute onions in butter until onions are soft. In a large bowl, combine all the ingredients and toss to mix well. Place mixture into a lovely porcelain casserole, cover with foil and heat in a 300° oven until heated through. Serves 6.

*Note:* *Casserole can be made earlier in the day and refrigerated. Remove from the refrigerator and let noodles come to room temperature. Then sprinkle with about 1 ounce chicken broth to prevent noodles from sticking to the pan. Reheat as described above. If you do not cover the pan, top will get lightly crisped, which is very nice, too.*

## Toasted Pastina with Mushrooms & Onions

*Pastina is a small pasta that is an interesting alternative to rice or noodles. With mushrooms and onions it is a nice accompaniment to roast veal or chicken.*

| | |
|---|---|
| 1/2 | pound mushrooms, thinly sliced |
| 1 | onion, minced |
| 1 | tablespoon butter |
| | pepper to taste |
| 1 | package (8 ounces) pastina |

In a saucepan, saute together first 4 ingredients until onion is soft. Meanwhile, toast pastina in a 350° oven for about 5 minutes, or until it is just beginning to take on color. Place it in a pot with 2-quarts of rapidly boiling water until it is tender, about 10 minutes. Drain thoroughly in a large strainer, with small holes. Don't use a collander with large holes or the pasta will slip through. Stir pastina into saucepan with mushrooms and heat through. Serves 6 to 8.

## Brown Rice with Carrots & Onions

| | |
|---|---|
| 2 | carrots, grated |
| 1 | onion, chopped |
| 1 | tablespoon oil |
| 1 | cup brown rice |
| 2 1/4 | cups chicken broth |
| | pepper to taste |

In a saucepan, saute carrots and onion in oil until onion is soft. Stir in the remaining ingredients, cover pan and simmer mixture for 40 minutes, or until rice is tender. Serves 6.

## Brown Rice with Lentils, Mushrooms & Onions

*Brown rice and lentils are a wonderful pair. Add mushrooms and onions and the combination is truly delicious...and healthy, too.*

| | |
|---|---|
| 1/2 | cup brown rice |
| 1/2 | cup lentils, picked over for foreign particles |
| 2 1/4 | cups beef broth |
| 2 | teaspoons oil |
| 1/2 | pound mushrooms, sliced |
| 1 | large onion, sliced |
| 1 | teaspoon oil |

In a covered saucepan, simmer together first 4 ingredients for about 40 minutes, or until lentils are tender. Meanwhile, in a skillet, saute mushrooms and onion in oil until onion is tender. When rice is cooked, stir in mushrooms and onions and heat through. Serves 6.

## Yellow Chili Rice with Tomatoes & Chiles

*This rice is an excellent accompaniment to a Mexican-style dinner. If you like a stronger chili taste, add 1 teaspoon chili powder. It can be prepared earlier in the day, and reheated at time of serving. Do not freeze.*

|       |                                                        |
|-------|--------------------------------------------------------|
| 1     | can (10 1/2 ounces) beef broth                         |
| 3/4   | cup water                                              |
|       | salt and pepper to taste                               |
| 1     | teaspoon chili powder                                  |
| 1/2   | teaspoon turmeric (or more to taste)                   |
| 1/4   | teaspoon ground cumin                                  |
| 1     | large tomato, skinned, seeded and chopped coarsely     |
| 1     | tablespoon Ortega's Diced Green Chiles, or more to taste |
| 3     | tablespoons butter                                     |
|       |                                                        |
| 1     | cup long-grain rice                                    |

In a saucepan, bring first group of ingredients to a boil. Add rice, cover pan and reduce heat. Simmer rice over low heat until liquid is absorbed and rice is tender, about 30 minutes. Serves 6.

## Fried Rice with Scallions & Water Chestnuts

|     |                                    |
|-----|------------------------------------|
| 2   | tablespoons butter or margarine    |
| 1   | cup long grain rice                |
| 1   | can (10 1/2 ounces) beef broth     |
| 1   | cup water                          |
| 1   | tablespoon soy sauce               |
|     | salt and pepper to taste           |

Saute rice in butter until rice is lightly browned. Add remaining ingredients and stir. Cover pan, lower heat and gently simmer rice until liquid is absorbed and rice is tender. When rice is cooked, add:

|     |                                                 |
|-----|-------------------------------------------------|
| 1/2 | cup leftover chicken, beef or pork, cut into small dice |
| 3   | scallions (green onions), finely chopped        |
| 6   | water chestnuts, thinly sliced                  |

Mix these into the rice and toss them to combine evenly. Heat through. Serves 6.

## Curry Rice Indienne with Raisins & Almonds

- 2 cups chicken broth
- 1 cup long grain rice
- 1 tablespoon oil
  salt and pepper to taste
- 1 teaspoon curry powder or to taste

Stir together all the ingredients in a saucepan. Cover pan and simmer mixture over low heat until liquid is absorbed and rice is tender, about 30 minutes. When rice is cooked, toss in the following:

- 1 onion, chopped
- 1 teaspoon oil
- 1/4 cup golden raisins, plumped in orange juice
- 1/4 cup slivered or chopped toasted almonds
- 1/4 cup chopped chives

Saute onion in oil until tender. Toss into rice with the remaining ingredients and heat through if necessary. Sprinkle top with additional minced chives. Serves 6.

## Golden Mexican Rice with Tomatoes & Chiles

- 1 medium tomato, chopped
- 1 can (3 ounces) diced green chiles
- 1 tablespoon oil

- 1 1/2 cups rice
- 3 cups chicken broth
- 1 teaspoon turmeric
- 1/4 teaspoon ground cumin
  salt and pepper to taste

In a saucepan, cook tomato and chiles in oil for 2 minutes, stirring. Stir in the remaining ingredients, cover pan, and simmer mixture for 30 minutes, or until rice is tender and liquid is absorbed. This is excellent to serve with Chili con Carne or Red Hot Lentil Chili. Serves 8.

# Rice with Pepper, Beef, Onion & Sun-Dried Tomatoes

*This recipe can be expanded with extra beef, and will serve 6 as a main course.*

- 1 can (10 1/2 ounces) beef broth
- 3/4 cup water
- 1 tablespoon oil
  salt and pepper to taste
- 1 cup long-grain rice

- 1/2 pound sirloin steak, cut into thin strips
- 1 tablespoon oil

- 1 green or red bell pepper, seeded and cut into strips
- 1 onion, chopped
- 2 sun-dried tomatoes, chopped

In a saucepan, stir together first 6 ingredients and bring mixture to a boil. Lower heat, cover pan and simmer mixture for about 30 minutes, or until rice is tender and liquid is absorbed.

Meanwhile, in a skillet, saute steak in oil until meat loses its pinkness. Remove from pan and set aside. In same pan, saute pepper, onion and sun-dried tomatoes until pepper and onion are soft. Stir beef and vegetables into the rice and heat through. Serves 8.

## Pink Rice with Tomatoes & Chives

*This is a very tasty way to prepare rice. Do not use any more than 3 tablespoons tomato sauce, or the rice can get sticky.*

- 1 can (10 1/2 ounces) chicken broth
- 3/4 cup water
- 1 tablespoon oil
- 1 tomato, seeded and coarsely chopped.
- 3 tablespoons tomato sauce
- 1 tablespoon chopped parsley
- 3 tablespoons chopped chives
  salt and pepper to taste

- 1 cup long-grain rice

In a saucepan, bring first group of ingredients to a boil. Stir in rice, cover pan and simmer rice over low heat until liquid is absorbed and rice is tender, about 30 minutes. Serves 6.

## Pink Rice with Artichokes & Cheese

1 1/2   cups long-grain rice
3   cups chicken broth
1   medium tomato, peeled, seeded and chopped
1   tablespoon oil
   salt and pepper to taste

1   jar (6 ounces) marinated artichoke hearts, drained, and
      cut into fourths.  Reserve marinade.
3   tablespoons grated Parmesan cheese

In a saucepan, stir together first 6 ingredients, cover pan, and simmer mixture for about 30 minutes, or until rice is tender and liquid is absorbed.  Stir in artichokes hearts and heat through.  Place in serving bowl and sprinkle top with grated cheese.  Drizzle a little marinade over all. Serves 6.

## Mushroom Rice with Onion & Shallots

1   cup rice, long-grain
1   can (10 1/2 ounces) beef broth
3/4   cup water
   salt and pepper to taste

1   small onion, finely chopped
2   shallots, minced
1   tablespoon butter
1/4   pound sliced mushrooms

In a saucepan, stir together the first 5 ingredients.  Cover pan and simmer mixture until liquid is absorbed and rice is tender.

Meanwhile, in a skillet, saute onion and shallots in butter until onions are soft.  Add mushrooms and continue cooking until mushrooms are tender.  Stir mushroom mixture into rice and heat through.  Serves 6.

# Royal Rice Pudding with Apricots & Raisins

*Rice pudding has been coming back into popularity...but, not the plain kind with a spot of cinnamon on top. This one is elevated with the added flavors of apricots and raisins.*

3 eggs
1/2 cup sugar
3/4 cup low-fat sour cream

3 ounces dried apricots, chopped
1/4 cup yellow raisins
1/2 orange, grated. Use fruit, juice and peel, about 3 tablespoons.
3 cups cooked long grain rice

2 teaspoons cinnamon sugar

Beat together first 3 ingredients until blended. By hand, stir in the next 4 ingredients until blended. Place mixture into an oiled 9x9-inch baking pan and sprinkle top with cinnamon sugar. Bake at 350° for 45 minutes, or until pudding is set. This is a nice accompaniment to chicken or veal. However, it can be served for a family dessert with a spoonful of apricot sauce on top. Serves 8.

Apricot Sauce:
1 cup apricot preserves, strained through a seive
1/4 cup orange juice
2 tablespoons apricot brandy

In a saucepan, heat together all the ingredients for 3 minutes or until slightly thickened. Serve sauce warm or chilled.

# Tomato Rice & Onions

1 onion, finely minced
2 medium tomatoes, peeled, seeded and chopped
2 tablespoons butter

1 cup long-grain rice
1 can (10 1/2 ounces) chicken broth
3/4 cup water
1 tablespoon tomato sauce
salt and pepper to taste

Saute onion and tomatoes in butter until onion is soft. Stir in remaining ingredients and bring to boil. Lower heat, cover pan and gently simmer rice until it is tender and liquid is absorbed, about 30 minutes. Serves 6.

# Kasha with Mushrooms & Onions

*Kasha is a healthy and wholesome alternative to rice or noodles. With onions and mushrooms it is truly delicious.*

| | |
|---|---|
| 1 | cup medium grain kasha |
| 1 | egg, beaten |
| 2 | cups chicken broth |
| 1 | tablespoon butter |
| 1 | medium onion, chopped |
| 1/2 | pound mushrooms, sliced |

In a saucepan, cook kasha with egg, stirring all the while, until kasha grains are dry and nicely separated. Stir in the broth, cover pan, and simmer mixture for about 20 minutes, or until kasha is tender and liquid is absorbed.

Meanwhile, saute onion in butter until tender. Add mushrooms and continue sauteing until mushrooms are tender and liquid rendered is absorbed. Stir mushroom mixture into kasha and heat through. Serves 6.

# Toasted Barley with Mushrooms & Onions

| | |
|---|---|
| 1 | cup toasted egg barley |
| 1 | can (10 1/2 ounces) beef broth |
| 1 1/4 | cups water |
| 1 | tablespoon oil |
| | salt and pepper to taste |
| 1/2 | pound mushrooms, sliced |
| 1 | large onion, chopped |
| 2 | tablespoons butter |

In an 8x3-inch round baking pan, stir together first 6 ingredients, cover pan tightly with foil and bake at 350° for 45 to 50 minutes, or until barley is tender and liquid is absorbed. Meanwhile, in a large skillet, saute together next 3 ingredients until onion is soft and most of the liquid rendered is absorbed. Fluff barley with a fork and stir onion mixture into the barley. Nice to serve with roast chicken or lamb. Serves 6.

Orzo, rice-shaped pasta, can be found in some markets or in Greek groceries. It comes in 3 sizes. The smallest size is found is most supermarkets and is O.K. for soup, but it lacks the glamor of the larger size for casseroles. I prefer the larger size for soups, too. In the recipes that follow, the orzo is toasted in the oven, or sauteed in a little oil. This helps to reduce the starchiness when cooking. Use the method you prefer as both work well.

---

## Pink Orzo with Tomatoes

1  cup orzo (large-size rice-shaped pasta)
1  tablespoon oil

2  cups chicken broth
   salt and pepper to taste

2  tomatoes, peeled, seeded and chopped
1  small onion, chopped
2  cloves garlic, minced
1  teaspoon oil

In a Dutch oven casserole, saute orzo in oil, stirring all the while, until orzo is just beginning to take on color. Carefully pour in (it will splatter) the chicken broth and seasonings. Cover pan, and simmer mixture for 40 minutes, or until orzo is tender and liquid is absorbed. Meanwhile in a covered saucepan, simmer together last 4 ingredients until onion is soft. Stir tomato mixture into cooked orzo until nicely mixed and heat through to serve. Serves 6.

## Toasted Orzo with Mushrooms & Onions

1  cup large-size orzo (rice-shaped pasta)

1  tablespoon oil
2  cups chicken broth
   salt and pepper to taste

1  onion, chopped
1  pound mushrooms, sliced
1  tablespoon oil

Place orzo in a shallow pan and toast at 350° for 8 minutes, or until orzo is beginning to take on color. In a Dutch oven casserole, place toasted orzo with the next 4 ingredients, cover pan and simmer orzo for 40 minutes, or until orzo is tender and liquid is absorbed. Meanwhile, in a large skillet, saute together onion and mushrooms in oil until onion is tender and liquid rendered is evaporated. Stir mushroom mixture into cooked orzo and heat through. Serves 6.

# Cous Cous with Raisins & Pine Nuts

*Precooked cous cous can be purchased in most markets and it takes minutes to prepare. I urge you to try it soon. It is great with Moroccan lamb or chicken.*

|   |   |
|---|---|
| 1 | clove garlic, minced |
| 1 | tablespoon butter |

|   |   |
|---|---|
| 1 | cup chicken broth |
| 1 | cup precooked cous cous |
|   | pinch of salt |

|   |   |
|---|---|
| 1/4 | cup toasted pine nuts |
| 1/4 | cup raisins, plumped in orange juice and drained |

In a saucepan, saute garlic in butter for 1 minute, or until garlic is softened. Add chicken broth and bring to a boil. Stir in cous cous and salt, cover pan, lower heat, and cook for 2 or 3 minutes, or until cous cous is tender. Fluff with a fork and stir in pine nuts and raisins. Serves 6.

**Cous Cous with Dates & Almonds:**
Substitute chopped dates and almonds for the raisins and pine nuts.

# Vegetable Cous Cous with Chick Peas

*Cous cous with vegetables and chick peas is practically a complete meal. Add a little cooked chicken or lamb for a feast.*

|   |   |
|---|---|
| 1 | onion, chopped |
| 2 | zucchini, unpeeled and sliced |
| 2 | carrots, thinly sliced |
| 1 | can (15 ounces) chick peas (garbanzos), rinsed and drained |
| 1/2 | cup chicken broth |

|   |   |
|---|---|
| 2 | cups chicken broth |
| 2 | cups precooked cous cous |
|   | pinch of salt |

In a covered saucepan, simmer together first 5 ingredients until vegetables are firm tender. Uncover pan and cook until broth is almost evaporated.

In another saucepan, bring chicken broth to a boil. Stir in cous cous and salt, cover pan, lower heat and cook for 2 or 3 minutes, or until cous cous is tender. Fluff with a fork and stir in vegetable mixture. Serves 8.

# Cheese Ravioli in Sun-Dried Tomato Sauce

*Won ton wrappers, sometimes called "Won ton skins" are a good substitute for fresh pasta in the making of ravioli. It cuts preparation time to the lowest minimum and the results are very satisfactory. The combination of goat cheese and sun-dried tomatoes is especially delicious. Won ton wrappers come in squares and rounds. I like the rounds for ravioli, as it eliminates trimming down the won tons to size.*

Cheese Filling:
- 1/2 pound low-fat Ricotta cheese
- 1/2 pound Chevre (goat cheese, such as Montrachet)
- 1 egg, beaten
- 1/4 cup chopped chives
- 1 teaspoon sweet basil flakes or
  2 tablespoons fresh basil, chopped
- 1 teaspoon grated lemon peel
  white pepper to taste

- 1 package round won ton wrappers, fresh or frozen. Defrost in refrigerator if frozen. (1 package contains 55 to 60 wrappers.)

In a bowl, stir together filling ingredients until blended. On a floured pastry cloth, lay 1 won ton wrapper. Place 1 tablespoon Cheese Filling in the center, moisten the edge of the wrapper with water, and place another won ton wrapper on top. Press the edges gently to seal and place filled ravioli on a floured plate. Continue with the remaining wrappers. (Can be held, at this point, for several hours, stored in the refrigerator, covered with plastic wrap.)

When ready to serve, in a spaghetti cooker, bring 4-quarts water and 1 tablespoon oil to a gentle boil. Add the ravioli in 2 batches, and allow to cook for 3 to 4 minutes, or until ravioli are tender and float to the top. Serve with Sun-Dried Tomato Sauce on top and a sprinkling of grated Parmesan. Yields 30 ravioli and serves 6.

Sun-Dried Tomato Sauce:
- 1 medium red pepper, cut into slivers
- 6 cloves garlic, minced
- 1 tablespoon olive oil

- 1 can (28-ounces) Italian plum tomatoes, drained and chopped. Use 1/2 cup juice and reserve the rest for another use.
- 4 sun-dried tomatoes (packed in oil), drained and chopped
- 1 teaspoon dried sweet basil flakes or
  2 tablespoons fresh basil, chopped

In a saucepan, saute together first 3 ingredients until peppers are tender. Add the remaining ingredients and simmer sauce for 5 minutes.

# Spinach & Cheese Ravioli in Pesto Sauce

*The combination of spinach and cheese with pesto is a delicious blend of flavors. Each serving of pesto contains 1 tablespoon oil. This can be reduced by substituting 6 tablespoons of chicken broth for 3 tablespoons of oil. The results are a little lighter and less caloric.*

**Spinach & Cheese Filling:**

| | |
|---|---|
| 1 | package (10 ounces) frozen chopped spinach, defrosted and pressed dry in a strainer |
| 1/2 | pound low-fat Ricotta cheese |
| 1/2 | cup grated Parmesan cheese |
| 1 | egg, beaten |
| 2 | tablespoons bread crumbs |
| | pepper to taste |
| | |
| 1 | package round won ton wrappers, fresh or frozen. Defrost in refrigerator if frozen. (1 package contains 55 to 60 wrappers.) |

In a bowl, stir together filling ingredients until blended. On a floured pastry cloth, lay 1 won ton wrapper. Place 1 tablespoon Spinach & Cheese Filling in the center, moisten the edge of the wrapper with water, and place another won ton wrapper on top. Press the edges gently to seal and place filled ravioli on a floured plate. Continue with the remaining wrappers. (Can be held, at this point, for several hours, stored in the refrigerator, covered with plastic wrap.)

When ready to serve, in a spaghetti cooker, bring 4-quarts water and 1 tablespoon oil to a gentle boil. Add the ravioli in 2 batches, and allow to cook for 3 to 4 minutes, or until ravioli are tender and float to the top. Serve with 2 tablespoons of Pesto Sauce on top and a sprinkling of grated Parmesan. Yields 30 ravioli and serves 6.

**Pesto Sauce:**

| | |
|---|---|
| 8 | cloves garlic |
| 1/4 | cup pine nuts |
| 1/2 | cup chopped fresh basil leaves |
| 2 | ounces grated Parmesan cheese (about 2/3 cup) |
| | |
| 6 | tablespoons olive oil |

In the bowl of a food processor, blend together first 4 ingredients, until finely chopped. With the motor running, slowly drizzle in the oil until thoroughly blended. Yields about 3/4 cup pesto.

# Turkey Ravioli in Light Tomato Sauce

*Using ground turkey, instead of ground beef, reduces markedly the fat content of this recipe. The taste difference is hardly perceptible. These can be frozen, uncooked, in separated layers of plastic wrap.*

**Turkey Filling:**

| | |
|---|---|
| 1 | medium onion, chopped |
| 2 | cloves garlic, minced |
| 1 | tablespoon olive oil |
| 1 | pound ground turkey |
| 1 | egg, beaten |
| 1/3 | cup bread crumbs |
| 1 | package round won ton wrappers, fresh or frozen. Defrost in refrigerator if frozen. (1 package contains 55 to 60 wrappers.) |

In a skillet, saute together first 3 ingredients until onion is soft. Add the turkey and cook and stir until meat loses its pinkness. Place turkey mixture in a bowl and stir in egg and bread crumbs.

On a floured pastry cloth, lay 1 won ton wrapper. Place 1 tablespoon Turkey Filling in the center, moisten the edge of the wrapper with water, and place another won ton wrapper on top. Press the edges gently to seal and place filled ravioli on a floured plate. Continue with the remaining wrappers. (Can be held, at this point, for several hours, stored in the refrigerator, covered with plastic wrap.)

When ready to serve, in a spaghetti cooker, bring 4-quarts water and 1 tablespoon oil to a gentle boil. Add the ravioli in 2 batches, and allow to cook for 3 to 4 minutes, or until ravioli are tender and float to the top. Serve with Light Tomato Sauce on top and a sprinkling of grated Parmesan. Yields 30 ravioli and serves 6.

**Light Tomato Sauce:**

| | |
|---|---|
| 1 | medium onion, chopped |
| 6 | cloves garlic, minced |
| 1 | tablespoon olive oil |
| 1 | can (1 pound 12 ounces) Italian plum tomatoes, chopped. Do not drain. |
| 1/4 | cup tomato paste |
| 1 | teaspoon, each, Italian Herb Seasoning and dried sweet basil flakes pepper to taste |

In a saucepan, saute onion and garlic in oil until onion is soft. Add the remaining ingredients and simmer sauce for 5 minutes.

# Vegetables

More →

# Artichokes with Mushrooms & Shallots

| | |
|---|---|
| 1 | package (10 ounces) frozen artichoke hearts |
| 1 | pound mushrooms, sliced |
| 1 | medium onion, minced |
| 4 | shallots, minced |
| 4 | cloves garlic, thinly sliced |
| 1 | tablespoon butter |
| 1/4 | cup chicken broth |
| 2 | tablespoons lemon juice |
| 2 | tablespoons minced chives |

In a covered saucepan, cook together first group of ingredients until onion is soft. Uncover pan and continue cooking until liquid rendered is almost all absorbed. Place in a serving bowl and sprinkle top with chives. Serves 6.

# Artichokes Provençal
# with Potatoes, Tomatoes & Onions

| | |
|---|---|
| 1 | can (1 pound) stewed tomatoes, chopped. Do not drain. |
| 2 | packages (10 ounces, each) artichoke hearts |
| 8 | baby potatoes, peeled and sliced (about 1 pound) |
| 1 | onion, very finely chopped |
| 1 | clove garlic, minced |
| 2 | tablespoons lemon juice |
| 1 | teaspoon olive oil |
| 1/2 | teaspoon sugar |
| | salt and pepper to taste |

In a covered Dutch oven casserole, place all the ingredients, and simmer mixture for 30 minutes, or until potatoes and artichokes are tender. This is a nice homey dish to serve with roast chicken. Serves 8.

# Asparagus with Yogurt, Lemon & Chives

        2    packages (10 ounces, each) frozen asparagus, cooked in 1/2 cup
               boiling water for 5 minutes and drained
        1    tablespoon melted butter

      1/2    cup non-fat yogurt
      1/4    cup chopped chives
        3    tablespoons lemon juice

        2    tablespoons bread crumbs
        2    tablespoons grated Parmesan cheese

Arrange cooked asparagus in a shallow baking dish and brush with melted butter. Stir together yogurt, chives and lemon juice and spread over the asparagus. Combine crumbs and cheese and sprinkle on top. Bake at 350° for 15 minutes, or until heated through. Broil for a few seconds to brown crumbs and serve at once. Serves 8.

# Asparagus in Lemon Sauce with Garlic Crumbs

        1    pound cooked asparagus spears
      1/4    cup low-fat sour cream
      1/4    cup low-fat, non-cholesterol mayonnaise
        2    tablespoons lemon juice, freshly squeezed
      1/4    cup chopped chives
      1/2    teaspoon grated lemon peel
               salt to taste
      1/2    cup garlic croutons, rolled into coarse crumbs

Lay drained asparagus in an oval porcelain baker. Combine remaining ingredients, except the croutons, and spread mixture over the asparagus. Sprinkle top with garlic crumbs. Heat in a 350° oven, until heated through. Brown under the broiler for a few seconds, or until crumbs are lightly browned. Serves 4.

**To Prepare Fresh Asparagus:**
Start by snapping off the tough ends of each stalk. Rinse under cold water to remove every trace of sand. With a vegetable peeler, peel off the bottoms of the stalk, if they are tough. In the case of baby stalks, do not peel. With white kitchen twine, tie asparagus into a bundle. Place upright in a stock pot with 2 to 4-inches of boiling water or in a steamer with 1-inch of boiling water, and cook until firm tender. Cooking times will vary from 2 to 10 minutes, depending on the thickness of the stalks.

# Asparagus with Low-Fat Lemon Creme Fraiche

*Using the low-fat sour cream and light cream still produces a very flavorful Creme Fraiche. A little goes a long way for flavor.*

Low-Fat Lemon Creme Fraiche:
- 1/4 cup low-fat sour cream
- 1/4 cup half and half
- 3 tablespoons chopped chives
- 2 tablespoons lemon juice

- 1 pound cooked fresh asparagus (page 197)
- 2 teaspoons melted butter
- salt and white pepper to taste

- 1/8 cup toasted chopped almonds
- 1/8 cup Ritz cracker crumbs or Waverly cracker crumbs

In a small bowl, mix together the sour cream, cream, chopped chives and lemon juice, and allow to stand at room temperature for 1 hour. Arrange cooked asparagus in a baking dish. Brush with melted butter and sprinkle lightly with salt and pepper.

Spread Low-Fat Lemon Creme Fraiche evenly over the asparagus. Sprinkle with chopped almonds and cracker crumbs. Heat through in a 325° oven. Do not overcook. Broil for a few seconds to brown the crumbs. Serves 4.

# Asparagus in Low-Fat Cheese Hollandaise

*Hollandaise, normally made with butter, is lighter and quite flavorful made with low-fat cream cheese. A bit unorthodox, I admit, but still a delicious sauce.*

- 4 ounces low-fat cream cheese, at room temperature
- 2 tablespoons half and half cream
- 1 egg yolk
- 1 1/2 tablespoons lemon juice
- 1/2 teaspoon finely grated lemon peel
- pinch of salt and white pepper

- 2 pounds cooked fresh asparagus (page 197)

Beat all the ingredients together, except the asparagus, until they are blended. Place mixture in the top of a double boiler over hot water. Cook, stirring until heated through. Place asparagus in a baking pan. Spoon warm sauce over hot asparagus and broil until lightly browned. Serves 8.

## Asparagus with Swiss Cheese and Parmesan

2   pounds cooked fresh asparagus (page 197)
    salt and white pepper to taste

3   tablespoons low-fat, non-cholesterol mayonnaise
2   tablespoons lemon juice
1/4  cup grated Parmesan cheese
1/2  cup grated Swiss cheese (2 ounces)

Arrange cooked asparagus in a baking dish. Season with salt and pepper to taste. Stir together mayonnaise and lemon juice and spread evenly over the asparagus. Sprinkle top with Parmesan and Swiss Cheese.

Bake the asparagus in a preheated 350° oven for about 15 minutes or until heated through and cheese is melted. Broil for a few seconds to brown top and serve immediately. Serves 6.

*Note:* ♥ *Entire dish can be assembled earlier in the day and brought to room temperature before heating.*

## Broccoli with Hollandaise Sauce

*The Hollandaise in this recipe is the "real" sauce and while you may not use it often, it should be part of your repertoire. Usually made with egg yolks, it is very good made with a whole egg. Sorry, there's no substitute for butter, but you can reduce the amount of butter to 1/4 cup and add 1/4 cup rich chicken broth. It won't be authentic, but it will be a very yummy sauce.*

1   egg
2   tablespoons lemon juice
    pinch of salt and white pepper
1/2  cup butter (1 stick)

2   packages (10 ounces, each) frozen broccoli, cooked firm, or
    2 pounds cooked fresh broccoli (page 200)

Place the egg, lemon juice, salt and pepper in the blender container. Blend for 10 seconds at high speed.

Heat butter until it is sizzling hot and bubbly, but be careful not to brown it. Add the hot, sizzling butter very slowly, in a steady stream, while the blender continues running at high speed. When the butter is completely incorporated, sauce is ready. Spoon warm sauce over hot broccoli. Serve at once. Serves 8.

# Broccoli with Garlic & Shallot Yogurt Sauce

2    packages (10 ounces, each) frozen broccoli or 2 pounds fresh
1/2  cup chicken broth

3    cloves garlic, minced
3    shallots, minced
2    tablespoons white wine
1    teaspoon butter

2    tablespoons chopped chives
2    tablespoons lemon juice
2    tablespoons non-fat yogurt

In a Dutch oven casserole, cook broccoli in chicken broth for 5 minutes or until tender. Remove broccoli from pan and place in a shallow baking pan. Add the next 4 ingredients to the Dutch oven casserole and simmer mixture for 10 minutes or until shallots are soft. Stir in remaining ingredients until blended and pour sauce over the broccoli. Heat at 350° for about 15 minutes, or until heated through. Serves 8.

# Broccoli in Yogurt Cheese Sauce

2    packages (10 ounces, each) frozen broccoli, or 2 pounds fresh, cooked in 1/2 cup boiling water for 5 minutes and drained. Brush with 1 tablespoon melted butter.

1/2  cup unflavored non-fat yogurt
1/4  cup grated Parmesan cheese
1/4  cup chopped chives
1/8  teaspoon garlic powder
1    tablespoon lemon juice
1    teaspoon grated lemon peel

3    tablespoons crumbled garlic croutons

Arrange broccoli in a shallow baking dish. Stir together the next group of ingredients and spread over the broccoli. Sprinkle top with garlic crouton crumbs. Heat at 350° for 15 minutes or until heated through. Broil crumbs for a few seconds to brown and serve at once. Serves 8.

**To Prepare Fresh Broccoli:**
Rinse broccoli in cold water to remove every trace of sand. Cut off the tough bottom part of each stalk. With a vegetable peeler, peel the tough bottoms of the stalk. With white kitchen twine, tie broccoli into a bundle. Place upright in a stock pot with 2 to 4-inches of boiling water, or in a steamer with 1-inch boiling water, and cook until firm tender. Cooking times will vary from 5 to 10 minutes, depending on the thickness of the stalks. Broccoli florets will cook in 3 minutes.

# Brussel Sprouts with Lemon & Garlic Crumbs

- 2 packages (10 ounces, each) frozen Brussel sprouts
- 1/2 cup chicken broth
- 2 tablespoons lemon juice
  salt and pepper to taste

- 2 cloves garlic, minced
- 2 tablespoons butter
- 1/3 cup fresh bread crumbs
- 1 tablespoon lemon juice

In a saucepan, simmer together first group of ingredients until sprouts are tender but firm, and drain. In a skillet, saute garlic in butter until garlic is softened, but not browned. Stir in the bread crumbs and lemon juice and toss until nicely blended. Add the sprouts and toss until sprouts are coated with crumb mixture. Heat through and serve 6.

# Cabbage with Apples, Raisins & Wine

*Earthy cabbage is heightened with the addition of apples, raisins and wine. This is a nice accompaniment to a hearty pot roast, roast goose or roast chicken. Cabbage can be prepared earlier in the day and stored in the refrigerator. Heat before serving.*

- 1 onion, chopped
- 1 tablespoon butter
- 1 teaspoon sugar

- 1 small head cabbage (about 3/4 pound), cored and shredded
- 2 apples, peeled, cored and grated
- 1/3 cup raisins, dark or light
- 1 cup dry white wine
- 2 tablespoons lemon juice
- 2 teaspoons sugar
  salt to taste

In a Dutch oven casserole, saute together first 3 ingredients, stirring now and again, until onions are soft, but not browned, about 5 minutes. Stir in the remaining ingredients, cover pan, and simmer mixture for about 30 minutes, or until cabbage is tender. Serves 6.

# Cabbage with Onions & Brown Rice

*Just delicious for an informal Sunday night dinner with family and friends.  Serve with roast chicken or veal.*

|     |                            |
|-----|----------------------------|
| 1   | cup finely shredded cabbage |
| 1   | large onion, chopped       |
| 2   | shallots, minced           |
| 2   | cloves garlic, minced      |
| 2   | tablespoons butter         |

|       |                     |
|-------|---------------------|
| 2 1/4 | cups chicken broth  |
| 1     | cup brown rice      |
|       | salt and pepper to taste |

In a Dutch oven casserole, cook together first 5 ingredients, for 20 minutes, stirring now and again, until vegetables are soft.  Stir in the remaining ingredients, cover pan, and simmer mixture for 40 to 45 minutes, or until rice is tender and liquid is absorbed.  Fluff rice with a fork and serve 6.

# Sweet & Sour Cabbage
# with Lemon, Tomato & Onion Sauce

*The simplicity of this dish in no way indicates how deep and flavorful it is.  It tastes just like stuffed cabbage without the dumplings.*

|     |                                             |
|-----|---------------------------------------------|
| 1   | head cabbage (about 1 pound), cored and shredded |
| 1   | can (1 pound) stewed tomatoes, chopped.  Do not drain. |
| 1   | large onion, chopped                        |
| 4   | tablespoons lemon juice                     |
| 1   | teaspoon sugar                              |
| 1/2 | cup chicken broth                           |
| 1   | tablespoon minced parsley leaves            |
|     | salt and pepper to taste                    |

In a covered Dutch oven casserole place all the ingredients and simmer mixture for about 40 minutes, or until cabbage is tender.  Serves 6.

## Honey Red Cabbage with Sauerkraut & Raisins

*Serve this unusual sweet and sour cabbage dish with pot roast, short ribs, or brisket. Potato pancakes add the perfect balance.*

| | |
|---|---|
| 1 | jar (1 pound) sauerkraut, drained |
| 1 | small head red cabbage, about 1 pound, shredded |
| 4 | cloves garlic, minced |
| 1 | can (1 pound) stewed tomatoes, chopped. Do not drain. |
| 1/4 | cup honey |
| 1/3 | cup raisins |
| 1 | teaspoon paprika |
| | salt and pepper to taste |

In a covered Dutch oven casserole, place all the ingredients and simmer mixture for about 45 minutes or until cabbage is soft.   Serves 8.

## Carrots with Apples and Raisins

| | |
|---|---|
| 1 | package (1 pound) fresh or frozen baby carrots |
| 1 | tablespoon butter |
| 1 | teaspoon sugar |
| 1 | teaspoon lemon juice |
| 1/2 | cup golden raisins, plumped overnight in orange juice |
| 1 | apple, peeled and grated |
| 1 | tablespoon finely minced parsley |
| | salt and pepper to taste |

Cook carrots in boiling water until tender, and drain.  In a skillet, melt the butter and add the carrots and remaining ingredients.  Continue cooking and stirring until apples are tender and carrots are glazed.  Serves 6.

## Glazed Carrots with Lemon & Dill

| | |
|---|---|
| 1 | pound fresh or frozen baby carrots, cooked for 5 minutes in boiling water and drained |
| 1 | tablespoon butter |
| 1 | tablespoon sugar |
| 2 | tablespoons chopped parsley |
| 2 | tablespoons lemon juice |
| 1/4 | teaspoon dried dill weed |
| | salt to taste |

Prepare carrots and refresh under cold water.  In a large skillet, heat together the remaining ingredients.  Add the carrots and cook, tossing and turning, until carrots are shiny and glazed.  Serves 6.

# Carrot Pudding with Raisins

1    can (1 pound) julienned carrots (or sometimes called Carrots French Style) drained and dried on paper towelling

1/2    cup sweet butter
1/2    cup brown sugar
1/4    cup sugar
2    eggs
1    tablespoon lemon juice

1    cup flour
1    teaspoon baking powder
1/2    teaspoon baking soda
    pinch of salt

1    teaspoon vanilla
1/2    cup yellow raisins, plumped in orange juice

Drain carrots and pat them dry with paper towelling. Beat together the butter, sugars, eggs and lemon juice until the mixture is smooth, about 2 minutes. Add dry ingredients and beat until blended, about 1 minute. Add vanilla and yellow raisins and beat until blended. Stir in the carrots.

Place mixture in a heavily greased and floured 2-quart ring mold. Bake at 350° for about 50 minutes or until a cake tester, inserted in center, comes out clean. Remove from the oven, loosen edges and carefully invert onto a serving platter. Fill center with wholeberry cranberry sauce or buttered peas. Serve with turkey or chicken. Serves 8 to 10.

# Honey Carrots with Chives

*Tender carrots are delicious when sweetened with honey and accented with chives. These are the carrots I prepare for Thanksgiving. Often I add a few dried currants and omit the chives.*

1    pound fresh or frozen baby carrots, cooked for 5 minutes in boiling water and drained

1    tablespoon butter
2    tablespoons honey
2    tablespoons chopped parsley
3    tablespoons chopped chives
    salt to taste

Prepare carrots and refresh under cold water. In a large skillet, heat together the remaining ingredients. Add the carrots and cook, tossing and turning, until carrots are shiny and glazed. Serves 6.

# Cauliflower with Apples & Noodles & Buttered Crumbs

- 1     onion, chopped
- 2     apples, peeled, cored and grated
- 1     teaspoon sugar
- 2     packages (10 ounces, each) frozen cauliflower cut into small florets
- 2     tablespoons butter

- 1/4     pound medium egg noodles, cooked until tender and drained
- 2     tablespoons lemon juice
      salt to taste

- 1/3     cup dry bread crumbs
- 1     tablespoon melted butter

In a Dutch oven casserole, saute together first 5 ingredients until apples are tender, about 20 minutes. Stir in next 3 ingredients until blended and heat through. In a skillet, toast bread crumbs in butter for 2 or 3 minutes and sprinkle over the cauliflower before serving. Serves 8.

# Cauliflower with Onions & Potatoes

*This is a fine way to serve cauliflower. A bit unusual with the addition of potatoes but they add a sweet and mellow touch to the assertive cauliflower.*

- 2     potatoes, peeled and diced
- 1     cup chicken broth
- 1     onion, minced
- 1     can (1 pound) stewed tomatoes, drained and chopped
- 2     packages (10 ounces, each) frozen cauliflower, cut into florets
- 2     tablespoons lemon juice
- 1     tablespoon minced parsley leaves
      salt and pepper to taste

In a covered Dutch oven casserole, place all the ingredients and simmer mixture for about 30 minutes or until potatoes are tender. Serves 8.

## Instant Oven-Fried Eggplant

1    eggplant (1 pound) peeled and cut into 3/8-inch slices
     low-fat, non-cholesterol mayonnaise, to lightly coat eggplant

20   Ritz crackers, rolled into crumbs
1    cup grated Parmesan cheese

Spread each slice of eggplant on both sides with mayonnaise. Dip each slice into mixture of crumbs and cheese so that they are well coated on both sides.

Place eggplant slices on a greased cookie sheet and bake at 400° until golden brown, about 20 minutes. Carefully turn and brown other side. Serves 6.

**To Make Oven-Fried Zucchini:**
Slices or strips of zucchini can be substituted for the eggplant. Delicious.

## Eggplant with Sun-Dried Tomatoes

*This versatile dish can be served hot or cold, as a vegetable accompaniment to lunch or dinner, or as a spread on crusty Italian bread. Or use it on pizza dough and top with some low-fat Mozzarella cheese. It is also delicious tossed with pasta. This is much like Caponata but I have omitted the olives.*

1    small eggplant (about 1 pound), peeled and cut into fourths. Cut
     each fourth into thin slices.
1    tablespoon olive oil

1    onion, chopped
4    shallots, minced
4    cloves garlic, minced
6    sun-dried tomatoes, chopped
1    tablespoon capers, rinsed and drained
3    tablespoons red wine vinegar
1    tablespoon olive oil
1    teaspoon sugar
3    sprinkles cayenne pepper
     salt and pepper to taste

Place eggplant in a 9x13-inch baking pan and drizzle with the oil. Cover pan tightly with foil and bake at 350° for 30 minutes, or until eggplant is soft. Meanwhile, in a covered Dutch oven casserole, simmer together the remaining ingredients until onions are soft. Stir in the cooked eggplant and heat through. Place in a covered bowl and refrigerate for several hours. Bring to room temperature before serving with thin slices of French bread. Lavosh crackers are good with this, too.

# Eggplant Stuffed with Ricotta Cheese

*This is a dish my mother made often. She loved to stuff vegetables and fill them with all manner of good things. This one is practically a perfect food, containing vegetables, cheese, eggs, and bread. A good vegetarian choice.*

 3 eggplants ( 1 pound, each) cut in half lengthwise
 1 tablespoon oil

**Stuffing:**
 1 pound Ricotta cheese
 1/2 cup grated Parmesan cheese
 2 eggs
 1/2 cup bread crumbs
 salt and white pepper to taste

**Topping:**
 1 egg, beaten, for brushing tops
 1/4 cup bread crumbs
 1/4 cup grated Parmesan cheese

Cut eggplants in half, lengthwise, and scoop out the vegetable, leaving a 1/2-inch thick shell. Set shells aside. Take scooped out eggplant and finely chop it. Place it in a 9x13-inch baking pan, drizzle it with oil, cover pan tightly with foil and bake it in a 400° oven for 20 minutes or until it is soft.

In a large bowl, beat together stuffing ingredients until mixture is blended. Beat in soft eggplant. Divide mixture evenly between the 6 eggplant shells. Brush tops generously with beaten egg and sprinkle them with bread crumbs and grated Parmesan cheese. Bake in a 350° oven for about 45 minutes or until filling is set and tops are golden brown. Serves 6.

# Green Beans with French Fried Onions

 1 pound fresh or frozen whole green beans
 1 tablespoon butter
 1/4 cup beef broth
 1/4 pound sliced mushrooms
 pinch of salt and pepper to taste

 1 can (3 ounces) Real French Fried Onions

In a Dutch oven casserole cook together first 6 ingredients over low heat until the green beans are firm tender. Place mixture in a shallow baker and sprinkle top with onions. Cover and refrigerate. When ready to serve, heat in a 350° oven until heated through. Serves 6.

# Winter Compote of Chestnuts, Apples, Apricots & Raisins

*This is one of the most delicious compotes and filled with some of my favorite things…chestnuts, apricots, apples and orange. This lovely dish will elevate a simple dinner to gastronomical heights.*

|       |                                                                |
|-------|----------------------------------------------------------------|
| 1     | can (15 1/2 ounces) chestnuts, drained and sliced              |
| 4     | apples, peeled, cored and very thinly sliced                   |
| 1     | bag (6 ounces) dried apricots, cut into halves                 |
| 1/2   | cup yellow raisins                                             |
| 1     | cup orange juice                                              |
| 1/2   | medium orange, grated. Use fruit, juice and peel (about 3 tablespoons.) |
| 1/4   | cup sugar                                                     |
| 1     | teaspoon pumpkin pie spice                                     |
|       |                                                                |
| 1/2   | cup chopped walnuts                                            |

In a 9x13-inch baking pan, stir together first group of ingredients and bake, uncovered, at 350° for 40 minutes, stirring now and again. Sprinkle the nuts on top and continue baking for 10 minutes. Delicious served with roast chicken or veal. Serves 8.

# Green Beans Italienne with Tomatoes, Onions & Parmesan

|       |                                                                |
|-------|----------------------------------------------------------------|
| 1     | pound fresh green beans, ends snapped and left whole - or - 1 bag (1 pound) frozen whole green beans |
| 3     | tomatoes, chopped, fresh or canned                            |
| 1     | onion, finely chopped                                         |
| 1/2   | cup rich chicken broth                                        |
| 1/2   | cup tomato sauce                                              |
| 1     | tablespoon lemon juice                                        |
| 1/2   | teaspoon Italian Herb Seasoning salt and pepper to taste      |
|       |                                                                |
| 2     | tablespoons grated Parmesan cheese                            |

In a Dutch oven casserole, simmer together first group of ingredients until green beans are tender, but firm, about 15 minutes for the fresh or 10 minutes for the frozen. Sprinkle top with grated cheese before serving. Serves 6.

# Confit of Honeyed Onions

2 large onions, thinly sliced
2 tablespoons oil

1/4 cup dry white wine
3 tablespoons honey
1 tablespoon Sherry
2 tablespoons vinegar

In a large skillet, over low heat, cook onion in oil, stirring now and again, until onions are very soft and limp, but not fried. Add the wine, and continue cooking until most of the wine has evaporated. Stir in the remaining ingredients and cook for another 2 minutes. Serve with roast chicken or broiled meats. Serves 4.

# Onions Carmelized in Brown Sugar

4 large onions, cut in half and thinly sliced
4 tablespoons butter
1/4 teaspoon paprika
2 tablespoons brown sugar
salt and pepper to taste

Saute onions in butter until they are transparent. Add remaining ingredients and continue sauteing until onions are glazed and golden brown. Serve with steak, London broil, hamburgers.

# Green Peas with Onions & Mushrooms

1/2 onion, finely chopped
1 tablespoon butter
1/4 pound mushrooms, cleaned and sliced

1/4 cup rich chicken broth
salt and pepper to taste
1/4 cup half and half cream

1 package (1 pound) frozen peas

Saute onion in butter until onion is transparent. Add mushrooms and saute until mushrooms are tender. Add broth, seasonings and cream and cook for 5 minutes, uncovered, or until sauce is slightly thickened. Add peas and cook for a few minutes or until peas are tender. Serves 6.

# Parsnips with Apples

*Parsnips are an unsung vegetable. Outside of sometimes being used in soups, it rarely appears on restaurant menus and I do believe, is rarely used in the home. Here I pair it with apples, sprinkle it with sugar and cinnamon and bake it in orange juice...interesting and delicious. Peel parsnips as you would carrots.*

- 2 apples, peeled, cored and thinly sliced
- 1 pound parsnips, peeled and thinly sliced on the diagonal
- 1/2 cup orange juice
- 2 tablespoons cinnamon sugar

In a 8x12-inch baking pan, place the apples and parsnips, drizzle with orange juice and sprinkle with cinnamon sugar. Cover pan with foil and bake at 350° for 40 minutes or until apples and parsnips are tender. Uncover pan, add a little orange juice, if it appears dry, and continue baking for 15 minutes, or until top is lightly browned. Serves 8.

# Old-Fashioned Candied Sweet Potatoes with Butter & Brown Sugar & Glazed Walnuts

*These are the sweet potatoes I make every Thanksgiving. They are the simplest and the best for my taste. The chopped walnuts are optional, but very good. A little more butter or brown sugar can be used.*

- 4 large sweet potatoes, about 2 1/2 pounds
- 1/4 cup butter, melted
- 1/3 cup dark brown sugar
- 1/2 teaspoon cinnamon
- 1/2 cup coarsely chopped walnuts

Scrub the sweet potatoes and cook them in boiling water until tender, but firm. Rinse them in cold water and allow to cool, so they can be handled, and peel. Cut into 3/4-inch thick slices. Place sweet potato slices, in one layer, in a shallow baker. Stir together the remaining ingredients and drizzle over the top. Bake at 350° for 20 minutes or until top is candied and glazed. Serves 6.

# Green Peppers Stuffed with Beef & Rice

*This is another one of my Mom's specialties. It often amazed me how, without a recipe, everything she made was always perfectly consistent.*

- 6 green peppers, medium sized, cut in half lengthwise (from top to bottom). Remove seeds and membranes. You will have 12 half peppers.

- 2 pounds ground beef or ground turkey
- 1 cup rice, parboiled in boiling water for 10 minutes and drained
- 1 tablespoon chopped parsley
- 1/4 teaspoon paprika
- 1/8 teaspoon garlic powder
  salt and pepper to taste

Wash peppers and drain. Combine remaining ingredients until blended and stuff peppers with this mixture. In a 9x13-inch pan, place a little Tomato Sauce. Place peppers in pan and pour remaining sauce over the tops. Cover pan tightly with foil and bake at 350° for about 30 minutes or until peppers and rice are tender. Uncover pan, and bake an additional 20 minutes, basting now and again, until tops are lightly browned. Serves 6.

Tomato Sauce:
- 1 tablespoon oil
- 1 can (1 pound 12 ounces) crushed tomatoes in puree
- 1 small onion, grated
- 1 teaspoon sugar
- 1 clove garlic, minced
- 2 tablespoons parsley
  salt and pepper to taste

Combine all the ingredients and cook sauce for 10 minutes.

# Roasted Potatoes with Rosemary & Garlic

- 2 pounds small red potatoes, scrubbed and cut into fourths
- 6 cloves garlic, very thinly sliced
- 2 teaspoons dried rosemary, crumbled
- 4 tablespoons margarine, melted
- 1/4 cup chicken broth
  pinch of salt and pepper to taste

In a 9x13-inch baking pan, toss together all the ingredients until potatoes are nicely coated. Roast them in a 350° oven for about 45 minutes, turning now and again, until potatoes are tender and golden brown. Add a little broth, if potatoes appear dry. Serves 8.

# Potatoes Baked without Skins

*The simplicity of this recipe in no way even hints at how delicious these potatoes are. They are perfect plain, but extra seasonings can be added (see note.) Try these soon. They're wonderful.*

6   potatoes, medium-sized, peeled
    salt to taste
4   tablespoons butter, 1/2 stick, melted

In a 9x13-inch baking pan, brush the peeled potatoes with the melted butter, being careful to cover the entire potato. Bake uncovered in a 350° oven, basting and turning every 15 minutes until potatoes are tender and outside is golden and crusty, about 45 minutes.. Keep warm in a low oven until ready to serve. (Can be held for at least 1/2 hour.)

*Note: ♥ There are several variations to the above basic recipe. When the potatoes are about half cooked, you can sprinkle them with paprika and onion powder and proceed baking and basting as above. You can sprinkle them with parsley or your favorite herb or seasoning.*

# Potatoes with Onions & Mushrooms

6   potatoes, medium sized, peeled

1   large onion, finely chopped
6   tablespoons butter, (3/4 stick)
1/2   pound mushrooms, sliced
1/2   cup half and half
    salt and pepper to taste

Boil potatoes in salted water until barely tender. Do not overcook. Slice potatoes crosswise into 1/2-inch thick slices. Set aside.

Saute onion in butter until onion is soft. Add mushrooms and continue sauteing until mushrooms are tender. Add cream and seasonings and stir to mix. Place sliced potatoes in a shallow casserole and spread onion mixture evenly over the top. Bake in a 350° oven for about 20 minutes or until piping hot. Serves 6.

# Roasted Potatoes with Garlic, Lemon & Dill

*This potato casserole, in a Greek mood, is especially good with roast chicken or veal. Add a little broth, if potatoes appear dry, but most of the broth should be consumed at the end of baking. Usually made with a lot of oil and a little broth, this adaptation, with a little oil and lots of broth, works very well, too.*

- 2 pounds potatoes, peeled and cut into 1-inch slices
- 4 tablespoons olive oil
- 6 cloves garlic, minced
- 3 tablespoons lemon juice
- 2 cups chicken broth
- 1 teaspoon dried dill weed
  salt and pepper to taste

In a 9x13-inch pan, toss potatoes with olive oil. Stir together the remaining ingredients and pour evenly over the potatoes. Tent pan loosely with foil. Bake at 350° for 30 minutes. Remove foil and continue baking for 30 minutes or until potatoes are tender. Broil for a few seconds to brown the top. Serves 6 to 8.

# Creamed Potatoes & Onions

- 2 medium onions, cut into 1/4-inch rings
- 3 tablespoons butter
- 6 large potatoes, peeled and sliced

- 2 cups chicken broth
- 1/4 cup half and half cream
- 3 tablespoons grated Parmesan cheese
  salt and freshly ground pepper

Saute onions in butter until onions are soft. In an oven proof casserole layer the potatoes and onions. Combine the remaining ingredients and pour over the potatoes. Cover pan tightly with foil and bake at 350° for about 1 hour or until potatoes are tender. Uncover pan and sprinkle top with a little more grated Parmesan. Continue baking for 20 minutes or until top is lightly browned. Serves 8.

# Potato Pancakes

*(Made in a processor or blender)*

2  eggs
1/4  cup cream
2  heaping tablespoons flour
1/2  teaspoon baking powder
   salt and pepper to taste

2  cups potatoes, peeled and cubed
1  onion, sliced
   oil for frying

Place first six ingredients in a food processor or blender container. Blend for 5 seconds. Add potatoes and onion and blend for another 10 seconds or until potatoes and onions are very finely ground, but not pureed. Do not overblend.

Heat a 12-inch skillet with 1/4-inch oil. When a drop of water skitters around, start making the pancakes. Pour 1/4 cup batter for each pancake but do not crowd them in the pan. Fry until golden brown on one side; turn and brown other side. Keep warm in a low oven. Serve warm with a spoonful of Orange Apple Sauce (page 215). Serves 6.

# Paprika Parsley Potatoes

1  pound potatoes, peeled and boiled until firm tender
1  small onion, grated
1/4  cup melted butter (1/2 stick)
1/2  teaspoon paprika
1  tablespoon chopped parsley leaves
   salt and pepper to taste

Cut potatoes into 1/3-inch slices. In a skillet, toss together all the ingredients. Gently saute potatoes until lightly crisped. Serves 4.

# Potato & Onion Cake with Orange Apple Sauce

*There is a little recipe tucked in at the end that you might overlook, so I am bringing it to your attention. If you want to enhance the flavor of prepared applesauce, add the concentrated orange juice. It is truly wonderful served this way. I make all my apple sauce with orange juice.*

| | |
|---|---|
| 6 | potatoes, peeled and grated |
| 3 | small onions, grated |
| 2 | eggs, beaten |
| 1/2 | cup cracker meal |
| | salt and pepper to taste |
| 3 | tablespoons salad oil |
| 1 | tablespoon salad oil |

Grate potatoes just before cooking so that the batter does not darken. If you grate potatoes earlier, cover them with cold water and drain before using.

Combine onions, eggs, meal and seasonings. Add grated potatoes to onion mixture. Preheat oven to 350°. Place 3 tablespoons oil in a 9x13-inch baking pan and heat the pan in the oven. Add potato mixture to preheated pan and spread evenly. Drizzle 1 tablespoon oil over top.

Return pan to the oven and cook until potatoes are tender and crust is a golden brown, about 50 minutes to 1 hour. Cut into squares to serve. Serve with a spoonful of low-fat sour cream and Orange Apple Sauce. Serves 8.

Orange Apple Sauce:
|   |   |
|---|---|
| 1 | jar (1 pound) unsweetened apple sauce |
| 6 | tablespoons concentrated orange juice, undiluted |

Stir together apple sauce and orange juice until blended.

Note: ♥ *To serve this as an hors d'oeuvre, slice into 1-inch squares and serve with bowls of low-fat sour cream and apple sauce.*
♥ *Can be cooked earlier in the day and reheated at time of serving.*
♥ *Do not freeze.*

# Noodle & Spinach Mold

1    package, (8 ounces), medium noodles, cooked and drained
2    packages, (10 ounces, each), frozen chopped spinach, defrosted and pressed in a strainer to drain

1/4   cup butter (1/2 stick), melted
1/2   pound mushrooms, sliced
2    eggs, well beaten
1/2   cup low-fat sour cream
1/2   cup half and half
1/2   cup grated Parmesan cheese
     salt and pepper to taste

Prepare noodles and spinach. Saute mushrooms in butter until mushrooms are tender. In a large bowl, stir together all the ingredients. Butter a 2-quart ring mold and coat with bread crumbs. Place mixture in mold, cover with foil and bake in a 350° oven for 45 minutes. Remove from oven, loosen sides by running a knife along the edge, and invert immediately onto a platter. Decorate with additional mushroom caps that were sauteed in butter. Serves 8.

# Spinach with Rice & Garbanzos

*This is a dish my mother made often. It is an unusual group of ingredients, but the results are delicious and healthy. The spinach is flavored with onion and lemon and the rice and garbanzos add an interesting texture.*

1/2   cup rich chicken broth
1    small onion, minced
1    can (1 pound) garbanzos, rinsed and drained
3    tablespoons lemon juice
     salt and pepper to taste

1 1/2   cups cooked rice
2    packages (10 ounces, each) chopped spinach, defrosted

In a saucepan, cook together first group of ingredients until onion is soft, about 20 minutes. Stir in the remaining ingredients and continue cooking for 10 minutes, or until liquid is absorbed. Serves 8.

## Creamed Spinach with Chives

1   package frozen chopped spinach (10 ounces), defrosted
      and drained
3   ounces low-fat cream cheese
4   tablespoons finely minced chives
1   teaspoon lemon juice
3   sprinkles ground nutmeg
      salt to taste

Combine all the ingredients and heat over a low flame until spinach is hot and cream cheese is melted. Serves 4 or 5.

*Note:* ♥ *Don't be misled by the simplicity of this dish. It is delicious yet takes only moments to prepare.*

## Instant Creamed Spinach

1   package frozen chopped spinach, (10 ounces), defrosted
1   package cream cheese (3 ounces)
      dash of nutmeg
      salt and pepper to taste

Combine all the ingredients and heat over a low flame until mixture is hot and cream cheese has melted. Serves 4.

## Spinach Mini-Mornay

1   package frozen chopped spinach, (10 ounces), defrosted and
      pressed in a strainer to drain
1/4 cup half and half
1/3 cup grated Parmesan cheese
1   teaspoon lemon juice
      salt and pepper to taste

Stir together all the ingredients until blended. Spread mixture evenly in a buttered 1 1/2-quart souffle dish and bake in a 325° oven until heated through. Serves 4 or 5.

# Tomatoes Stuffed with Beef
# in Tomato Cheese Sauce

*This is another one of my Mom's specialties. Be certain to grate the onion. Chopping it will not do. A good main course served with Pink Rice.*

| | |
|---|---|
| 12 | firm medium tomatoes |
| 2 | pounds ground beef or ground turkey |
| 1/2 | cup cracker meal |
| 1 | egg |
| 1 | small onion, grated |
| 2 | tablespoons chopped parsley |
| | salt and pepper to taste |

Cut tops off tomatoes and scoop out tomato pulp. Chop tomato pulp coarsely and set it aside for the sauce. Mix together remaining ingredients until blended and stuff tomatoes loosely with meat mixture.

In an 8x12-inch baking pan, place a little Tomato Cheese Sauce. Set tomatoes in one layer over the sauce, and spoon remaining sauce over them. Bake uncovered in a 350° oven for about 40 minutes or until meat is cooked through. Serves 6.

Tomato Cheese Sauce:

| | |
|---|---|
| 1 | tablespoon oil |
| | reserved tomato pulp |
| 1 | can (8 ounces) tomato sauce |
| 2 | teaspoons sugar |
| | salt and pepper to taste |
| 1/4 | cup grated Parmesan cheese |

Stir together all the ingredients until blended.

# Broiled Tomatoes with Parmesan & Chives

| | |
|---|---|
| 8 | slices tomatoes, about 1/2-inch thick |
| 8 | teaspoons low-fat mayonnaise |
| 8 | teaspoons grated Parmesan cheese |
| 4 | tablespoons chopped chives |
| | pepper to taste |
| 8 | teaspoons cracker crumbs |

Place tomatoes on a cookie sheet. Mix together next 4 ingredients until blended. Spread cheese mixture evenly over tomato slices. Sprinkle tops with cracker crumbs. Broil tomatoes until crumbs are lightly browned. Serves 4.

# Zucchini Stuffed with Beef in Tomato Sauce

6 6-inch zucchini, peeled and cut in half crosswise. Each half should be about 3-inches long. Scoop out the pulp leaving a ring, 1/3-inch thick. Reserve pulp for sauce.

1 1/2 pounds ground beef or ground turkey
1 small onion, grated
1 clove garlic, minced
2 tablespoons chopped parsley
2 eggs
1/2 cup bread crumbs
 salt and pepper to taste

Topping:
1 egg, beaten
12 teaspoons bread crumbs

Prepare zucchini and set aside. Coarsely chop pulp and set aside for the sauce. Blend together the remaining ingredients and fill zucchini shells with meat mixture. In a large casserole place the Tomato Sauce. Set filled zucchini over the sauce, filled side up.

Brush tops of stuffed zucchini with beaten egg and sprinkle with 1 teaspoon bread crumbs. Bake in a 350° oven for 40 minutes or until zucchini are tender and beef is cooked through. Serve with Pink Rice. Serves 6.

Tomato Sauce:
1 tablespoon oil
 reserved zucchini pulp (from above)
2 cans (8 ounces each) tomato sauce
1 teaspoon sugar
1 small onion, minced
1 clove garlic, minced
1 tablespoon parsley, chopped
1 teaspoon sweet basil flakes
1/2 teaspoon Italian Herb Seasoning
 salt and pepper to taste

In a saucepan, stir together all the ingredients and cook for 10 minutes.

# Zucchini, Chile, Tomato Casserole

       1   onion, thinly sliced
       1   tablespoon butter
    1 1/2  pounds zucchini, peeled and sliced on the diagonal
           salt and pepper to taste
       2   tomatoes, cut into medium slices
       1   can (4 ounces) diced green chiles

     1/2   cup low-fat sour cream
     1/2   cup grated Jack cheese

Saute onion in butter until onion is tender. Add zucchini and seasonings and continue sauteing until zucchini are cooked but still firm.

In an 8x12-inch pyrex baking dish, layer the zucchini-onion mixture, tomatoes and chiles. Cover vegetables evenly with the sour cream and sprinkle top with the Jack cheese. Bake in a 350° oven until heated through and cheese is melted and bubbly, about 20 or 25 minutes. Serves 6.

# Zucchini Frittata with Tomatoes and Herbs

*This is a lovely little luncheon dish, very light and satisfying. It is an attractive choice for a buffet. Entire dish can be assembled earlier in the day and refrigerated. Bake before serving. Do not bake it earlier. Do not freeze.*

       1   large onion chopped
       6   shallots, minced
       2   teaspoons margarine
       1   pound zucchini, sliced. Do not peel.

       6   eggs
     1/2   cup half and half cream
     1/4   cup chopped chives
       1   tablespoon chopped parsley leaves
     1/2   teaspoon sweet basil flakes
     1/4   cup grated Parmesan cheese
     1/2   cup grated Swiss cheese (2 ounces)
           pepper to taste

       6   slices tomatoes
       2   tablespoons grated Parmesan cheese

Saute onion and shallots in margarine until onion is transparent. Add zucchini and continue sauteing until zucchini and onion are tender. Beat together next 8 ingredients until blended. In a lightly oiled 8x12-inch porcelain baking pan, place zucchini mixture. Pour egg mixture evenly over all. Lay tomatoes on top and sprinkle with grated cheese. Bake at 325° for about 40 minutes or until eggs are set. Serves 6.

# Desserts

More →

### (Desserts, Cont.)

Old Fashioned Hot Fudge Sauce, 248
Strawberry Iced Cream, 248
After Dinner Cold Cappuccino, 249
Instant Velvet Sherbert with Champagne, 249
Instant Frozen Chocolate Mousse, 250
Vanilla, Strawberry, Biscuit Tortoni Variations, 250
Nutcracker Chocolate Chip Pie, 251
Lemon Cloud Torte, 251
Old-Fashioned Country Apple Tart, 252
Strawberry Cream Cheese Pie with Raspberry Syrup, 253
Peach Pie, Apricot Pie, Blueberry Pie Variations, 253
Tarte Tartin, 254
Easiest Apple Pie in Crisp Cookie Crust, 255
Flaky Pastry Peach & Cranberry Pie, 256
Italian Plum Tart on Almond Macaroon Cookie Crust, 257
Viennese Apple Tart with Rummy Whipped Cream, 258
Apple Cream Cheese Pie, 259
Apple Tart with Sour Cream, 259
Strawberry Cheese Pie in Almond Pie Shell, 260
Fruity Bread Pudding & Creme Fraiche Vanilla, 261
Quick Puff Paste, 262
Apricot Strudel with Walnuts, 263
Chocolate Chip Danish, 263
Crescents with Cinnamon & Walnuts & Vanilla Glaze, 264
Old-Fashioned Apple Strudel, 265
Cinnamon Raisin Danish, 265
Strawberry Walnut Raisin Strudel, 266
Honey Almond Maple Sauce, 267
Chocolate Chocolate Chip Sauce, 267
Honey Cinnamon Vanilla Sauce, 267
Instant Hot Fudge Sauce, 268
Instant Butterscotch Sauce, 268
Maple Walnut Sauce, 268
Instant Strawberry Sauce, 268

# Chocolate Torte a la Sacher
# with Apricot & Chocolate Glaze

*This is one of my very favorite chocolate cakes. The combination of apricots and chocolate is like a marriage made in chocolate heaven. This torte is a little moister than the original Sacher, but I am only mentioning it for the sake of the purists. It is very simple to prepare and a joy to serve.*

|       |                        |
|-------|------------------------|
| 5     | eggs                   |
| 1     | cup sugar              |
| 1 1/3 | cups walnuts           |
| 1     | teaspoon vanilla       |
| 4     | tablespoons flour      |
| 4     | tablespoons cocoa      |
| 1     | teaspoon baking powder |

In a food processor, blend together all the ingredients for 1 minute, or until nuts are very finely ground. Pour batter into a wax-paper-lined 10-inch springform pan and bake at 350° for 25 to 30 minutes, or until a cake tester, inserted in center, comes out clean. Do not overbake. Remove from pan and place on a footed platter.

Spread top evenly with warmed apricot jam and with a teaspoon, swirl top with warm Chocolate Glaze, allowing some of the jam to show. Allow chocolate to set at room temperature, about 1 hour. Serves 12.

Topping:
   1/2   cup apricot jam, warmed

Chocolate Glaze:
   1/2   cup semi-sweet chocolate chips
   1/4   cup butter (1/2 stick), at room temperature
   1/2   teaspoon vanilla

In the top of a double boiler, over hot water, melt chocolate. Stir in butter until blended. Stir in vanilla until blended. Spoon over cake immediately while warm.

# The Best Apricot & Walnut Coffee Cake

*This is a great cake to serve. Even purists with great palates have raved about this cake before they knew its simple beginnings. When I bring this cake for a pot luck or barbecue, I glaze the top. It dresses the cake for a party.*

- 1 package (18 1/2 ounces) Duncan Hines yellow cake mix.
  (Use a cake mix with no pudding added.)
- 1 cup sour cream
- 3 eggs
- 1/4 cup water
- 1/3 cup oil

- 1/2 cup dried apricots, coarsely chopped in food processor

- 1/3 cup sugar
- 1 teaspoon cinnamon

- 1/2 chopped walnuts

In the large bowl of an electric mixer, beat together first 5 ingredients for 2 minutes or until batter is light. Beat in apricots until blended.

Spread 2/3 of the dough on the bottom of a greased 10-inch tube pan (with a removable bottom.) Stir together sugar and cinnamon and sprinkle on top of the batter. Spoon remaining batter over the cinnamon mixture and spread to even. Sprinkle top with chopped walnuts and press them gently into the batter to prevent them from burning.

Bake at 350° for 45 minutes, or until a cake tester, inserted in center, comes out clean. Allow to cool in pan. When cool, remove from pan and serve 12. If you are preparing this for a special occasion, brush top with Apricot Glaze.

**Apricot Glaze:**
- 2 tablespoons finely chopped dried apricots
- 1 tablespoon orange juice
- 1/2 cup sifted powdered sugar

Stir together all the ingredients until blended.

# Easiest & Best Walnut & Raspberry Torte
## with Lemon Glaze

*This marvellous nut cake, accented with raspberry jam and complemented with lemon is a beautiful balance of flavors. Best of all, it can be prepared in minutes in a food processor. The results will truly amaze you.*

|        |                          |
|--------|--------------------------|
| 5      | eggs                     |
| 1      | cup sugar                |
| 1 3/4  | cups walnuts             |
| 1/2    | cup flour                |
| 1      | teaspoon baking powder   |
| 1      | teaspoon vanilla         |
|        |                          |
| 3/4    | cup seedless red raspberry jam, heated |

In the bowl of a food processor, blend together first 6 ingredients until the nuts are very finely ground, about 45 seconds to 1 minute. Pour the batter into a greased 10-inch springform pan, and bake at 350° for 30 minutes or until top is browned and a cake tester, inserted in center, comes out clean. Allow to cool in pan.

When cool, remove from pan and place on a lovely platter. Spread raspberry jam evenly over the top and then drizzle with Lemon Glaze in a decorative and lacy pattern. Cut into wedges to serve. Serves 12.

Lemon Glaze:
|     |                          |
|-----|--------------------------|
| 1   | tablespoon lemon juice   |
| 2/3 | cup sifted powdered sugar |

Stir together lemon juice and powdered sugar until blended. Add a little more sugar or lemon juice to make glaze a drizzling consistency. This glaze should hold its shape and should not be too loose.

# Hungarian Red Cherry Almond Sponge Cake

*This is one of the easiest cakes to make. A few ingredients, quickly beaten, and Voila!, a light, delicious cake. This little cake uses no fat and low-fat milk was used in testing. Red cherries are very tart, and using Bing cherries produces a totally different cake. If you use Bings, then substitute 1 teaspoon vanilla for the almond extract and 1/2 cup chopped walnuts for the almonds. This is not a sweet, rich cake. It is light and low-fat.*

|        |                                       |
|--------|---------------------------------------|
| 2      | eggs                                  |
| 1      | cup sugar                             |
| 1/2    | cup non-fat yogurt                    |
| 1/2    | cup low-fat milk                      |
| 1      | teaspoon almond extract               |
|        |                                       |
| 2 1/2  | cups flour                            |
| 3      | teaspoons baking powder               |
| 1      | cup frozen red pitted cherries (not Bing) |
| 1/2    | cup chopped almonds                   |

In the large bowl of an electric mixer, beat together eggs and sugar until mixture is lightened, about 2 minutes. Beat in the yogurt, milk and almond extract until blended. Beat in the flour and baking powder until nicely blended, about 1 minute. Stir in the cherries.

Place batter in a greased 10-inch springform pan and sprinkle top with almonds. Press almonds gently into the batter. Bake at 350° for 45 minutes, or until a cake tester, inserted in center, comes out clean. Tent top loosely with foil, if top is browning too rapidly. Drizzle top in a decorative fashion with Almond Cream Glaze. Serves 10.

Almond Cream Glaze:
|      |                            |
|------|----------------------------|
| 1/2  | cup sifted powdered sugar  |
| 1    | tablespoon cream           |
| 1/4  | teaspoon almond extract    |

Stir together all the ingredients until blended.

# Viennese Apple & Orange Pecan Torte
## with Orange Peel Glaze

*This little gem was fashioned after a delicious cake we enjoyed in Vienna. It is a rather dense cake, very moist and fruity. Not the least of its virtues is the fact that it can be prepared in minutes in the food processor...including chopping the fruit and nuts. The Orange Peel Glaze adds a little tartness, which is a lovely balance.*

|       |                                           |
|-------|-------------------------------------------|
| 6     | eggs                                      |
| 1     | cup sugar                                 |
| 1 3/4 | cups pecans                               |
| 3/4   | cup flour                                 |
| 1     | teaspoon baking powder                    |
| 1     | teaspoon vanilla                          |
|       |                                           |
| 1     | apple, peeled, cored and cut into 8 pieces |
| 1/2   | medium thin-skinned orange, cut into 8 pieces |

In the bowl of a food processor, blend together first 6 ingredients until the nuts are very finely chopped, about 45 seconds. Add the fruit and process for about 15 seconds more, or until the fruit is finely chopped, but not pureed. You should see little flecks of orange and apple.

Pour batter into a greased 10-inch springform pan and bake at 350° for about 40 to 45 minutes, or until top is browned and a cake tester, inserted in center comes out clean. Allow to cool in pan.

When cool, remove from pan and place on a lovely serving plate. Spread top with Orange Peel Glaze and let a little drip down the sides. Beautiful and delicious. Serves 12.

**Orange Peel Glaze:**

|     |                                                          |
|-----|----------------------------------------------------------|
| 2   | tablespoons grated orange peel. (A little of the white can be used.) |
| 1   | tablespoon orange juice                                  |
| 1/2 | cup sifted powdered sugar                                |

Stir together all the ingredients until blended.

# Fresh Country Carrot and Raisin Cake

*This cake, for all its simplicity, has wonderful taste and texture. Carrot cakes can be moistened with pineapple, sour cream, cream cheese and lots of oil. This one uses water...lowering the calories, but not the taste.*

| | |
|---|---|
| 1/4 | cup butter |
| 1 1/2 | cups sugar |
| 3 | large carrots, peeled and grated (about 1 1/2 cups) |
| 1 1/3 | cups water |
| 2 | teaspoons pumpkin pie spice |
| 1 | cup yellow raisins |
| 3 | tablespoons grated orange. (Use peel, juice and fruit. Remove any large pieces of membrane.) |
| 1 | egg, beaten |
| 2 | cups flour |
| 2 | teaspoons baking soda |
| 1 | teaspoon vanilla |
| 1 | tablespoon cinnamon sugar |
| 1 | cup chopped walnuts |

In a saucepan, bring first 7 ingredients to a boil. Remove from heat and refrigerate until cold. Remove from the refrigerator and beat in the egg until blended. Beat in the next 3 ingredients until blended.

Spread batter evenly into a greased 9x13-inch baking pan, sprinkle top with cinnamon sugar and press walnuts gently on top. Bake at 350° for 35 to 40 minutes, or until a cake tester, inserted in center, comes out clean. Allow to cool in pan and cut into 24 2-inch squares.

# Cranberry Orange Tea Cake with Orange Glaze

*This is one of the most delicious cakes. The texture is marvelous. Please note that it does not contain eggs. The Orange Glaze may seem a little like gilding the lily, but it does add a tart, orange flavor to the cake. The glaze also adds a decorative touch which is so nice during the holidays.*

| | |
|---|---|
| 1/2 | cup butter |
| 1/2 | cup sour cream |
| 1 | cup sugar |
| 1/4 | cup orange juice |
| 3 | tablespoons grated orange (1/2 medium orange) |
| | |
| 2 | cups flour |
| 1 | teaspoon baking powder |
| 1 | teaspoon baking soda |
| | |
| 1 | cup cranberries, fresh or frozen, coarsely chopped |
| | |
| 1/2 | cup chopped walnuts |

Beat together first 5 ingredients until nicely blended. Beat in next 3 ingredients until blended. Carefully, stir in the cranberries just until blended. Do not overmix or cranberries will discolor the batter. Spread batter evenly into a greased 10-inch tube pan (with a removable bottom) and sprinkle top with walnuts. Press the walnuts gently into the batter. Bake in a 325° oven for about 45 minutes, or until a cake tester, inserted in center, comes out clean. Allow to cool in pan. When cool drizzle top with Orange Glaze. Serves 10.

Orange Glaze:

| | |
|---|---|
| 1 | tablespoon orange juice |
| 1/2 | cup sifted powdered sugar |
| 1 | teaspoon grated orange rind |

Stir together all the ingredients until blended.

# The Best Walnut Torte with Raspberry Jam on Butter Cookie Crust

*From the traditional soft-centered Southern Pecan Pie, to this chewy walnut creation, I love nut pies and tortes. For me, this one is so pleasurable, that even a small portion is very satisfying.*

**Butter Cookie Crust:**

| | |
|---|---|
| 1 | cup butter, (2 sticks) |
| 1/2 | cup sugar |
| 2 | cups flour |
| | |
| 1 | egg |
| 1 | tablespoon water |
| | |
| 3/4 | cup seedless raspberry jam, heated |

In the bowl of a food processor, blend together first 3 ingredients until butter is the size of small peas. Beat together the egg and water, and add all at once, blending until dough clumps together. Place dough on floured wax paper and press together to shape into a disc. Pat the dough on the bottom and 2-inches up the sides of a lightly greased 10-inch springform pan and bake at 350° for 20 minutes, or until crust is golden brown.

Spread crust with raspberry jam and spread Nut Torte Filling on the top. Bake at 350° for 40 minutes or until top is golden brown. (It is not easy to test with a cake tester.) Allow to cool in pan. Decorate with a sprinkle of sifted powdered sugar. Serves 12.

**Nut Torte Filling:**

| | |
|---|---|
| 2 | cups walnuts |
| 1/4 | cup sugar |
| | |
| 3 | eggs |
| 3/4 | cup sugar |
| 1/2 | cup flour |
| 1 | teaspoon baking powder |
| 1 | teaspoon vanilla |

In a food processor, grind walnuts with sugar until nuts are very finely chopped. Beat together the remaining ingredients until blended. Beat in walnuts until blended.

# Spiced Applesauce Cake

*There are few cakes you can make that are more delicious than this one. It is especially satisfying with a mug of hot cider and great to serve between Thanksgiving and Christmas.*

|       |                           |
|-------|---------------------------|
| 1/2   | cup butter                |
| 1     | cup sugar                 |
| 1     | egg                       |
| 1/4   | cup sour cream            |
|       |                           |
| 1 1/2 | cups cake flour, sifted   |
| 1     | teaspoon baking soda      |
| 1     | teaspoon baking powder    |
| 1 1/2 | teaspoons pumpkin pie spice |
|       | pinch of salt             |
|       |                           |
| 1     | cup applesauce            |
|       |                           |
| 1/4   | cup cake flour            |
| 1/2   | cup golden raisins        |
| 1/2   | cup currants              |
| 1     | cup chopped walnuts       |

Cream butter with sugar until light and fluffy. Add egg and beat until blended. Add sour cream and continue beating until blended.

Stir together dry ingredients, flour, soda, baking powder, pumpkin pie spice and salt. Beat in dry ingredients and applesauce alternately to creamed mixture, beating well after each addition. Dredge raisins, currants and walnuts in 1/4 cup flour and beat these into the batter until blended.

Place batter in a lightly greased 10-inch tube pan (with a removable bottom) and bake at 350° for about 45 or 50 minutes or until a cake tester inserted in center comes out clean. Allow to cool in pan. When cool, remove from the pan and drizzle top with Orange Glaze, allowing some of the glaze to run down the sides. Serves 12.

Orange Glaze:

|     |                           |
|-----|---------------------------|
| 1   | tablespoon orange juice   |
| 1/2 | cup sifted powdered sugar |

Stir together orange juice and powdered sugar until blended.

# Country Home Banana Cake with Walnuts

*While this cake does contain a little butter, it is moistened with water and bananas and is a fine tasting cake. Ingredients are basic to most pantries and it is a good recipe for a country place, where you want to keep things simple. As with most banana cakes, don't puree the bananas, or cake may become gummy.*

| | |
|---|---|
| 1/3 | cup butter, softened |
| 1 1/4 | cups sugar |
| 2 | eggs |
| 1/4 | cup water |
| | |
| 2 | large bananas, coarsely mashed |
| | |
| 1 2/3 | cups flour |
| 1 | teaspoon baking powder |
| 1 | teaspoon baking soda |
| 2 | teaspoons cinnamon |
| | |
| 1 | tablespoon cinnamon sugar |
| 1/2 | cup coarsely chopped walnuts |

In the large bowl of an electric mixer, beat together first 4 ingredients until blended. Stir in the bananas. Stir in the next 4 ingredients until blended. Do not overmix. Spread batter into a lightly greased 10-inch tube pan and sprinkle top with cinnamon sugar and walnuts. Press the walnuts lightly into the batter to prevent them from burning. Bake at 350° for about 40 minutes, or until a cake tester, inserted in center, comes out clean. Allow to cool in pan. Serves 12.

# Chocolate Chip Chocolate Cake

| | |
|---|---|
| 1 | package (18-1/2 ounces) chocolate cake mix |
| 1 | cup sour cream |
| 4 | eggs |
| 1/2 | cup oil |
| 1 | package (3-3/4 ounces) instant chocolate pudding |
| | |
| 1 | cup chocolate chips, semi-sweet, coarsely crushed |

In your electric mixer beat together all the ingredients except the chocolate chips. Beat mixture for 4 minutes at medium speed. Add the chocolate chips and beat until blended.

Place batter in a lightly buttered and floured 10-inch tube pan. Bake in a 325° oven for about 50 minutes or until a cake tester inserted in center comes out clean. Cool cake in pan. Dust lightly with sifted powdered sugar when cool. Serves 12.

# Banana Fudge Devil's Cake

*This little treasure whips up in literally seconds and elevates a simple cake mix to gastronomical heights. Everybody loves this cake. It is moist, delicious and has a very fine texture.*

  1  package (18 1/2 ounces) Duncan Hines Devil's Cake Mix
       (regular cake mix without pudding)
1/2  cup oil
1/2  cup water
  1  cup sour cream
  3  eggs

  1  large banana, coarsely mashed, not pureed
1/3  cup chopped walnuts (for the top)

Beat together first 5 ingredients for about 4 minutes, or until batter is nicely blended and light. Stir in the bananas. Spread batter into a greased 10-inch tube pan and sprinkle walnuts on top. Press them gently into the batter (so that they do not burn.)

Bake at 350-degrees for about 45 minutes or until a cake tester, inserted in center, comes out clean. Allow to cool in pan. When cool, remove from pan and place on a lovely platter. Sprinkle top lightly with sifted powdered sugar. Serves 10.

# Chocolate Chip Sour Cream Cake

  1  package (18-1/2 ounces) yellow cake mix (without pudding added)
3/4  cup water
  1  cup sour cream
  2  eggs
  1  cup chocolate chips, semi-sweet, coarsely crushed

  3  tablespoons chocolate flavored Nestle's Quik

In your electric mixer, beat together the cake mix, water, sour cream and eggs. Beat at medium speed for 4 minutes. Add chocolate chips and mix until blended.

Place half the batter in a greased and floured 10-inch tube pan. Sprinkle the chocolate powder evenly over the batter. Pour the remaining batter evenly over the chocolate powder. With your scraper, cut into the batter at 2-inch intervals.

Bake in a 325° oven for about 50 minutes or until a cake tester inserted in center comes out clean. Dust lightly with sifted powdered sugar when cool. Serves 12.

# Darling Carrot Cake

*While some may feel that the old-fashioned carrot cake is passé, this one is still a favorite among so many of our friends. In fact, one of them, has established quite a reputation with this recipe and this was the cake her son chose to serve for his wedding. Properly wrapped in double thicknesses of plastic wrap and foil, this freezes well.*

|   |   |
|---|---|
| 2 | eggs |
| 3/4 | cup oil |
| 1/4 | pound cream cheese (4 ounces), at room temperature |
| 2 | teaspoons vanilla |

|   |   |
|---|---|
| 1 | cup flour |
| 1 | cup sugar |
| 1 | teaspoon baking powder |
| 1/2 | teaspoon baking soda |
|   | pinch of salt (optional) |
| 1 | teaspoon cinnamon |

|   |   |
|---|---|
| 1/2 | cup chopped walnuts |
| 1 1/2 | cups grated carrots |

Beat together the eggs, oil, cream cheese and vanilla until nicely blended. Beat in the next 6 ingredients until blended. Beat in the carrots and the walnuts until blended. Do not overbeat.

Pour batter into a lightly greased and floured 10-inch tube pan and bake in a 350° oven for about 35 to 40 minutes, or until a cake tester, inserted in center, comes out clean. Allow to cool in the pan. When cool, remove from the pan and swirl Cream Cheese Frosting on the top. Serves 12.

**Cream Cheese Frosting:**

|   |   |
|---|---|
| 1/4 | cup (1/2 stick) butter, softened |
| 1/4 | pound cream cheese (4 ounces), at room temperature |
| 1 | teaspoon vanilla |
| 1 | cup sifted powdered sugar |

Beat butter and cream cheese together until well blended. Add vanilla and sugar and beat until smooth.

# Velvet Cheesecake
## with Strawberry Orange Syrup

*There are few cheesecakes that are creamier and more velvety than this one. It is one of my favorites. It is beautiful with either the almond flavoring or the lemon accent. Do not overbeat cheesecakes, unless you like them very light and fluffy. I prefer a denser cheesecake.*

**Crust:**

| | |
|---|---|
| 1 1/4 | cups graham cracker crumbs |
| 2 | ounces butter, (1/2 stick), melted |
| 1/2 | cup coarsely chopped walnuts |
| 2 | tablespoons cinnamon sugar |

**Filling:**

| | |
|---|---|
| 1 | pound cream cheese, softened |
| 1 | cup sugar |
| 3 | eggs |
| 3 | cups sour cream |
| 2 | teaspoons vanilla |

| | |
|---|---|
| 1 1/2 | teaspoons almond extract **or** |
| 3 | tablespoons lemon juice and |
| 2 | teaspoons grated lemon zest |

Stir together the crust ingredients until blended. With your fingers, press mixture evenly on the bottom and 1/2-inch up the sides of a 10-inch springform pan that is lined with waxed paper. In the large bowl of an electric mixer, beat together the filling ingredients until blended. Do not overbeat. Pour mixture into the prepared crust.

Bake in a 350° oven for about 50 minutes or until top is just beginning to take on color. Do not overbake. Cool in pan and then refrigerate for at least 4 to 6 hours. Overnight is good, too. Remove from pan and serve with a spoonful of Strawberry Orange Syrup. Serves 12.

**Strawberry Orange Syrup:**

| | |
|---|---|
| 1 | package frozen strawberries in syrup, (10 ounces), defrosted |
| 3 | ounces (1/2 can) frozen orange juice, undiluted and defrosted |
| 1 | teaspoon finely grated orange zest |

Combine all the ingredients and refrigerate until serving.

*Note:* ♥ *Lemon Zest is obtained by grating the outer skin of the lemon It does not include the white part (the pith).*

# Cheese Cake with Cookie Crust & Glazed Strawberries

**Cookie Crust:**
- 1 cup flour
- 1/4 cup sugar
- 1/2 cup butter, softened

- 1 tablespoon grated lemon peel
- 1 egg yolk

Beat together flour, sugar and butter, until butter is evenly distributed. Beat in lemon peel and egg yolk just until blended. Gather dough, and work it lightly with your fingers until smooth. Pat dough on the bottom and 1-inch up the sides of a 10-inch springform pan. Bake at 400° for 15 minutes or until lightly browned. Cool.

**Cream Cheese Filling:**
- 1 1/4 pounds cream cheese, softened
- 3/4 cup sugar
- 1 1/2 tablespoons flour
- 4 teaspoons grated lemon peel
- 1 teaspoon vanilla
- 3 eggs
- 1 egg yolk
- 2 tablespoons heavy cream

Beat together all the filling ingredients until blended. Pour Cream Cheese Filling into prepared crust and bake at 250° for 1 hour and 20 minutes or until just firm. Do not overbake. Refrigerate for at least 4 hours. Overnight is good, too. Remove from pan and place on a lovely footed platter.

**Topping:**
- 2 pints fresh strawberries, cleaned and stemmed

Top cake with plump strawberries and brush strawberries with Currant Jelly Glaze. Refrigerate until serving time. Serves 12.

**Currant Jelly Glaze:**
Heat 3/4 cup currant jelly and simmer for 3 minutes until slightly thickened.

# Cherry Nut Mandelbread Cookies

*This cookie is not like the traditional mandelbread. It is a little softer and chewier but truly delicious. By spreading the batter into foil pans, shaping the dough into loaves is eliminated, saving a good deal of time and work. Cookies can be stored in a cookie jar or frozen in double plastic bags.*

|       |                              |
|-------|------------------------------|
| 1/2   | pound butter, (2 sticks)     |
| 2 1/2 | cups sugar                   |
| 6     | eggs                         |
| 2     | teaspoons vanilla            |
| 4     | cups flour                   |
| 3     | teaspoons baking powder      |
| 3     | cups chopped walnuts         |
| 1     | pound glaceed cherries, chopped |

Cream butter with sugar until light. Add eggs, one at a time, beating well after each addition. Beat in the vanilla, flour and baking powder until blended. Beat in the walnuts and the cherries until blended.

Divide dough into 6 greased and lightly floured foil loaf pans, 6x3x2-inches. (The foil pans make it easy to remove the cookie.) Bake in a preheated 350° oven for about 30 minutes or until top is lightly browned. Remove from oven and cool for 5 minutes. Remove from pans and invert on a cutting board. Slice with a very sharp knife and cut cookies about 1/2-inch thick.

Place cookies, cut side up, on a cookie sheet and return to oven to lightly toast on both sides. To serve, sprinkle lightly with sifted powdered sugar. Makes about 72 cookies.

# The Best Oatmeal Chocolate Chip Cookies

|     |                              |
|-----|------------------------------|
| 1   | cup butter or margarine, softened |
| 2   | cups brown sugar             |
| 2   | teaspoons vanilla            |
| 2   | eggs                         |
|     |                              |
| 1   | cup flour                    |
| 1   | teaspoon baking soda         |
| 3   | cups quick-cooking oats      |
| 1/2 | teaspoon salt                |
|     |                              |
| 1   | cup semi-sweet chocolate chips |
| 1   | cup chopped pecans           |

More →

(The Best Oatmeal Chocolate Chip Cookies, Cont.)

In the large bowl of an electric mixer, cream together butter, sugar and vanilla until mixture is light. Beat in eggs until blended. Combine next 4 ingredients and beat until blended. Stir in chocolate and pecans.

Drop batter by the heaping tablespoon onto an ungreased cookie sheet and bake at 375° for 8 to 9 minutes for soft cookies or 10 minutes for crisp ones. Remove cookies from the pan and allow to cool on brown paper. Yields about 30 to 36 cookies.

**Variations:**
**Blondies:**
Substitute butterscotch chips for the chocolate chips. Prepare with or without nuts.

**Oatmeal Raisin:**
Substitute raisins for the chocolate chips. Prepare with or without nuts.

# Raspberry Button Cookies

*This recipe appeared in the original "Joy of Eating" as a recipe that was given to me "20 years ago by a dear friend." Alas and alack!, it is now 35 years ago and it is still one of my favorites.*

| | |
|---|---|
| 1/2 | cup butter (1 stick) |
| 1/4 | cup brown sugar |
| 1 | egg yolk |
| 1/2 | teaspoon vanilla |
| 1 | cup flour |
| | |
| 1 | egg white, beaten slightly |
| 1/2 | cup finely chopped walnuts |
| | raspberry jam, sieved |

Cream butter and sugar together. Beat in egg yolk and vanilla until blended. Beat in flour until blended. Refrigerate dough for 1 hour.

Shape dough into 1/2-inch balls. Dip into egg white and then into the chopped nuts. Place on a greased cookie sheet. Make an impression in the center of each cookie with your thumb or index finger.

Bake at 325° about 20 minutes. Press center down again, if they have puffed up. Fill center with 1/2 teaspoon raspberry jam when cool.

*Note:* ♥ *Cookies can be frozen with or without the jelly centers. However, I would recommend filling the jelly centers after defrosting.*
♥ *You can substitute your favorite jelly or jam for the raspberry jam.*

# The Best Apricot Cookies on Butter Cookie Crust

**Butter Cookie Crust:**
- 3/4 cup butter
- 1 1/2 cups flour
- 3/8 cup sifted powdered sugar
- 1 tablespoon grated lemon peel

**Topping:**
- 1 cup dried apricots, soaked in boiling water for 10 minutes, drained and chopped
- 3 eggs
- 1 1/2 cups sugar
- 4 tablespoons flour
- 3/4 teaspoon baking powder
- 1 teaspoon vanilla
- 3/4 cup chopped walnuts

In the large bowl of an electric mixer, beat together first 4 ingredients until blended. Pat mixture into a lightly buttered 9x13-inch baking pan. Bake crust at 350° for about 20 to 25 minutes, or until lightly browned.

Meanwhile, beat together topping ingredients until blended. Pour mixture on baked crust and continue baking an additional 30 minutes or until topping is set. Cool in pan and cut into squares. Sprinkle with sifted powdered sugar. Yields 4 dozen cookies.

 # Butter Pecan Balls

- 1/2 pound butter, (2 sticks)
- 1/2 cup sugar
- 2 cups cake flour
- 2 teaspoons vanilla

- 1 cup finely chopped pecans
  sifted powdered sugar

Cream butter with sugar. Beat in flour and vanilla until blended. Beat in pecans. Shape dough into 3/4-inch balls. Bake at 300°, on a lightly greased cookie sheet, for about 25 to 30 minutes, or until just beginning to take on color. Roll in powdered sugar when hot and again when cold. Makes about 60 cookies.

*Note: ♥ These cookies freeze beautifully. Roll them in the sifted powdered sugar after defrosting.*

# Date Nut Chewies

*These are great to take to a pot luck or to a brunch meeting. They are intensely chewy. Whole wheat flour can be substituted for the all-purpose flour.*

|       |                          |
|-------|--------------------------|
| 3/4   | cup flour                |
| 1     | cup sugar                |
| 1/2   | teaspoon baking powder   |
|       | pinch of salt            |
|       |                          |
| 2     | eggs, beaten             |
| 1/2   | cup oil                  |
| 1     | teaspoon vanilla         |
|       |                          |
| 1     | cup chopped pitted dates |
| 1     | cup chopped walnuts      |

In the large bowl of an electric mixer, place first 4 ingredients. Add eggs, oil and vanilla all at once and beat until blended. Stir in dates and nuts. Spread mixture into a 9x13-inch lightly greased baking pan and bake at 350° for 25 minutes.

Remove pan from the oven and cut into squares while warm. Remove cookies from the pan immediately and cool on brown paper. When cool, wrap securely in plastic wrap to prevent drying. Makes about 48 cookies.

# Swiss Butter Crescents

*This delightful cookie recipe was given to me by a friend's Swiss cook who was an extraordinary baker. Her directions were to "put your hand in the sugar bin and take out 1 handful of sugar." I followed her instructions and came up with the 3 heaping tablespoons of sugar. It worked fine.*

|       |                                      |
|-------|--------------------------------------|
| 1/2   | cup butter, (1 stick)                |
| 3     | heaping tablespoons sifted powdered sugar |
| 1     | cup flour                            |
| 1/2   | cup very finely chopped walnuts      |

Cream butter and sugar together. Beat in flour until blended. Beat in nuts until blended.

Shape 1 teaspoonful of dough into tiny crescents. Place on a lightly greased cookie sheet and bake at 350° until just beginning to take on color. Do not let them brown. They should be pale and delicate. When cool, sprinkle with powdered sugar. Makes about 40 cookies.

## Best Raspberry Bars on Almond Cookie Crust

| | |
|---|---|
| 1 3/4 | cups flour |
| 3/4 | cup sugar |
| 3/4 | cup ground almonds (can be purchased at health food stores) |
| 1/2 | cup butter |

| | |
|---|---|
| 1 | egg, beaten |
| 1/2 | lemon, grated. Use peel, juice and fruit. Remove any large pieces of membrane. |

| | |
|---|---|
| 1 | cup raspberry jam |

In the large bowl of an electric mixer, beat together first 4 ingredients until mixture resembles coarse meal. Beat in egg and lemon until just blended. Set aside 3/4 cup dough. With floured hands, pat the remaining dough into a lightly buttered 9x9-inch baking pan. Dough is very soft. Spread raspberry jam evenly over the dough.

Divide the reserved dough into 8 balls and with floured hands, roll and pat dough out to 9-inch strips. Lay the strips over the jam lattice-fashioned. Bake at 350° for about 30 to 35 minutes or until top is golden brown. Allow to cool and cut into bars. Yields 18 cookies.

## Easiest & Best Apricot Nut Bars

*This is an easy cookie that is tart and crunchy. Whenever I make it, everyone asks for the recipe. It is intensely "apricot" and for the apricot lover.*

| | |
|---|---|
| 1 | package (6 ounces) dried apricots |
| 1/2 | cup of sugar |

| | |
|---|---|
| 1 | cup butter, softened |
| 1/2 | cup sugar |
| 1 | cup brown sugar |
| 2 | eggs |
| 2 | teaspoons vanilla |

| | |
|---|---|
| 2 1/4 | cups flour |
| 1/2 | teaspoon baking powder |
| 1/2 | teaspoon baking soda |
| 1 | cup chopped walnuts |

In food processor, finely chop apricots with sugar. Beat together next 5 ingredients until blended. Beat in apricot mixture until blended. Beat in next 4 ingredients until blended. (Batter will be thick.) Spread batter evenly into a greased 10x15-inch jelly roll pan and bake at 375-degrees for 20 minutes or until top is lightly browned. Cool in pan and cut into 1 1/2-inch squares. Yields about 60 cookies.

# Mother's Lemon Cloud Cookies

*These were one of our favorite cookies when we would rush home after school. It still is one of the best. It is a tangy and refreshing cookie with an excellent after-taste.*

|       |                             |
|-------|-----------------------------|
| 3/4   | cup butter                  |
| 1 1/2 | cups flour                  |
| 1/3   | cup powdered sugar          |
|       |                             |
| 3     | eggs                        |
| 1 1/2 | cups sugar                  |
| 3     | tablespoons flour           |
| 3/4   | teaspoon baking powder      |
|       | grated zest of 1 1/2 lemons |
| 1/4   | cup lemon juice             |

Beat butter, flour and sugar together until blended. Pat mixture into a lightly buttered 9x13-inch baking pan. Bake for 15 minutes in a 350° oven.

Beat together the remaining ingredients until blended. Pour this mixture on a baked crust. Bake for an additional 25 to 30 minutes, or until top is lightly browned. Allow to cool. Cut into 1 1/2-inch squares and sprinkle with sifted powdered sugar. Yields 72 cookies.

# Chocolate Chip Chewies

*These are very rich, so I kept the portions small.*

|       |                               |
|-------|-------------------------------|
| 1     | can (14 ounces) condensed milk |
| 1     | package (6 ounces) milk chocolate chips |
| 1/2   | cup chopped walnuts           |
| 1 1/2 | cups graham cracker crumbs    |

Combine all the ingredients and mix together until well blended. Heavily grease a pan measuring 6x12x1-inches. Place batter in pan and spread evenly. Bake in a preheated 350° oven for about 30 minutes. Cool for 5 minutes and then cut into 1-inch squares. Remove from pan immediately and allow to cool on a brown paper bag. When cool, dust lightly with sifted powdered sugar. Yields 72 cookies.

# Pecan Apricot Pastries on Shortbread Crust

*This recipe is a simplified version of a Hungarian masterpiece that I included in an earlier work. The original was given to me by my mother-in-law and called for separating the eggs, beating them separately, grating the nuts, etc., etc. In this version, all these steps have been eliminated. A little flour and baking powder have been added in lieu of these steps, but the result is surprisingly similar. These little nut cookies are welcomed around the holidays, as they are easy to prepare, you can keep the portions really small, and this recipe will yield at least 4 dozen cookies. The topping, a delicious nut cake, is a perfect balance of texture on the cookie crust. The original contained apricot jam. Raspberry jam is also very good.*

**Pecan Topping:**

| | |
|---|---|
| 6 | eggs |
| 3 | cups dark brown sugar |
| 1/4 | cup flour |
| 1/2 | teaspoon baking powder |
| 3 | cups pecans, finely chopped |
| 2 | teaspoons vanilla |

Beat together all the ingredients until blended. Spread mixture evenly into prepared Shortbread Crust and continue baking at 350° for 35 to 40 minutes, or until topping looks set and a cake tester, inserted in center, comes out clean. Allow to cool in pan. When cool, cut into 1 1/2-inch squares and decorate with a dusting of powdered sugar. Yields 48 cookies.

**Shortbread Crust:**

| | |
|---|---|
| 1 | cup margarine (2 sticks), cut into 8 pieces |
| 1/4 | cup sugar |
| 2 | cups flour |
| 3/4 | cup apricot jam, warmed |

In the large bowl of an electric mixer, beat together first 3 ingredients until mixture resembles coarse meal. Pat mixture on the bottom and 1-inch up the sides of a greased 9x13-inch baking pan and bake at 350° for 20 minutes, or until crust looks dry and is just beginning to take on color. Brush apricot jam over the baked crust.

243

# The Very Best Classic Chocolate Chip Brownies

This "toned down" recipe is the one I now make most often. I like the addition of walnuts, but my family prefers chocolate chips. Whenever I bring these to a meeting or a pot luck, I always hear those wonderful m-m-m-m's, culinary music to a cook's ears. I used to make these with two sticks of butter and have cut it down to one. It is still a very rich brownie, so keep the portions small. Using more chocolate and butter, these can be made richer, but not better.

A few words about brownies. There are many versions and techniques for preparing these delicious morsels, but I will tell you mine. My family and I like a brownie that is dense and fudgy, so I beat the ingredients just until blended. There are recipes that have you beat the eggs for 15 minutes (yes, that's true), but I like to incorporate as little air as possible. I am telling you this so that if you like a puffy, cakey brownie, this recipe is not for you.

Another important consideration is cooking time. It is difficult to test when brownies are done. At best, the top looks dry and a cake tester "appears" clean with a crumb or two. As oven temperatures and performance vary, you will have to experiment to find the perfect time. I bake my brownies for exactly 28 minutes, no more.

|       |                                   |
|-------|-----------------------------------|
| 4     | ounces unsweetened chocolate      |
| 4     | ounces butter (1 stick)           |
|       |                                   |
| 4     | eggs                              |
| 1 3/4 | cups sugar                        |
| 1     | tablespoon vanilla                |
| 1     | cup flour                         |
| 1/4   | teaspoon salt                     |
|       |                                   |
| 1     | cup semi-sweet chocolate chips or/and |
| 1 1/2 | cups chopped walnuts              |

Preheat oven to 350°. Grease a 9x13-inch baking pan. In the top of a double boiler, over hot, not boiling water, melt the chocolate with the butter, stirring now and again. Place chocolate mixture into the large bowl of an electric mixer. Beat in eggs, one at a time until blended. Beat in the sugar, vanilla, flour and salt until blended. Stir in the chocolate chips and/or walnuts.

Spread batter evenly into prepared pan and bake for 28 to 30 minutes, or until a cake tester, inserted in center, comes out barely clean. Do not overbake. Allow brownies to cool and then cut into small squares to serve. (It is easier to cut the brownies if you refrigerate them.) Cover leftover brownies securely with plastic wrap to prevent them from drying out. Yields 48 brownies.

# The Best Apricot Walnut Chewies

*There are few cookies that give me more pleasure than this one. Outside of the fact that it does not contain chocolate (but it can), it is perfect for my taste. Very chewy, with the flavor of apricot and textured with walnuts and oats...very satisfying. They are a little tricky to handle as they are very soft when removed from the oven. They do firm up when cool. Do not overbake or they will get too crisp. These are very large cookies. If you choose to make them half the size, then bake for 7 to 8 minutes.*

| | |
|---|---|
| 1 | cup (2 sticks) margarine, at room temperature |
| 3/4 | cup dark brown sugar |
| 3/4 | cup sugar |
| 2 | eggs, at room temperature |
| 1 | teaspoon vanilla |
| | |
| 1 | cup flour |
| 3 | cups oats |
| 1 | teaspoon baking soda |
| | |
| 2/3 | cup finely chopped apricots |
| 3/4 | cup finely chopped walnuts |

To cool the cookies, lay brown paper (from a roll or use large clean paper bags) on the kitchen counter. (Cookies are too soft to cool on racks.)

In the large bowl of an electric mixer, cream together margarine and sugars. Beat in eggs and vanilla until blended. Beat in the next 3 ingredients until blended. Beat in apricots and walnuts until blended. Drop batter by the heaping tablespoon on a greased cookie sheet. These cookies spread, so allow 2-inches between cookies. Bake at 375° for about 9 to 11 minutes, or until edges are beginning to take on color. Allow cookies to cool in pan for 3 to 4 minutes and then, with a wide spatula, remove them onto the brown paper to finish cooling. Yields 30 large cookies.

**To make Chocolate Chip Chewies:**
Substitute 1 cup semi-sweet chocolate mini-chips for the apricots.

**To make Raisin Walnut Chewies:**
Substitute 1 cup yellow raisins for the apricots.

**To make Date Nut Chewies:**
Substitute 1 cup chopped pitted dates for the apricots.

## Spiced Peaches with Walnuts

*This very tart and spicy fruit is nice to serve over low-fat vanilla ice cream or non-fat frozen yogurt. It is also great to serve with roast chicken or veal. It is attractive and colorful on a buffet. Can be prepared earlier in the day and heated before serving. Apples or apricots can be substituted for the peaches.*

    6    large peaches, (about 2 pounds) peeled, cut in half
           and stones removed
  1/2    cup orange juice
    3    tablespoons brown sugar
  1/2    teaspoon cinnamon
    3    sprinkles, each, ground nutmeg and ground cloves
  1/2    cup coarsely cut walnuts

Place peaches in one layer in a shallow baker and pour orange juice on top. Stir together brown sugar, cinnamon, nutmeg and cloves and sprinkle evenly over the fruit.

Cook peaches in a 350° oven, basting every now and again, about 20 minutes. Sprinkle top with walnuts and bake another 10 minutes. Serve warm or at room temperature. Serves 6.

**To make Spiced Apples with Walnuts:**
Substitute 2 pounds apples, peeled, cored and sliced, for the peaches. Total baking time is 45 minutes. Sprinkle with walnuts after 35 minutes. and then bake 10 minutes longer.

**To make Spiced Apricots with Walnuts:**
Substitute 2 pounds apricots, peeled, halved and stoned, for the peaches. Baking times are the same as for the peaches.

# Bananas Baked with
# Almonds & Orange Liqueur

    4    large firm bananas
    2    tablespoons lemon juice
    2    tablespoons butter
  1/4    cup brown sugar
  1/2    cup slivered toasted almonds
    2    tablespoons orange liqueur

Peel bananas and cut them into 1/2-inch slices on the diagonal. Place banana slices in a shallow baking dish and brush them thoroughly with lemon juice. In a saucepan, melt butter, add sugar, almonds and orange liqueur. Drizzle this mixture over the bananas and bake them in a 350° oven for about 15 minutes. Serves 6.

# Chocolate Iced Cream

*This, delightfully light and very delicious iced cream is as smooth as velvet.*

- 6 egg whites, beaten with a pinch of salt
- 8 tablespoons sugar

- 2 cups heavy whipping cream
- 3/4 cup chocolate syrup
- 2 tablespoons Creme de Cacao liqueur

- 1/2 cup semi-sweet chocolate chips, melted over hot, not boiling water

In an electric mixer, beat egg whites with a pinch of salt until soft peaks form. Add sugar slowly and continue beating until a stiff meringue. Set aside. In another bowl, beat the cream with the syrup and liqueur until stiff.

Combine beaten egg whites and whipped cream and beat together on low speed of your mixer until thoroughly combined.

Divide mixture between 24 paper-lined muffin cups. Swirl 1 teaspoon of melted chocolate over each top. Place muffin pans in freezer and freeze until solid. Remove ice cream cups from the muffin pans and store them in a box. Cover box securely with plastic wrap. Return to freezer.

When ready to serve, remove paper cup and place iced cream in a lovely stemmed glass or dessert dish. You can serve it plain or with a teaspoon of Creme de Cacao liqueur spooned over the top. Or you may enjoy a sprinkling of shaved chocolate (or both). Makes 24 servings.

**Chocolate Chip Chocolate Iced Cream:**
Follow the instructions for Chocolate Iced Cream, except chop the last 3 ounces of chocolate and fold it in at the end. Proceed in the same manner to freeze, store and serve.

# Ambrosia with Oranges and Pineapple

- 4 large navel oranges, peeled and cut into bite-size pieces. Make certain all the pith (white part) is removed.
- 1 can (16 ounces) pineapple chunks, thoroughly drained
- 1 cup coconut flakes or 1 cup coarsely chopped walnuts
- 1 pint sour cream
- 2 cups miniature marshmallows

Mix together all the ingredients and spoon into a 2-quart ring mold. Refrigerate overnight. (Mold does not get too firm but does hold its shape.) Unmold onto a large serving platter and decorate with orange slices and green leaves. Serves 8.

# Vanilla Iced Cream

6 egg whites, beaten with a pinch of salt
8 tablespoons sugar

2 cups whipping cream
4 tablespoons sugar
1 teaspoon vanilla
2 tablespoons orange liqueur

Follow instructions for Chocolate Iced Cream with the substitutions listed above. Proceed in the same manner to freeze and store. Serve with Old Fashioned Hot Fudge Sauce and toasted slivered almonds.

# Old Fashioned Hot Fudge Sauce

2 tablespoons butter
2 squares unsweetened chocolate
1 cup sugar
1/2 cup boiling water
2 tablespoons light corn syrup
1/8 teaspoon salt
1/2 teaspoon vanilla

In top of a double boiler, melt butter and chocolate over hot water. Add sugar, boiling water, corn syrup and salt. Place pan over direct heat and bring mixture to a boil. Cook for about 4 minutes or until sauce is thickened. Stir in vanilla. Serve hot over iced cream.

# Strawberry Iced Cream

6 egg whites, beaten with a pinch of salt
8 tablespoons sugar

2 cups heavy whipping cream
2 tablespoons sugar
2 tablespoons Grand Marnier liqueur
1 package (10 ounces) frozen strawberries in syrup, thawed

Follow instructions for Chocolate Iced Cream with the substitutions listed above. Proceed in the same manner to freeze and store. Serve with sliced fresh strawberries on top. Or a teaspoon of Grand Marnier liqueur and a sprinkling of shaved chocolate would be lovely. Yields 24 servings.

# After-Dinner Cold Cappuccino

*This is a great touch for dessert. It is delicious and refreshing to serve for a summer dessert or as a light ending to a meal. I made this up for a friend who would not consider a meal complete without a cup of cappuccino. Add a cookie and it is sheer perfection. Serve this in stemmed goblets with a pretty colored straw.*

- 2 cups low-fat vanilla ice cream
- 1 tablespoon Amaretto liqueur
- 1 tablespoon Creme de Cacao liqueur
- 1/2 teaspoon instant espresso or instant coffee

In the large bowl of an electric mixer, beat together all the ingredients until blended. Divide mixture between 4 stemmed glasses. Sprinkle a little ground chocolate over the top and add a little liqueur to taste (optional). Serve with a straw but have a spoon close by. Serves 4.

# Instant Velvet Sherbert with Champagne

- 2 cups orange sherbert, softened
- 2 egg whites
- 1 tablespoon sugar

Place sherbert in a large bowl. Beat egg whites until foamy. Continue beating, adding the sugar slowly until whites are stiff. Stir a little of the whites into the sherbert. Fold the remaining whites into the sherbert. Divide mixture between 6 paper-lined muffin cups and freeze until firm.

To serve, remove paper liner and place sherbert in balloon stemmed glasses. Add 2 ounces champagne to each glass and serve with a colorful straw. Serves 6.

# Instant Frozen Chocolate Mousse

*If you are looking for a frozen dessert that is light and luscious, this is a good one to consider. Vary it with any number of different flavors. My favorite is vanilla, but my family prefers chocolate.*

|   |   |
|---|---|
| 4 | egg whites, at room temperature |
| 4 | teaspoons sugar |
| 1 | teaspoon vanilla |
|   |   |
| 4 | cups chocolate ice cream, slightly softened |
| 12 | teaspoons ground chocolate |

In the large bowl of an electric mixer, beat egg whites until foamy. Continue beating, gradually adding the sugar, until whites are stiff, but not dry. Beat in vanilla.

Place ice cream in a large bowl, and add 1/4 of the beaten whites. Fold in remaining whites. Divide mixture between 12 paper-lined muffin cups and freeze until firm. To serve, remove paper liner, place mousse in a stemmed glass and sprinkle each top with 1 teaspoon ground chocolate. A teaspoon of liqueur is nice, but optional. Serves 12.

**Vanilla Mousse:**
Substitute vanilla ice cream for the chocolate and add 2 tablespoons Grand Marnier liqueur. Top with sliced strawberries or raspberries.

**Strawberry Mousse:**
Substitute strawberry ice cream for the chocolate and serve with sliced strawberries on top.

**Biscuit Tortoni:**
Substitute vanilla ice cream for the chocolate and add 1/4 cup macaroon crumbs, 4 tablespoons chopped maraschino cherries, and 2 tablespoons rum (optional).

# Nutcracker Chocolate Chip Pie

*This is my daughter's favorite pie. It ranks pretty high with our family and friends. Whenever I prepare it, the raves are very gratifying.*

    3   egg whites
    1   cup sugar

    22  Ritz crackers, coarsely crumbled
    1   cup coarsely chopped walnuts
    3/4 cup semi-sweet chocolate chips
    1   teaspoon vanilla

Beat egg whites until foamy. Add sugar, 1/4 cup at a time, beating, until egg whites are stiff and glossy. Beat in remaining ingredients just until blended. Spread mixture into a buttered 9-inch pie pan and bake in a preheated 350° oven for about 30 minutes or until top is dry and beginning to take on color. Top with Vanilla Whipped Cream and sprinkle with grated chocolate. Refrigerate for 6 hours. Overnight is good, too. Serves 8 to 10.

**Vanilla Whipped Cream:**
    3/4 cup whipping cream
    1   tablespoon sugar
    1   teaspoon vanilla
Beat cream with sugar and vanilla until cream is stiff.

# Lemon Cloud Torte

**Meringue Shell:**
    4   egg whites
        pinch of salt
        pinch of cream of tartar
    1   cup sugar

Beat egg whites with salt and cream of tartar until foamy. Beat in sugar, a little at a time, beating all the while, until the meringue is stiff and glossy. Spread meringue into a greased 9-inch pie pan and build up the sides to form a shell. Bake in a 275° oven for 1 hour. Cool.

**Lemon Filling:**
    4   egg yolks
    1/2 cup sugar
    1/4 cup lemon juice, freshly squeezed
    1   tablespoon finely grated lemon peel

    1   cup whipping cream whipped with 1 tablespoon sugar

In the top of a double boiler, over hot water, beat together first 4 ingredients. Cook and stir until mixture thickens. Allow to cool.

Whip the cream and fold it into the cooled lemon mixture. Spoon filling into prepared shell and refrigerate overnight or for at least 6 hours. Before serving sprinkle with some finely grated lemon peel. Serves 8.

# Old-Fashioned Country Apple Tart

*This delicious tart is one of the best. The cookie crust is perfect with the apples and the apricot jam. For a festive touch (and a very delicious one, too) serve with Creme Fraiche Vanilla. The Creme Fraiche is one of my variations, with a little less tartness.*

| | |
|---|---|
| 1/4 | pound butter (1 stick) |
| 1/4 | pound cream cheese |
| 1 | cup flour |
| 4 | tablespoons sifted powdered sugar |
| | |
| 1/2 | cup apricot jam |
| 3 | apples, peeled, cored and sliced thin |
| 1/4 | cup cinnamon sugar |
| | |
| 1/4 | cup apple jelly, melted |

In mixer, cream butter and cream cheese until thoroughly combined and blended. Add flour and sugar and beat at low speed until dry ingredients are well incorporated. Do not overbeat. Dough is quite soft.

Pat dough evenly on the bottom and 1-inch up the sides of a lightly greased 10-inch springform pan. Bake crust in a 400° oven for 20 minutes. Remove from oven and paint crust with 1/2 cup apricot jam.

Lay overlapping apple slices over the jam in a circular pattern. Sprinkle apples with cinnamon sugar and bake another 20 to 25 minutes or until apples are tender. Paint apples with melted jelly and bake another 5 minutes to set glaze. Cool in the pan. Serve warm or at room temperature. Serves 8.

Creme Fraiche Vanilla:
| | |
|---|---|
| 1 | cup whipping cream |
| 1/2 | cup sour cream |
| 1 | tablespoon sugar |
| 1 | teaspoon vanilla |

In a glass jar, mix the creams together until well blended. Leave uncovered and at room temperature for about 5 or 6 hours or until the creme has thickened. Stir in sugar and vanilla. Cover and refrigerate. This creme will keep, refrigerated, for a week to ten days. Makes 1 1/2 cups Creme Fraiche.

*Note: ♥ This sauce is incredibly delicious spooned over puddings or pies or fruits. Keep it on hand, for it can transform a quite ordinary dessert into a culinary delight.*

# Strawberry Cream Cheese Pie with Raspberry Syrup

*Very elegant, very lovely, this is one of my favorite pies. It can be served with any number of fresh fruits or berries.*

| | |
|---|---|
| 1 1/4 | cups graham cracker crumbs |
| 1/2 | cup chopped walnuts |
| 1/3 | cup butter, melted |
| 3 | tablespoons cinnamon sugar |

Combine all the ingredients and mix until blended. Pat mixture on the bottom and sides of a buttered 10-inch pie pan. Bake in a 350° oven for about 8 minutes or until crumbs are beginning to take on color. Cool before filling.

**Creamy Cream Cheese Filling:**

| | |
|---|---|
| 1 | package (8 ounces) cream cheese, at room temperature |
| 3/4 | cup sifted powdered sugar |
| 1 | teaspoon vanilla |

| | |
|---|---|
| 3 | tablespoons lemon juice |
| 1 | teaspoon lemon zest |
| 1 | cup whipping cream |

| | |
|---|---|
| 1 | pint fresh strawberries, hulled and halved |
| 1 | package (10 ounces) frozen raspberries in syrup |

Beat together the cream cheese, sugar and vanilla until the mixture is light and fluffy. Beat in the lemon juice and zest. In another bowl, beat the whipped cream until it is stiff.

On the low setting of an electric mixer, beat together the whipped cream and cream cheese mixture until blended. Spread into cooled pie shell. Cover top with strawberries, cut side down, cover with plastic wrap and refrigerate until serving time. Cut into wedges to serve and spoon a little raspberries and syrup on top. Serves 10.

**To Make Peach Cream Cheese Pie with Raspberry Syrup:**
Substitute 2 pounds fresh peaches, peeled, pitted and sliced, for the strawberries.

**To Make Apricot Cream Cheese Pie with Raspberry Syrup:**
Substitute 2 pounds fresh apricots, pitted and sliced, for the strawberries.

**To Make Blueberry Cream Cheese Pie:**
Instead of strawberries and raspberry syrup, top pie with 1 cup of blueberry pie filling.

# Tarte Tartin

This has been a popular dessert for many years and still ranks high at many of the best French restaurants. The original recipe calls for a crust of puff pastry. I have substituted frozen patty shells which greatly decreases the amount of preparation time and works just fine. I have adjusted the ratio of sugar and butter to allow for quicker carmelization.

Tarte Tartin is an open faced apple tart, where the apples have been carmelized. While the recipe is basically not difficult, it is a little tricky. Follow the instructions carefully and you should have a perfect tarte that is memorable. The Vanilla Cream Sauce is one of the easiest and the best.

| | |
|---|---|
| 1/2 | package Pepperidge Farms Frozen Patty Shells (3 patty shells) |
| 1/2 | cup butter, melted (1 stick) |
| 1 1/2 | cups sugar |
| 8 | large apples, peeled, cored and halved |

You will need a round baking pan, 8 to 9-inches wide and 2 1/2-inches deep. Place melted butter and sugar in pan. Arrange apples upright around the edge of the pan and place 2 apple halves in the center. Simmer apples over medium high heat until syrup is a golden caramel color (not browned), about 45 minutes.

Partially defrost patty shells, stack them and roll them out in a circle slightly smaller than the diameter of the baking pan. Place dough over the apples, pierce the crust and bake in a 400° oven for 30 minutes or until crust is golden. Cool for a few minutes.

Place a serving platter over the tart and carefully invert it. With a spatula, arrange apples if some have fallen away. Serve plain or with whipped cream or with Vanilla Cream Sauce as a lovely accompaniment. Serve tart warm or at room temperature. Serves 8.

Vanilla Cream Sauce:

| | |
|---|---|
| 1 | cup heavy whipping cream |
| 1 | tablespoon sugar |
| 1 | teaspoon vanilla |
| 1 | cup vanilla ice cream, softened |

Whip cream with sugar and vanilla until stiff. Fold whipped cream into the ice cream. Refrigerate until ready to serve. You can make this up to 2 hours before serving time. Makes 3 cups sauce.

# Easiest Apple Pie in a Crisp Cookie Crust

*This is one of the simplest of apple pies in the fullest sense of the word, and to my mind and taste, one of the best. A delicious crisp cookie crust filled with a tart fruity filling is a pure pleasure.*

**Crisp Cookie Crust:**
- 1 cup butter
- 2 cups flour
- 1/3 cup sugar

- 1/4 cup water
- 1 teaspoon cinnamon sugar

In a food processor, blend butter, flour and sugar until butter particles are the size of small peas. (Do not overprocess or the flakiness will be lost.) Add water and pulsate 4 or 5 times, or until dough clumps together. Place dough on floured wax paper and shape into a ball.

Pat 2/3 of the dough onto the bottom and up the sides of a greased 10-inch heart-shaped pan with a removable bottom. Bake in a 375-degree oven for 20 minutes, or until crust is lightly browned. Place Apple Pie Filling evenly over the crust. Divide remaining dough into thirds, pat each into a 6-inch circle and place on top of pie. Sprinkle top with 1 teaspoon cinnamon sugar. Continue baking for about 30 minutes, or until top is golden brown. Serves 8.

**Apple Pie Filling:**
- 6 large apples, peeled, cored and thinly sliced
- 1/2 cup sugar
- 1/3 cup yellow raisins
- 1 teaspoon grated lemon peel
- 1 tablespoon flour

In a bowl, toss together all the ingredients until nicely mixed.

*Note:* ♥ *The crust can be prepared in a mixer using the instructions described above. Simply beat the butter with the flour and sugar until butter is the size of small peas. Then add the water and beat until dough clumps together around the beaters.*

# Flaky Pastry Peach & Cranberry Pie

*Peaches and cranberries are paired in this ultra-delicious pie. Very fruity and tart, it also serves beautifully, with large petals of flaky pastry surrounded by peaches and cranberries. It is further simplified with the preparation of a softer dough that can be pressed into the pan, avoiding the need to refrigerate and roll the pastry.*

**Flaky Pastry:**
- 1 cup butter (2 sticks)
- 2 cups flour
- 1/4 cup sugar

- 1 egg
- 1 tablespoon water
- 1 teaspoon cinnamon sugar

In a food processor, blend butter, flour and sugar until butter particles are the size of small peas. (Do not overprocess or the flakiness will be lost.) Lightly beat together the egg and water until blended. Add to the butter mixture and pulsate 4 or 5 times, or until dough clumps together. Place dough on floured wax paper and shape into a ball.

Pat 2/3 of the dough onto the bottom and up the sides of a greased 10-inch heart-shaped pan with a removable bottom. Bake in a 375-degree oven for 20 minutes, or until crust is lightly browned. Place Peach & Cranberry Filling evenly over the crust. Divide remaining dough into thirds, pat each into a 6-inch circle and place on top of pie. Sprinkle top with 1 teaspoon cinnamon sugar. Continue baking for about 30 minutes, or until top is golden brown. Serves 8.

**Peach & Cranberry Filling:**
- 4 large peaches, peeled, stoned and thinly sliced
- 1/2 pound frozen cranberries, picked over. Do not defrost.
- 1/2 cup sugar
- 2 tablespoons flour
- 1/2 small orange, grated (optional)

In a bowl, toss together all the ingredients until nicely mixed.

# Italian Plum Tart on
# Almond Macaroon & Cookie Crust

**Cookie Crust:**
- 1 1/2 cups flour
- 1/2 cup butter
- 3 tablespoons sugar
- 3 tablespoons water

In a food processor, beat together flour, butter and sugar until mixture resembles coarse meal. Add the water and beat just until dough clumps together. Do not overbeat. Gather dough onto floured wax paper and knead 2 or 3 times to combine. Press dough on the bottom and 1-inch up the sides of a lightly greased 10-inch springform pan and bake at 375° for 20 minutes, or until crust is lightly browned. Remove from oven and cool.

Spread Almond Macaroon filling over the bottom of the crust and lay Plum Topping on top in a decorative fashion, allowing some of the macaroon to show. Bake at 375° for 35 to 40 minutes or until top is browned. Allow to cool in pan and cut into wedges to serve. Serves 10.

**Almond Macaroon:**
- 1/2 cup almonds
- 2 tablespoons sugar

- 1/4 cup butter, softened
- 2 tablespoons sugar
- 1 tablespoon flour
- 1 egg
- 1/2 teaspoon almond extract

In a food processor, grind almonds with sugar. Add the remaining ingredients and beat until blended. Do not overbeat.

**Plum Topping:**
- 1/2 pound purple plums, pitted and thinly sliced
- 1 tablespoon sugar

Toss together plums and sugar until blended.

# Viennese Apple Tart
## with Rummy Whipped Cream

**Crust:**

- 1 cup flour
- 4 tablespoons sifted powdered sugar
- 1 teaspoon grated lemon peel
- 6 tablespoons butter

- 3 tablespoons orange juice, about

In the large bowl of an electric mixer, beat together first 4 ingredients, until mixture resembles coarse meal. Continue beating, and add only enough orange juice until a dough forms around the beaters, about 12 to 15 seconds. Shape dough into a ball, flatten slightly, wrap in plastic wrap and refrigerate for 1 hour.

Roll dough out on a lightly floured board and place it in a buttered 10-inch tart pan; preferably one with a removable bottom. Prick crust with the tines of a fork, line it with foil and weigh it down with rice.

Bake crust at 400° for 20 minutes. Remove foil and rice. (Reserve rice for future use.) Continue baking crust until it is lightly browned, about 10 minutes. Cool.

Fill cooled pie shell with Apple Pie Filling. Decorate top with Rummy Whipped Cream piped over the pie, lattice-fashion. Refrigerate until serving time. Serves 6 or 8.

**Apple Pie Filling:**

- 6 tart apples, peeled, cored and thinly sliced. Toss in 2 tablespoons lemon juice.
- 1 cup sugar
- 1/2 cup apricot jam
- 1/2 cup coarsely chopped toasted pecans

Combine apples, sugar and apricot jam and cook over low heat, stirring now and again, until mixture thickens and apples are tender but still firm. Remove from heat and add chopped pecans. Cool.

**Rummy Whipped Cream:**

Beat together until stiff, 1 cup whipping cream, 2 tablespoons sifted powdered sugar, and 1 tablespoon rum.

# Apple Cream Cheese Pie

| | |
|---|---|
| 1 | 10-inch Vanilla Wafer Lemon Crust |

| | |
|---|---|
| 1 | package (8 ounces) cream cheese, softened |
| 1/2 | cup sour cream |
| 3/4 | cup sifted powdered sugar |
| 1 | teaspoon grated lemon rind |
| 1 | tablespoon fresh lemon juice |

Prepare crust. Beat together the remaining ingredients until blended. Pour mixture into Vanilla Wafer Lemon Crust and spread evenly. Cover cream cheese mixture with Apple Topping and sprinkle with cinnamon sugar to taste. Refrigerate for at least 4 hours. Overnight is good too. Serves 6 to 8.

**Apple Topping:**

| | |
|---|---|
| 1 | can apple pie filling, cut into small pieces |
| 1/2 | cup apricot jam |
| 1/2 | cup golden raisins, soaked overnight in orange juice and drained |

Combine all the ingredients and mix to blend.

**Vanilla Wafer Lemon Crust:**

| | |
|---|---|
| 1 1/4 | cups vanilla wafer crumbs |
| 1/2 | cup chopped walnuts |
| 1/3 | cup butter, melted |
| 1 | tablespoon grated lemon peel |
| 3 | tablespoons sugar |

Combine all the ingredients and pat them on the bottom and sides of a lightly buttered 10-inch pie pan. Bake in a 350° oven for about 8 minutes or until top is very lightly browned. Set aside to cool.

# Apple Tart with Sour Cream

*This is very much like the Viennese Apple Cream Tart, but the crust is made easy using prepared cake mix.*

| | |
|---|---|
| 2 | cups regular yellow cake mix (without the pudding added) |
| 6 | tablespoons butter |
| 1/2 | cup chopped walnuts |
| 2 | apples, peeled and grated |
| 1 | cup sour cream |
| 1 | egg |
| 3 | tablespoons sugar |

More →

(Apple Tart with Sour Cream, Cont.)

In the large bowl of an electric mixer, beat cake mix with butter until mixture resembles coarse meal.  Add nuts and mix well.  With your fingers, pat mixture on bottom and sides of an ungreased 10-inch tart pan with a removable bottom.  Bake crust in a preheated 350° oven for 8 minutes.

Place apples evenly over warm crust.  Beat together the sour cream, egg and sugar.  Pour mixture evenly over the apples.  Return to oven and continue baking at 350° for 35 minutes or until top is lightly browned.  Serves 8.

# Strawberry Cheese Pie in an Almond Pie Shell

Almond Shell:
- 2 cups grated almonds (almond meal).  Can be purchased at most health food stores.
- 1/3 cup cinnamon sugar
- 1/3 cup butter, melted

Combine grated almonds, cinnamon sugar and melted butter.  Pat mixture on bottom and sides of a buttered 9-inch pie pan.  Bake in a 350° oven for about 8 minutes or until shell is lightly browned.  Set aside to cool.

Pour Cream Cheese Filling into cooled pie shell and spread evenly.  Place strawberries cut side down over the filling.  Melt the currant jelly with the orange liqueur and brush the strawberries until nicely glazed.  Refrigerate. Serves 6 or 8.

Cream Cheese Filling:
- 1 package cream cheese (8 ounces) softened
- 1/2 cup sour cream
- 1 teaspoon grated lemon peel
- 1 tablespoon lemon juice
- 1/2 cup sifted powdered sugar

Beat together all the ingredients until the mixture is blended.

Strawberry Topping & Currant Glaze:
- 1 pint strawberries, cleaned, thoroughly dried and cut in halves
- 1/2 cup currant jelly
- 1 tablespoon orange liqueur

# Fruity Bread Pudding & Creme Fraiche Vanilla

Creme Fraiche, back in the "old days", was made with cream that was heated with buttermilk and allowed to stand at room temperature to thicken. In the early 50's, I devised a simpler (and equally delicious) way of making Creme Fraiche by just stirring together equal parts of cream and sour cream, and allowing it to ripen at room temperature. My method is commonly used today in most cookbooks.

I called it Creme Vanilla in those days, because I felt that purists might not consider it a true Creme Fraiche. Also, at that time, hardly anyone even knew of Creme Fraiche. Today, Creme Fraiche is known by most cooks, so I am giving the sauce its proper name. I have relied on it often throughout the years to prepare sweet or savory sauces, and as a base for cream soups. I have varied the ratio in dozens of ways, too numerous to mention. The following is a "skinny" Creme Fraiche, using low-fat sour cream and half and half.

| | |
|---|---|
| 6 | slices stale egg bread, remove crusts and cut into cubes |
| 2/3 | cup orange juice |
| 2 | bananas, peeled and sliced |
| | |
| 2/3 | cup golden raisins |
| 1 | cup brown sugar, loosely packed |
| 1 | apple, peeled and grated |
| 2 | peaches, peeled and thinly sliced, fresh or frozen |
| 1 | teaspoon orange zest |
| 1/2 | teaspoon vanilla |
| | |
| 1 | tablespoon cinnamon sugar |
| 1/2 | cup chopped walnuts |

In a large bowl, place bread, orange juice and bananas and toss to mix well. Add raisins, sugar, apple, peaches, orange zest and vanilla and mix together. Place mixture into a 2-quart casserole. Sprinkle top with cinnamon sugar and chopped walnuts and gently press the walnuts into the pudding.

Bake at 325° for 25 to 30 minutes or until piping hot. Serve warm (not hot) or at room temperature with Creme Fraiche Vanilla. Serves 6.

Creme Fraiche Vanilla:

| | |
|---|---|
| 1/2 | cup low-fat sour cream |
| 1/2 | cup half and half |
| 1 | tablespoon sugar |
| 1/2 | teaspoon vanilla |

In a glass jar with a tight fitting lid, place all the ingredients and stir until blended. Allow mixture to stand at room temperature for 4 hours and then refrigerate. Stir before using. This is a grand sauce to keep on hand for spooning over puddings, pies or stewed fruits. Yields 1 cup.

*Puff paste in an instant?? No way . . . they say. And they are probably right. Puff pastry is one of the most majestic of doughs, but its preparation is an arduous task that requires a great deal of time. Rolling, folding, turning, refrigerating, 6 times for Danish pastry, 8 times for the classic pastry, is a labor of much love and adoration. And it is well worth it too, if you happen to have the time.*

*However, if you do not, Quick Puff Pastry is a little treasure that I hope you will enjoy. It is an amazingly simple dough, that is assembled in minutes and produces an incredibly delicate and flaky pastry very much like the regal puff paste. It handles so easily and requires so little attention that even the most inexperienced beginner will produce masterful results every time.*

*The number and combinations of fillings are inexhaustable. I have included, in the following, a few of my very favorites.*

# Quick Puff Paste

1    cup butter, salted
2    cups flour
1    cup sour cream

Cut butter into flour in your electric mixer until the mixture resembles coarse meal. (You can do this in your electric mixer with perfect results.) Add sour cream and beat for 15 seconds. Turn mixture out onto wax paper that is heavily dusted with flour. Sprinkle a little more flour over the dough for ease of handling. Shape into a ball and wrap in the floured wax paper. Refrigerate for several hours or overnight. (Dough will keep for one week.)

**To Assemble:**
Divide dough into 4 parts. Working one part at a time, roll it out on a floured pastry cloth until dough measures about 10x10-inches. Spread 1/4 of the filling evenly over the dough. Roll jelly roll fashion ending with a strudel that measures 3x10-inches and seam side down.

Place strudel in a lightly greased pan. (Use a 12x16-inch pan so that you can bake the four strudels at one time.) Repeat with the remaining 3 parts of dough. Bake in a preheated 350° oven for about 30-35 minutes or until golden. Remove from the pan and cool. Sprinkle generously with sifted powdered sugar. Cut when cool.

## Apricot Strudel with Walnuts

1    recipe Quick Puff Paste

1    cup apricot jam
1    cup chopped walnuts

Divide dough into 4 parts. Working one part at a time, roll it out on a floured pastry cloth until the dough measures about 10x10-inches. Spread 1/4 cup of apricot jam over the dough. Sprinkle with 1/4 cup of chopped walnuts. Roll jelly roll fashion ending with a strudel that measures 3x10-inches and is seam side down.

Place strudel on a lightly greased 12x16-inch pan. (You can bake the four strudels at one time.) Repeat with the remaining 3 parts of dough and filling.

Bake in a preheated 350° oven for about 30 minutes or until top is golden. Cool in the pan for 10 minutes and then cool strudels on a rack or on a brown paper bag. Sprinkle generously with sifted powdered sugar. Cut when cool. Makes 24 to 30 slices.

## Chocolate Chip Danish

1    recipe Quick Puff Paste

12    tablespoons Nestle's Quik
1    package (6 ounces) milk chocolate or semi-sweet chocolate chips

Divide dough into 4 parts. Working one part at a time, roll it out on a floured pastry cloth until the dough measures about 10x10-inches. Spread 1/4 of the chocolate powder over the dough. Sprinkle with 1/4 of the chocolate chips. Roll jelly roll fashion, ending with a roll that is about 3x10-inches and is seam side down.

Place Danish roll on a lightly greased 12x16-inch pan so that you can bake the four pastries at one time. Repeat with the remaining 3 parts of dough and filling.

Bake in a preheated 350° oven for about 30 minutes or until top is golden. Cool in the pan for 10 minutes. Remove from pan and continue cooling on a rack or a brown paper bag. Sprinkle generously with powdered sugar. Cut when cool. Makes 24 to 30 slices.

*Note:* ♥ *Danish can be frozen after they are baked. Place them uncut on a piece of cardboard and wrap them in plastic wrap and foil. Defrost uncovered. Do not freeze with the powdered sugar on top.*

# Crescents Filled with Cinnamon & Walnuts & Vanilla Glazed

| | |
|---|---|
| 1/2 | pound butter |
| 1/2 | cup sugar |
| 1 | egg yolk |
| 3/4 | cup sour cream |
| 2 | cups flour |

Beat butter and sugar at medium speed until mixture is creamy. Beat in egg yolk and sour cream just until blended. Add flour and continue beating until the dough collects around the beaters. Turn dough out onto wax paper that is heavily dusted with flour. Sprinkle a little more flour over the dough for ease of handling. Shape into a ball, flatten it slightly and wrap in the floured wax paper and then foil. Refrigerate overnight.

Take dough from the refrigerator and divide it into 4 parts. Working one part at a time, roll it out on a floured pastry cloth until the dough measures about a 12-inch circle. Sprinkle 1/4 of the filling over the dough. Pat it down gently. With a knife, cut circle in half, then half again. Cut it like you would a pie until you have 12 triangular wedges. Roll each triangle from the wide side toward the center.

Place them on a lightly buttered baking pan and bake them at 350° for about 25 minutes or until they are lightly browned. When they are cool, brush them lightly with Vanilla Glaze or with a sprinkling of sifted powdered sugar. Yields 48 crescents.

Filling:
| | |
|---|---|
| 1 | teaspoon cinnamon |
| 3/4 | cup chopped walnuts |
| 1/2 | cup sugar |

Toss together all the ingredients until blended.

Vanilla Glaze:
| | |
|---|---|
| 1/2 | cup powdered sugar |
| 1 | teaspoon vanilla |
| 1 | tablespoon cream |

Stir together all the ingredients until blended.

# Old Fashioned Apple Strudel

1 recipe Quick Puff Paste

2 apples, peeled and grated
3/4 cup apricot jam
1 cup chopped walnuts
4 tablespoons cinnamon sugar

Divide dough into 4 parts. Working one part at a time, roll it out on a floured pastry cloth until the dough measures about 10x10-inches. Spread 1/4 of the apricot jam over the dough. Spread 1/4 of the apples evenly over the jam. Sprinkle 1/4 of the chopped walnuts over the apples. Sprinkle 1 tablespoon of the cinnamon sugar over all. Roll jelly roll fashion ending with a roll that is about 3x10-inches and is seam side down.

Place strudel on a lightly greased 12x16-inch pan so that you can bake the four pastries at one time. Repeat with the remaining 3 parts of dough and filling.

Bake in a preheated 350° oven for about 30 minutes or until top is golden. Cool in the pan for 10 minutes. Carefully remove from the pan and continue cooling on a rack or on a brown paper bag. Sprinkle generously with Vanilla Sugar. Cut when cool. Makes 24 to 30 slices.

**Vanilla Sugar:**
Place 1 pound of sifted powdered sugar into a cannister or jar with a tight lid. Snap two vanilla beans sharply in thirds and bury them in the sugar. Use on pastries, cakes and where powdered sugar is called for. This will give the sugar a gentle hint of vanilla which is just marvellous.

# Cinnamon Raisin Danish

1 recipe Quick Puff Paste

1/2 cup cinnamon sugar
1 cup finely chopped walnuts
1 cup golden raisins

Divide dough into 4 parts. Working one part at a time, roll it out on a floured pastry cloth until the dough measures about 10x10-inches. Sprinkle the top with 2 tablespoons cinnamon sugar, 1/4 the walnuts and 1/4 the raisins. Roll jelly roll fashion ending with a roll that is about 3x10-inches and is seam side down.

Place Danish roll on a lightly greased 12x16-inch pan so that you can bake the four pastries at one time. Repeat with the remaining 3 parts of dough.

More →

Bake in a preheated 350° oven for about 30 minutes or until top is golden. Cool in the pan for 10 minutes. Carefully remove from the pan and continue cooling on a rack or on a brown paper bag. Sprinkle lightly with sifted powdered sugar. Yields 32 slices.

**Cinnamon Sugar:**
Combine 1 cup sugar and 3 teaspoons cinnamon in a jar with a tight lid. Shake and roll until sugar and cinnamon are evenly mixed.

# Strawberry Walnut Raisin Strudel

| | |
|---|---|
| 2 | cups flour |
| 1/2 | pound cream cheese |
| 1/2 | pound butter |
| 2 | egg yolks |
| 1 | teaspoon grated lemon peel |
| 4 | tablespoons sugar |

Place all the ingredients in your mixer bowl. Beat at medium speed until the dough collects around the beaters and then 30 seconds more. Turn dough out onto wax paper that is heavily dusted with flour. Sprinkle a little more flour over the dough for ease of handling. Shape into a ball and wrap in the floured wax paper and then foil. Refrigerate overnight.

Take the dough from the refrigerator and divide it into 4 parts. Working one part at a time, roll it out on a floured pastry cloth until the dough measures about 10x10-inches. Spread 1/4 of the filling evenly over the dough. Roll jelly roll fashion ending with a strudel that measures 3x10-inches and seam side down.

Place strudel on a lightly greased 12x16-inch pan so that you can bake the four strudels at one time. Repeat with the remaining 3 parts of dough. Bake in a preheated 350° oven for about 30 to 35 minutes or until top is lightly browned. Remove from the pan with two pancake turners and cool on a brown paper bag. Sprinkle with sifted powdered sugar when cool.

**Walnut Raisin Filling:**

| | |
|---|---|
| 1 | cup strawberry jam |
| 1 | cup chopped walnuts |
| 1/2 | cup golden raisins, plumped overnight in orange juice |
| 1/4 | cup coconut flakes |
| 1/2 | cup marshmallow creme |

Stir together all the ingredients until blended.

# Low-Calorie Dessert Sauces

The following are a few dessert sauces that can be prepared in minutes. Using the non-fat yogurt helps keep the calories down. These are tasty, not as rich as their roly-poly cousins, but they will satisfy you at dessert time.

## Honey Almond Maple Sauce:

- 1 cup non-fat unflavored yogurt
- 3 tablespoons honey
- 1/2 teaspoon pure maple extract
- 3 tablespoons chopped toasted almonds

Stir together all the ingredients until blended. Serve over low-fat ice cream or non-fat frozen yogurt. Yields 1 1/4 cups sauce.

## Chocolate Chocolate Chip Sauce:

- 3/4 cup non-fat unflavored yogurt
- 2 tablespoons sifted cocoa
- 3 tablespoons brown sugar
- 1/2 teaspoon vanilla

- 1/4 cup mini-semi-sweet chocolate chips

In a sauce pan, over low heat, stir together first 4 ingredients until mixture is nicely blended and sugar has melted. Do not allow to boil. Chill in the refrigerator for 1 hour and then stir in the chocolate chips. Serve over low-fat ice cream or non-fat frozen yogurt. Yields 1 1/4 cups sauce.

## Honey Cinnamon Vanilla Sauce:

- 1 cup non-fat unflavored yogurt
- 3 tablespoons honey
- 1 teaspoon vanilla
- 1/2 teaspoon cinnamon

Stir together all the ingredients until blended. Yields about 1 1/4 cups sauce.

# Dessert Sauces

## Instant Hot Fudge Sauce:

*This little recipe has all the properties of hot fudge sauce. It is very thick, and will firm up when it comes into contact with the ice cream. Unused sauce should be stored in the refrigerator and warmed in the top of a double boiler before serving.*

- 1  can (14 ounces) sweetened condensed milk
- 4  ounces unsweetened chocolate
   pinch of salt
- 2  teaspoons vanilla

In the top of a double boiler, over hot water, heat the condensed milk. Add the remaining ingredients, and stir until chocolate is melted. Mixture will be very thick. Place in a sauce boat and serve over ice cream, or frozen desserts. Yields 2 1/4 cups sauce.

## Instant Butterscotch Sauce:

- 1  can (14 ounces) sweetened condensed milk
- 1  package (6 ounces) butterscotch chips
- 1  teaspoon vanilla

In the top of a double boiler, over hot water, heat the condensed milk. Add the remaining ingredients, and stir until butterscotch is melted. Mixture will be very thick. Place in a sauce boat and serve over ice cream, or frozen desserts. Unused sauce should be stored in the refrigerator and heated in the top of a double boiler before serving. Yields 2 1/2 cups sauce.

## Maple Walnut Sauce:

- 1  cup maple syrup
- 1/2  cup toasted chopped walnuts

In a saucepan, heat together all the ingredients for 2 minutes. Serve over low-fat ice cream or non-fat frozen yogurt. Yields 1 1/2 cups sauce.

## Instant Strawberry Sauce:

- 1  cup low-fat sour cream
- 1/4  cup strawberry jam
- 1/2  cup sliced strawberries

Stir together all the ingredients until blended. Serve over non-fat frozen yogurt or sponge cake. Yields 1 1/2 cups sauce.

# The Index

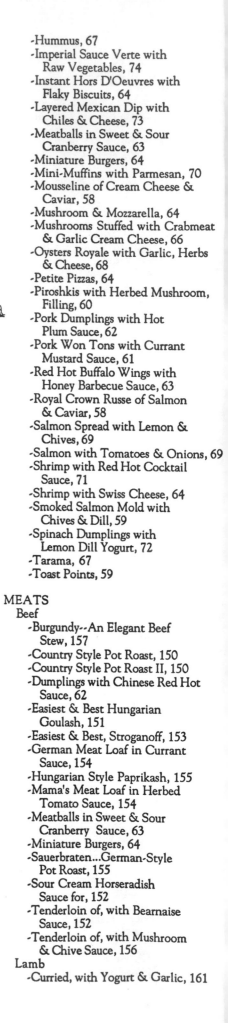

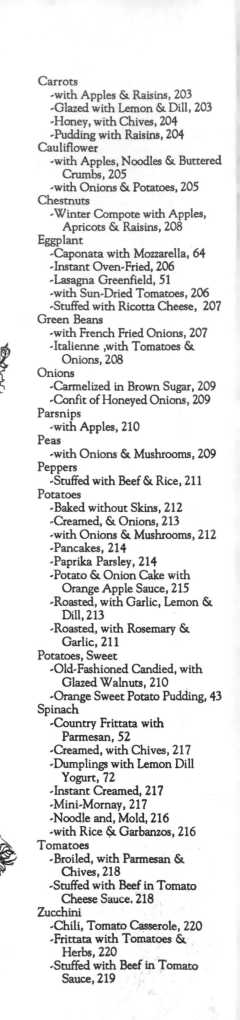